This book is the original book written by Nicholas De Vere before it was edited by Tracy Twyman

From Transylvania to Tunbridge Wells

Original manuscript by Nicholas de Vere (1957–2013).
Edited and republished by Abbe de Vere through Dragon Publishing.

Published by Dragon Publishing

Cover design by Abbe de Vere
Printed in the United Kingdom by Amazon KDP

Editor & Publisher's Note

This edition of *From Transylvania to Tunbridge Wells* presents the original manuscript of Nicholas de Vere, preserved as he wrote it between 1996 and 1999. It is published here without alteration to his voice, vision, or structure, allowing readers to encounter his work in its most authentic form.

As his daughter, I have chosen to bring this manuscript back into print so that his insights, wit, and scholarship may be preserved for future generations. Through **Dragon Publishing**, under the auspices of **The Sovereign Grand Duchy of Drakenberg Ltd, London**, this release marks the beginning of a wider effort to safeguard and republish rare historical, genealogical, and esoteric works connected to the Dragon Court tradition.

In presenting this text, my purpose is not only to honour my father's legacy, but also to establish a publishing line dedicated to the preservation of history, heritage, and truth — ensuring that voices like his continue to be heard, studied, and remembered.

— *Abbe de Vere*
Editor & Publisher

Welcome to the Realm of the Shining Ones!

From Transylvania to Tunbridge Wells

The history and etiquette of Vampirism in the Home Counties~

A collection of essays on the ***Derkesthai Culture*** with

accompanying extracts from the Dragon Court archives

by

Nicholas de Vere
Sovereign Grand Master - The Imperial and Royal Dragon Court

Edited and Illustrated by

- H.E. Michael Hunter B.A. -

Archaeological and Anthropological Consultant

- Baron Richard Dufton B.A. -

Dedication

This work is dedicated to the memory

of an Elven Princess of the House of

Llewelyn who opened her heart in love,

threw the doors of Elphame wide and gave

birth to the Sovereign Dragon Nation once more;

and to the Grail Maidens and Dragon Princesses

who are the sole and rightful custodians of Eternity'

Extracts from this collection first appeared in **Mr. Laurence Gardner**'s book '*Genesis of the Grail Kings*' with the kind permission of HI&RH **Prince Nicholas de Vere**, who also formerly permitted further extensive essay and research material, and archival extracts from the *Dragon Collection* to form the bulk of **Mr. Gardner**'s September 1999 '*Nexus Lectures*' and his next book '*Ring Lords of the Dragon*' which, although due to be published by Element Books in September 2000, has now apparently either been abandoned or renamed'

From Transylvania to Tunbridge Wells
Frontispiece

"***The Beast, the Dragon***, the terrible monster, is the disguise of the beloved; the horror to be overcome itself is, or contains, the Reward' Beauty and the Beast must be conjoined' The old tag that a serpent becomes not a Dragon save by devouring another serpent, has an Alchemical sense:

These are the two Dragons, male and female: they destroy one another, or one destroys the other and a new and mightier one is born, a fiery wonder: A ***Phoenix*** (traditionally depicted as having red and gold plumage*), a leaping glory, a STAR of dream ascending to the throne of the world. This was the Transmutation, the Great Work of the hidden glory of perfection".

Arthur Machen, Fr.GD.
(Frater of the Hermetic Order of the Golden Dawn)

The mating of Ravens is the rhythmic inhalation and exhalation of the breath of Ravens, one by the other. And in this way are the children of Ravens fashioned. (The Raven is the Phoenix of the Elven Kings)'

Traditional country folklore (England)

* (The red and gold field, symbolizing the plumage of the Phoenix - superimposed by the white Star - are the ***Arms of the Vere***, supported by two Dragons they historically become one of the Seals of the House. Red and gold are also the colors of other descendants of the ***Merovingian dynasty***, including

the ***Planagenets***, the ***Mandevilles***, the ***Spencers*** and the ***Royal House of Scotland***).

Acknowledgements and Credits

This book is a conversational and informal, organic, evolving work which will grow as ***the Dragon Court*** archives are converted into electronic data. Further chapters will include *The Origin of the Dragon Lords of the Rings* and a comprehensive discourse on the ancient methods used in *The Rite of the Vampire*, accompanied by a detailed endocrinological schematic.

The author would like to acknowledge, thank and/or credit the following people for supportive and corroborative source material and for their encouragement throughout the years. These will be added to as time marches on. Anyone who feels that they have been forgotten should contact the site administrator and the oversight will be rectified if your work has been consulted.

- Carol Thomas
- Elizabeth Ward
- Ian Inskipp
- Jiddu Krishnamurti
- Richard Dufton
- Michael Hunter
- Chris Hall
- Kenneth Grant
- Ward Rutherford
- David Wood
- Yatri
- Pennethorne Hughes
- H.T.F. Rhodes
- Yuri Stoyanov
- David Barker
- George Reilly-Scott
- Peter Anderson
- Sabine Baring-Gould
- Ulick Beck
- Ean Begg
- Margaret Murray
- Richard Gregory
- Drs. Walter Pierpaoli & William Regelson
- Miranda Green
- Vivian Green
- David Day
- Prof. Ray McNally
- Austin Osman Spare
- George Woodcock
- Verily Anderson
- James Anderson
- Prof. Morton Smith
- J. H. Brennan
- Israel Regardie

- Francis King
- Colin Wilson
- MacGregor Mathers,
- Jack Parso
- John Matthews
- Jehovah (author of the bestselling novel The Holy Bible)
- and a bunch of Irish and Welsh Monks for variously fiddling with the Annals of Irish History and for committing to parchment the Mabinogion and the Liebher Gabhala.

In all other respects the bulk of this work was anticipatory and derived from the application of the *Derkesthai phenomenon.* It would be pretty pointless writing about it if it hadn't and the reader would just be confronted with yet another rehash of the same old material that has been doing the rounds for years.

Grateful thanks are also extended to my mother, about whom my father says "that she is the only woman I have ever known to have suffered from post-natal depression for more than thirty years".

Introduction

A New Age Critique

The etymology of the word 'dragon' comes to us via the Latin but is derived ultimately, it is thought, from the Greek, though the origin of the word and its definition is probably much older. The word in Greek is *drakon* (drakon); as in *edrakon* (edrakon), an aorist of *derkesthai* (derkesthai), which means '<u>to see clearly</u>'.

A ***dragon*** was one who saw clearly, and clarity of vision engendered and was always classically associated with wisdom, which itself produced power. Today we say that knowledge is power, so nothing has changed in that respect, except that it is actually wisdom - the ability to predict or intuit and synthesize knowledge - a prerequisite of druidic or fairy ***neuro-physiology***, that actually affords the greatest power of all.

In a progression of logic that naturally suggests itself, we are therefore entering in upon the linguistic territory of the seer, the witch and the magus, with whom the foregoing qualities have always been closely identified, a state of affairs with which etymologists concur.

From there, in the Gaelic realms, we encounter the '***Merlins***', a name which, like '***Dragon***', literally means '***seer***', and who furthermore, were of a class of druid priests or '*philosophus*' or 'magi', as they were also known in classical times. Anciently the foregoing regional epithets were all attributed to one royal, priestly tribe originally known in Indo-European as the Arya: The 'race of the wise ones', a caste who were described in Latin as the '*nobilis*', a name which originated from the Greek root *gno* (***gno***) meaning '*to know*'.

Similarly the word king is derived from the related Gothic word *kuningzam*, meaning both "knowing one" and "*scion of the noble, (meaning wise), race*". In addition we have the associated word ***siddhis***, meaning '***the powers***' and from this word or vice versa, was derived the tribal name 'the Scythians' the '*Arya-Sidhe*' or '*Sidheans*'. The '*siddhis*' were a range of psychic or paranormal phenomena which manifested themselves as the attributes of those Tantric priests in Eurasia who had attained '*samadhi*' or '*enlightenment*'.

These people, coterminously the ***Aryans*** or ***Scythians***, who are thought to have developed *Tantra* in ***Sumeria***, were known as the legendary **Tuadha d'Anu** (tribe of Anu and by a traditional, widely known derivation - "people of the stars") or *daouine sidhe* (meaning people of the powers) in the Gaelic countries. They were the 'wise ones', the ***elves*** or ***fairies***; and from this we can conclude that by correct definition, a Dragon was originally, (by blood descent from the race of the wise), an overlord, an *archdruid* or *bruidhina*, *magus* and a *seer*, an ***elven goddess-queen*** or ***god-king***.

Such are not to be confused with the warrior kings or tinker dynasties installed by the ***Roman Church*** over the last 1500 years, nor with any modern royal family. The ***druidhe*** were kings above kings.

The ***dragon*** or ***fairy gene*** was very rare and true *archdruidic*, royal dragon families were rarer still. Persecutions excepted, if this were not the case anyway, then perhaps many fairy stories of the popular genre which originated from outside the dragon culture would never have taken hold, because the reality would have been constantly staring people in the face.

Traditionally and consistently, the symbol of both wisdom (*Sophia*) and healing was the serpent or, as it was also known, ***the dragon***. In keeping with this the kings and queens of pre-catholic history were noted for their healing capabilities and as such, in Judaic mythology, were called, perhaps after the **archangel Raphael**, the ***Repha'im*** or ***Rapha'Elohim;*** the healing gods of ***the Anunnaki.*** **Raphael** was the Prince who appeared to **Adam** in *Eden* according to **Milton**.

No mention of this is made in *Genesis* and one suspects that of the two entities that did appear to **Adam**, **Enlil** and **Enki**, or if you like: *God* and the *Catholic Satan*. **Raphael** - the *Angel of the Rising Sun* - must have been **Enki** who gave Kingship to man in the form of the ***Elven Overlords*** and after whom, by various related epithets; including '***The Repha'im***', the Elven Kings are known.

Authorities believe that these people were identical to both the ***Nephilim*** and the ***Anakim of Idumea*** and ***Canaan***. In early heraldry, derived from ancient sources, the dragon was depicted as a serpent with the wings of a swan. This image was also given the wings of a bat.

The dragon nevertheless was humanoid and so the symbolism in the dragon glyph ought rather be interpreted to substantiate the etymology of the word itself. The serpent stands for the wisdom and healing powers of the sacred king or queen whose regalia often consisted of serpent-like scale armour and whose consciousness soars above that of humanity as if carried on wings, which were symbolized by shamanic swan's feather cloaks.

The nocturnal habits of the dragon people, typically those of the ***Cimmerian Scythians***, were noted by their contemporaries and the swan's wings of the ***dragon glyph*** attributed to them were either interchangeable with, or substituted by, those of the bat to signify this.

One of their earlier names - ***Anunnaki*** - means "*heaven meets earth*". Lots of fanciful notions have been put forward to suggest that the Anunnaki were from outer space, but a far simpler way of understanding the name is to ask a simple question: "when do the heavens - the ***An*** or ***Stars*** - meet the Earth?". The answer is of course - "at night time".

When considering the nature of ***the elves*** or ***the Anunnaki***, rather than believing they came from a different planet, it might be worth considering that they occupied a different dimension. If this sounds equally as fanciful and implausible, consider this. A multitude of different animal species on this planet can be seen and touched.

However, because of their physiology and chemical make-up were different and these differences in synaptic connections and hormone levels altered their perceptions of their universe, these species actually lived in another dimension and at a ***higher frequency***, where time and the environment for them were totally different to the way humans perceived them. The level to which ***the fairies*** experienced life was far deeper than the level to which humans experienced it.

In real terms the fairies inhabited an entirely alien world but occupied the same planet. In this sense they were from a different dimension, characterized and regulated by their body chemistry which enabled them to see more in the environment than humans could. In this they were no more remarkable than any other non-human species we are able to study today.

Flies, Sharks, Dolphins and a host of other lifeforms have attributes and abilities humans do not possess and the way in which they interact with the planet is completely alien to the way in which humans do. For a fly time is completely different and for a *Shark*, any warm blooded creature glows with a blue, electro-chemical haze or aura, proving to some extent, the veracity of the theory of ***Kirlian photography***.

The ***Fairies*** were ***dragons*** and this means that they 'saw clearly', they saw subtler emanations than man could. In order to be able to do this the fairy would have to have their senses tuned into a higher frequency than man, meaning that the fairies, perforce, were tuned to a higher frequency of perception and activity generally.

In cybernetic terms, any system that is faster and consequently higher than a given base is called a ***nautonnier*** or ***navigator*** and in cybernetics these systems are set over and in control of the slower functional operations within any given mechanical or organic arrangement.

If we transpose this theory onto human society we get leaders and followers, where the ***leaders*** are supposed to be able to function at a faster rate than the followers and thereby anticipate any given direction the system might go in and plan sensible strategies that the system might adopt for its well-being.

Today this is a joke and incompetent, self-seeking, middle class idiots more often find themselves voted into control of vast social systems which, once upon a time, no-one would trust to anyone but ***the Elves***.

In the past therefore, because the ***Fairies*** were, for millennia, physiologically bred and exhaustively trained to operate at a higher level than men, humans often invited them to become social *navigators* or *nautonniers*. The ***Sumerian word*** for a navigator is a ***GALL***, which sounds a bit like a ***Gael***, doesn't it? The language of the western Royal Scythians was ***Gaelic*** and the ***Royal Scythians*** were the fairies, the Elves: ***The Dragons***.

The dragon's fiery breath symbolized the *pneuma*, the spirit of the divine, which coalesced into the ***Torah*** or cosmic law that the ***Dragon queens*** and ***kings*** delivered as their pronouncements in the affairs of man. Thus the image of the dragon of myth and legend is complete, as a set of symbolic attributes belonging to an ancient magical race of praeter-natural beings, the *vampyr overlords* or *fairy overkings*.

Though humanoid, ***Dragons*** were not Homo Sapiens but from the far ***older elven race*** sometimes called in literature - the ***Elda*** or ***Eldar***, probably suggested or derived from the name of an ancient queen and her ancient, former habitation in ***Mesopotamia*** and possibly intended, in its attribution as a simile for ***Elder*** perhaps, to imply some form of racial primogeniture.

Reflected upon within the context of early Sumerian historical records, such a synonym would indeed seem to be apposite, inasmuch as this ancient and mysterious people claimed that ***the Dragons***, with **Queen Hawah Elda**'s assistance, made mankind.

Homo Sapiens?

From the ***OED*** *(Oxford English Dictionary)* we learn that the prefix ***homo*** (from whence comes '*man*'), is derived from the same root as the prefix in *homo-genous*, and it means '*common*', '*the same*' or '*the same as*', '*average*', '*mediocre*'.

The word ***sapiens*** is itself derived from the Latin word '***sapienta***' meaning understanding - but it was a word which was used in a solely pejorative and derogatory context - from as far back as the Middle English period - explicitly in the sense of artful, deceitful, contrived or would-be wisdom; meaning sophistry or low cunning and hypocrisy. From ***sapienta*** we derive the slang derogative ***Sap*** which has been used throughout the English-speaking world to taunt *idiots* and *fools*.

Hereto, in contemporary currency the phrase homo sapiens therefore, simply defines a common, undistinguished hominid species, the members of which (rather like sheep), within a limited field of conscious responses and conditioned reflexes, all act in the same manner and think the same self-deluding thoughts, whilst relating to each other through a veil of deception.

Taken in relation to what man has done to the planet and to his fellow creatures, the author doesn't think that this is an unwarranted or unsubstantiable attack, but a justifiable observation. Man aptly named himself: ***homo = mediocre + sapiens = cunning.***

As such, applying the correct, literal definition within the *Oxford English Dictionary*, the entire membership of that species are all as mediocre and erroneous in their behavior, perceptions and understanding as each other. Because, continuing with this accepted definition: "*homo sapiens*", it says, "is the genus of which man is the only species".

Therefore man is defined currently by the *Oxford English Dictionary*, the recognized authority on, and arbiter of the English language, as being uniquely, thoroughly stupid and dim witted, and his species description has incorporated within it a clear indication that this condition is genetically inherited. Nurture seems unable to ameliorate what nature has here ordained.

Here the idealist might argue that a *eugenic solution*, mediated through genetic engineering could produce a more passive, thoughtful population by weeding out the stupid gene and replacing it with something that would make us all less wasteful, aggressive and acquisitive.

Take a look around you, who runs the planet? That's right - the multi-national corporations, and what is their raison d'etre? To force people to produce rubbish for the same people to buy. Where does the funding come from for scientific research grants? From the multi-national corporations or via governments who are subservient to, because they are paid for by, those same corporations. Would either support any form of research that would make people refuse to fight their wars for them or consume less of their pointless crap? No.

In any case, at present, ***genetic engineering*** for the most part is becoming yet another manifestation of human megalomania within a cosmos or world socio-economic system that owes its very existence to the continued cultivation and promotion by the corporate elites, of mass psychosis on an international scale.

This, as they are wont to say, is a sad indictment upon the entire human race, but nevertheless the evidence speaks for itself and after several millennia of wars and destruction, culminating in the present series of precipitative social and ecological disasters, it doesn't seem that homo sapiens will ever be anything other than what they are and that furthermore, this is a profitable, and therefore a protected and encouraged, irremediable and irreversible, genetic condition.

In contrast ***the Dragons*** or ***Draco Sentiens***, according to the most ancient definitions, were, once upon a time, long long ago, genetically "clear sighted" members of the ***elder race***, the "race of the wise".

It therefore follows in conclusion that, because of the neurophysiological, and consequently the cognitive, cogitative and psychological differences between the two, neither were of the same species as the other and the ***ancient Sumerian texts*** would uphold this view without question.

Grail Code - What Grail Code? A personal view

People enter relationships that serve their own interests or the interests of the 'extended self' which, beyond the immediate level of everyday materialism, they externalize as pecuniary acquisitiveness, as political ambition or an abstracted spiritual ideal, as manifestations of or tools to service that same materialistic greed, but operating on a sublimated level of personal and social deceit. In the end therefore, all human endeavor is self centered, and all is 'egotism'.

Beyond this there may be something of greater merit dwelling in the depths of the silence beyond their own chattering minds and feeble aspirations, but because such dwells in stillness and silence it cannot be either comprehended with, or eulogized about, by an unquiet mind and it therefore transcends the limits of petty human understanding.

However 'bigger' any greater, non-personalized aim might be, it is still serving itself and its own interests through the drives it instills in them. The universe eats the universe as a manifestation of a larger cosmic egotism which cares nothing for the 'rights' of Man.

A greater merit then may be the compassion life has for itself but even so, ultimately this does not necessarily serve the interests of Man, who is merely one species amongst many, one component of consciousness with which life perceives itself through those interactive experiences that cause each other, but which are no respecters of persons or of any individually or collectively projected egotism which we might define as a divine, consciously moral incentive.

This, in actuality and on mans' part, is merely a desire that the universe be nice to them and fulfill all their greedy ambitions and assuage all their fears for their well-being and continuity. The Universe has no contract with humanity and therefore no contract men have with each other has any valid basis in reality either.

In times past they would speak of the '*Covenant with God*', now certain individuals pontificate vacuously about '***The Grail Code***'. Both - then and now - can only be seen as fraudulent contracts which no party can uphold because neither party can fulfill the obligations or restrict themselves to the limits implied within them, because abiding, externalized, imposed contracts are not a part of natural law.

Individuals put up with *eachother's peccadilloes* if they have something to contribute to each other which is valued. Their degree of longsuffering is directly proportional to the value they place on the ethos or image they each project, or on each other's input or their potential or actual services.

In the particular instance being referred to in this essay the '***Grail Code***' of service to others is prominent in its absence because the relationships people have are driven by a financial imperative, making the statements of collective high idealism just that, a hollow mockery of something that died out long ago. The ***Grail Code*** today is just another *clichéd* phrase, a tatty piece of New Age verbosity aimed at selling contrived, pseudo-intellectual, academically amateur jingoism to frightened, greedy idiots.

Religious coercion is now replaced by these kinds of *jargonistic phrases*, which are geared towards promoting limp, new age philosophies that, like religion, are engineered to appeal to or coerce (for selfish motives) a higher sense in man that simply doesn't exist. For the ***Grail Code*** to work as it was envisaged or understood, everyone subscribing to it now would have to think with one mind and not consider individual gain before the welfare of the group. This is simply not happening nor will it.

Such a level of co-operation could only be achieved in the ability of all the subscribers to the 'code' being able to communicate at the same level of understanding and with the same degree of experiential intensity and the same semeiological and semantic inflection at the same time. ***Service to others*** without thought of self requires others to serve you with equal dedication and devotion if you and the group - collectively - are to survive.

The ***Grail Code*** in the distant past was not a contract nor an ideal. It was the manifestation of a type of behavior which was subsequent to a particular form of consciousness.

Hierogamy or ***enthea*** between the ***Dragon Prince*** and the ***Swan Maiden*** resulted in the creation of an extended mind, the development of an interaction where the bounds of individual consciousness were broken and two people joined together with an intensity that created a being greater than the sum of its parts. In ***alchemy*** this was called the breath of Ravens from which resulted the birth of the ***red-gold Phoenix***, conceived in the death of Dragons and born in the ascent of the white star. The way these two individuals treated each other was called ***True*** or ***Courtly Love***.

If this phenomena happened on a wider scale within ***the genome***, then it, along with other universal phenomena, was a part of the ***Web of Wyrd*** and its child was ***True Love*** manifest collectively, which was called the ***Grail Code.*** **Jesus** called it "*the Law of God written on the hearts of men in tongues of fire*". Genetic righteousness.

The ***Grail Code*** was the behavioral manifestation of an attuned group of empathic individuals working towards the common good of that group. This required a '***Hive Mind***' - a collective consciousness - or at least a heightened capacity towards sensitivity and the anticipation of the needs of all within the genome, that transcended common consciousness, being therefore a manifestation of the outworking of the ***Siddhis*** within the web of interrelated and interconnected points of consciousness that are manifest throughout all levels of life.

The ***Grail Code*** therefore, was a set of behavioral patterns that arose from within as a response to a particular endocrinologically mediated, psychological condition that has detachment as its hallmark. It was not imposed from without by people with vested interests who were attempting to manipulate circumstance by manipulating other peoples appetites or consciences for their own ends or for the ends of any other disassociated group of individuals' co-operative self interests.

Without the '***Hive Mind***' (symbolized in the ***Dragon Dynasty*** by the ***Merovingian Bee***, the ***Phoenician*** '***House of the Gods***' and the hexagonal figure of the ***Tree of Life*** of the ***Kabala***) the ***Grail Code*** is a meaningless set of unattainable social aspirations which can only serve nowadays to fill the gaping chasm left by people's apathy towards more traditional forms of judicial, spiritual or moral flannel.

In the hands of New Age style authors and their wannabee audiences the ***Grail Code*** becomes just another form of legalism. Without the brain physiology required to understand its implications, those who cannot share in the collective consciousness of the group (whose very being was founded on co-operation and whose mental condition created the ***Grail Code*** as a naturally occurring phenomenon) make a mockery of all the Code stands for.

To these - the people left outside the group who don't have the wiring or chemistry to participate and understand the collective mind - the ***Grail Code*** is just another mishmash of rules which, however prettily and romantically packaged, will inevitably be broken and which therefore are no better or worse than any other meaningless set of regulations.

The universe has features which are prime constants, the behavior of materials is one example, which we call the '*laws of physics*'. These we can term truths, because they don't vary under a given range of circumstances, even down at the sub atomic level, the weirdness is still a constant, inasmuch as it is constantly weird. Without these prime constants the universe would cease to exist.

The ***Grail Code***, as a worthy set of regulations or aspirations for the governance of people's behavior in relationship to each other is, quite frankly, an idealistic load of nonsense. It isn't that the ***Grail Code*** is a fantasy or a lie, it is simply a fact that it was and still is misapplied to the wrong people.

Relatively and contextually speaking the ***Grail Code*** is not a truth, because it is not a constant, and it cannot be applied to regulate human behavior in human societies and we know this because it caused, in part, the manifestation of a set of social conditions which were required in order to allow to occur the 1000 year genocide which is referred to in *the Family as the Elven Holocaust*, which resulted ultimately in the abandonment of the ***Grail Code*** itself.

What was the big mistake ***the Family*** made? They did unto others as they would have done unto themselves. In other words they used the transcendently inspired ***Grail Code*** they anciently applied to their own mystical race to order societies that were founded not upon transcendent perception, but upon animal instincts, where irredeemably materialistic individuals co-operated merely for personal gain and in constantly shifting temporary alliances that had no notion of a collective mind or group cohesion at the profound level which would have been needed to make the ***Grail Code*** manifest outside the genome and prove successful.

The ***Grail Code*** was applicable only to the ***Grail Blood.*** Elsewhere the only thing that worked was the law of the jungle and terrorism. The Family were seen as a soft touch because their empathy was extended to peoples who had no empathy themselves, only the desire to satisfy their own greed and assuage their own fears.

These peoples' selfish, individualistic motivations stood in direct opposition to the ***Grail Code*** of 'royal communism' and community service. Desire is a great motivator in any society and ***the Elves'*** desires were motivated by their transcendent consciousness, which could only operate in an environment of truth and empathy.

The more one sees the less one desires for oneself and the less attached one becomes. If one desires truth and sees only truth and gives instinctively for the common good because one can feel the common need, one becomes the target for opportunists and deceivers.

Faced with the violence and hostility of a group of myopic animals hell bent on their pursuing their own own interests and unable to see the bigger picture, the ***Elves*** had no chance of survival anyway, whatever the other circumstances might have been.

This alone was enough to destroy them. In a sense then, the ***Grail Code*** was a death sentence to the ***Dragon Families***. This, perhaps, is how the ***Mayors of the Palace*** took over, through exploiting what they perceived as the innate trust, complacency and weakness of the ***Merovingian*** kings.

One can appear dark or harsh in one's attitudes towards human beings and human behavior and one may make people wonder how one could possibly spout about ***the Grail*** on one hand and despise humans so much on the other. After all, isn't the ***Grail Code*** all to do with being nice to each other? Isn't it about being fair to one's fellow man? Doesn't it fit in with the overall ethos of the New Age? The answer to all these rhetorical questions is an absolute No. It isn't and it doesn't.

The ***Grail Code*** is the perfect example of an ill-advisedly applied series of innate laws arising from the profound depths of the genetic constitution of one species, applied to and completely misunderstood and abused by another, to the detriment of their originators and ultimately to the detriment of the abusers themselves, who thought to gain by killing their *nautonniers*, not realizing that they, the usurpers, were too thick to organize society themselves. In this statement wrong?

Look around you and judge for yourself. After a thousand years of tyrannical misrule, European society is finally beginning to throw off the shackles of merchant class stupidity and disintegrate. Unfortunately this new found dissent and 'freedom' has no direction either and the path society is treading will inevitably become littered with the corpses of the fallen.

People aren't naturally '*nice*' to each other, they are simply conditioned to fear the consequences of not appearing to be nice to each other. Even so, this barrier is now breaking down and at the grassroots level society is becoming more violent as individuals embrace '*Aquarian Individualism*' (aka *selfish opportunism*) and disregard their conditioning.

There is a stark difference between the two concepts and conditions of natural empathy and social fear. One comes from within, the other is applied from without. If people were naturally co-operative and naturally empathic, the ***Grail Code*** would be a universal behavioral constant in an ordered world of ecological sensitivity and social harmony. This, plainly and manifestly is not, and never has been the case, certainly not since the Church came to power. The ***Grail Code*** arises naturally from, and is pertinent solely to, the ***Grail Blood***.

The ***Grail Code*** is the behavioral benchmark by which those of the ***Grail*** or ***Dragon Blood*** might be recognized, but it is not the code that efficiently orders the behavior of the ***Dragon Families*** in their dealings with those not of the ***Grail Blood***.

In '*Genesis of the Grail Kings*' **Gardner** commented on the love that ***the Anunnaki*** had for social order, which was echoed in ***Transylvania*** where vampires were said to have a reputation for pathological meticulousness and where nearby, **Dracula** ran his kingdom with the precision of a well oiled machine.

In the earlier days of ***the Anunnaki*** it is quite feasible to think that the collective empathic consciousness was particularly strong and we might see here the foundation of the ***Grail Code*** within the family of the Gods. Nevertheless, later there were still incidents of internecine strife.

However, where outsiders were concerned the ***Grail Code*** was only applied inasmuch as it related to maintaining order for the benefit of ***the Overlords***. Was there any question of *the Gods* being '*Nice*' to man or applying the ***Grail Code*** solely for man's benefit? There was a difference between the ***Grail Code*** for the ***Grail Blood*** and the ***Grail Code*** as it applied to man. One has to say that **Enlil** was right.

As the Blood devolved the capacity to apply empathy and co-operation appropriately weakened and this resulted formerly in family wars, and latterly in the kind of mental weakness, confusion and cultural misapplication which ended in the genocide of the race by Catholic opportunists.

These are pertinent lessons that ***the Bloodline*** would do well to learn if it is to rebuild itself again. It doesn't necessarily mean, because ***the Bloodline*** is at the end of the seventh millennium of its recorded history, that it is too late to turn back the clock. However, if ***the Dragon*** is to survive at all, it must learn the lessons of history, redefine its identity and strive to enrich its Blood once more. If it doesn't, it will die completely and the world will die with it.

An old saying from British folklore asserts that if the land loses its ***Elves***, the land dies. In two thousand years the face of the countryside in ***Britain*** and ***Ireland*** in particular has changed completely and there is now nowhere that man hasn't manipulated, exploited or raped. Compared to what it was, the land is indeed dead. Its spirit has almost gone.

The spirit of the land, its innate magic and mystery, has died because ***the Elves*** have all but died as well. The land consequently has no real voice anymore, no champions and no orators. Without the ***Dragon Queens*** and the El***ven Overlords*** to interpret the will of the Earth (and without ***Brehon Law*** to protect it from fools) man himself fails to hear the deeper message the land gives him.

The ancient forests of ***giant Oak*** and ***Beech*** are no more and the sacred places have been either built on in acts of blasphemy by greedy religion or torn up by the mindless merchant-class ancestors of today's mindless, middle-class consumer population.

In the theory of critical mass, sometimes called the "*99th Monkey Effect*" - based on **Jung**'s theory of *Collective Consciousness* working through **Rupert Sheldrake**'s '*Field of Morphic Resonance*' - the ***collective mind of a race*** creates a spiritual and cultural ***Archetype*** whose field of resonance can be felt in the material world. In the case of the ***Elves*** that ***Archetype*** was manifest in the Age of Magic. Simply put, when ***the Elves*** lived they created a field of magic around them whose power arose from the very sovereignty of the earth itself. However, when the Church killed the Elves, the ***Earth*** was silenced and the magic largely died.

Having assisted the *Church to kill off the Elves* man now stands alone against a being he uses with contempt for his own gain, but whose power against him is limitless and whose patience with him is not. The highest so-called authorities on Earth have finally realized what they have done and even they, the ***United Nations Organization***, say that the clock is ticking and time is running out.

The spirit of *True Romance and Magic* is all but dead. It diminished when the Church enslaved the spirit of mankind to a material, hateful god. Through scientific means, however, the ***Sundered Tribes*** can be reborn, the dragon blood can be restored and enriched, and the ***Dragon Queens*** and ***Elven Lords*** can rise once more to restore to people a sense of wonder, a sense of hope and an Age of Magic.

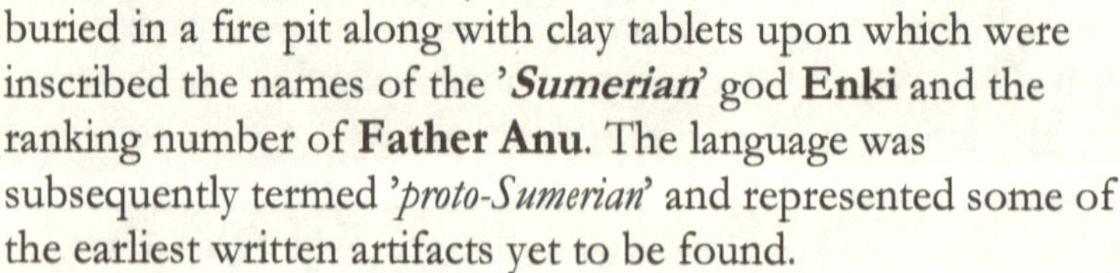

The Origins of Vampirism

Some of the earliest evidence of *Ritual Vampirism* comes from ***Tartaria*** in ***Transylvania*** and stems to the fifth millennium BC. Remains of a human body were found buried in a fire pit along with clay tablets upon which were inscribed the names of the '***Sumerian***' god **Enki** and the ranking number of **Father Anu**. The language was subsequently termed '*proto-Sumerian*' and represented some of the earliest written artifacts yet to be found.

The descendants of these early *vampires* were the ***Sacred Ubaid Race*** who, one millennium later, settled ***Mesopotamia*** and founded ***the Anunnaki*** religion of the Sumerians in 3500 BC. Their ***Transylvanian*** ancestors were **the Anunnaki Gods themselves**.

Various suggestions have been proposed in an attempt to

explain the origin and meaning of the word ***vampire***. One recent suggestion was that it was applied to a group of '*Watchers*' (*Seers - Derkesthai:* ***Dragons***) who had occupied a settlement near "***lake Van***", in ***Urartu*** - ***Armenia***. The original location - ***Greater Scythia*** - is faultless, the association is without error but the etymology is unresearched and the philology is completely absent.

Although that author's suggested identification between ***Watchers*** and ***Vampires*** is absolutely correct, the word ***vampire*** does not in any sense relate to their former geographical location or origin but, as we shall see, rather to the *vampires*' social and spiritual identity and status within a given cultural framework, which in this instance was ***Scythian***, overlaid on ***Celtic***.

In the journals of the 17th century cleric, the **Abbé Calmet**, the word *vampire* is transliterated into its most common, and its earlier, central European form which is spelt either ***oupire*** or ***oupere***. These spellings are common in literature of **Calmet**'s time and represent the original form of the word ***vampire***.

When the word migrated into *Latin* from *Anatolian* the ***u*** became a ***v*** because, as we will recall, there is no ***u*** character represented in the Latin alphabet. If there had been, then the Latinized western European construction of the word would have been *uampire*. By now bells should be ringing in the readers' heads as they remember hearing about ***wampires*** somewhere or another, perhaps in a humorous context.

The ***Romans*** didn't have a ***w*** and this letter appeared in *clerical Latin* during the medieval period as ***v v***, as presented in the ridiculous phrase *mortvvs svm*. The ***vv*** being used then as a <u>long vowel sound</u> to differentiate between ***u*** and ***v*** sounds which were both represented by the Latin ***v***.

So to recap, let's have a look at the linguistic migration so far: ***oupere - oupire - owpire - ovpire***. At this point we must remember that the word migrated from one language into another at a time when the most commonly used form of transmission was oral. This was bound to lead to confusion when the word was written down for the first time, as it has in numerous other instances.

By now we should be asking "If the word ***vampire*** was originally spelt ***oupire***, where on earth did the '***m***' come from?" All the author can say is thank heavens for the anomalous '***m***' because it is this component that really confirms the origin and meaning of the word ***vampire***, according to currently accepted scholarship.

Philologists would agree that the word ***vampire***, as ***oupere***, in its present form originated from the Turkish word ***uber***, which means '***witch***'. This would appear to present even more problems because in addition to an anomalous '***m***', we now also have a '***b***' to explain away! Nevertheless the author promises you that tenacity and perseverance will bring its own rewards, so be patient and do try and keep up.

Leaving the '***m***' aside for a moment, there would seem to be a serious linguistic problem in that ***oupere*** is spelt with a '***p***' and ***uber*** is spelt with a '***b***', which the reader might suspect would undermine the connection between both words. Especially as ***vampire*** or ***oupere*** is European and ***uber*** is Turkish and thus from a separate language group. However, this is not so.

As the Turkic-Uralic language is very different from Indo-European, it would appear that the word ***vampire*** in its original form is not Indo-European, but an Asiatic word that has changed in spelling and pronunciation during the passage of time and its migration northward.

It might then appear that the central Asian word for a ***witch*** - ***uber*** - would mean something entirely different to the European meaning of the word '***witch***' and would therefore bring with it an entirely different set of cultural and mythic associations. However, what the reader might not realize is that ***modern Turkey*** and its language is, like any other, an evolutionary compilation of historical, linguistic and cultural influences.

Prior to being named ***Turkey***, ***Asia Minor*** or ***Anatolia*** was the centre of the eastern Roman Empire of Byzantium. At the heart of Asia Minor, contemporary with ***Rome*** but originating from an earlier period still, was the vast region of ***Galatia*** at the heart of which was a region occupied in the Persian era by the ***Cimmerians of Scythia***, at a time when ***Galilee***, ***Gilead*** and ***Gaulatinis*** in northern Israel were Scythian territories named after their language.

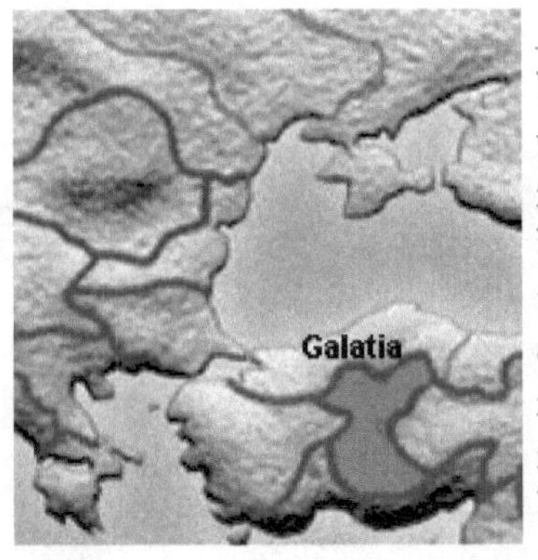

As ***Galatia*** spread northwards it bordered upon ***Phrygia*** and ***Troy*** and reached out further still to become ***Galati*** as it crossed the ***Bosphorus*** and encompassed ***Transylvania***. On its westward marches ***Galati*** assimilated both ***Bulgaria*** and ***Gaul***.

In consequence of this, a massive proportion of what is now called ***Turkey*** was in fact, along with most of Europe, a ***Gaelic*** or properly a Goidelic speaking, Scythian/Celtic civilization, comprising of independent tribal groups who spoke a number of *Gaelic dialects*, amongst which and most notably are what we now know as the so called '***P*' and '***Q*' or '***K*' Goidelic language variants.

The ***P*** and ***Q*** variants in *Brythonic-Cymric* (***Welsh***) and *Goidelic-Scotic* (***Irish Scots***), as an example, mean that the word '*son*' will be spelt ***map*** in Cymric and ***mac*** in Scotic. Furthermore there is a sub variant in this language group where '***P*' and '***B*' sounds also become interchangeable, as in the Welsh pen as in the mountain - *Penllithrig'y'wrach* - meaning "the *slippery hill of the witch*" in ***Snowdonia***, and the Scots ***ben*** as in ***Ben Nevis*** in Scotland - both of which mean '***head*' or '***peak*'. The ***Cymric language*** was originally Cimmerian or northern Scythian, whilst ***Scotic*** is a southern Scythian dialect.

The Galatian word ***uber*** is from the Scythian goidelic group whilst in Russia and Poland, which was influenced by the *Cimmerian* or Brythonic group, the same word for ***vampire*** is spelt ***upyr*** and ***upior*** respectively. There have been numerous ***Scythian migrations*** over the millennia and the Gaelic language has been carried across the Eurasian continent to influence the languages of many peoples. The ***Trojans*** who lived next door to the ***Galatians*** and were themselves ***Scythians*** moved to Italy and became ***the Latines***.

As we can see by this example, the ***b*** has consistently become a ***v*** and this is how we know that the word for a ***vampire uber***, is not a Turkish word at all but Gaelic or Galatian. Remember the anomalous '***m*' in *vampire*? Well it just so happens that in ***dialectic Gaelic*** the consonant group ***Mh*** is pronounced ***V***. The '***h*' became discarded over time and left the '***m*' in vampire where the '***u*' or '***v*' should be. If spelt literally vampire would be ***uavber***, ***uauber*** or ***uaupir***, which is the central European ***oupire*** or ***oupere***.

These variants stem from the *Sanskrit* ***upari*** (*Up-Ari* or *Up-*

Arya, meaning ***Over-Lord***) for which the *Greek* is ***uper*** - ***uper*** - which, as we have already seen, is a component of *super* in Latin. *Over* (*ME* - ***ouere***) began as a graphic variant of ***uuere*** which translates into the dynastic name ***Vere*** with the Latin ***V*** being interchangeable with the ***double U*** or hard Germanic ***W*** which became ***V*** - rendering ***Ver*** or ***Were***. This is pronounced as a soft ***F***, which we find in the ***Norse Yfari*** and the old English ***Uffara*** or ***Yffera***.

The Turkish, or properly *Galatian* word ***Uber***, meaning '***witch***' therefore linguistically corresponds to the foregoing variations found in *Gothic, German, Dutch, Norse English, Greek, Latin* and *Sanskrit*, where finally, as ***Upari***, we discover that originally ***Uber*** - ***Vampire*** - meant ***Overlord***. In the following paragraphs we shall investigate the cultural background behind the word '***witch***' as ***uber***, and discover that what holds true linguistically is supported by cultural and social evidence.

Contextually, when applied to an individual as a '***witch***', the word ***uber*** would suggest that the person referred to was in some way '***over***' or '***above***' others, as in the German *ubermensch* or *uberherren*. The Germanic languages, as with the others sampled here, are all Indo-European and the ***Sanskrit*** in particular, being of ***Aryan*** or ***Scythian*** origin is closest to the Galatian, and we shall see that the argument for ***overlordship*** is exactly the case.

From a cultural standpoint, we read the word '***witch***' and with it comes a large trolley of baggage that we have inherited from the popularly reinforced understanding of the word, influenced heavily by fairy stories and biased histories told from a protagonistic point of view. Today the specifically *Saxon word* '***witch***' tends to conjure up images of old hags prancing about on dark, spooky moors and cackling into cauldrons.

Witch is derived from the ***Saxon*** root word ***wicce*** (***feminine***) or ***wicca*** (***masculine***) and the Saxons used it to describe a class of persons whom they thought were inhabited by an *intelligence* or *spirit* - a ***daemon*** or ***genii*** - usually evil, because the Saxons took up catholicism pretty early on in their careers and were consequently biased.

Conversely, some people today would like us to believe, however, that '***witch***' meant a "*wise one*" and say that *witchcraft*, or in Saxon - ***wiccecraeft*** as they like to call it - means craft of the wise, failing completely to realize that the word ***wise*** in Saxon is ***wita***, not *wicca* or *wicce*.

Wicca is actually related to both '*wicker*' and '*Viking*' or *Wiking* as ***the Norse*** would pronounce it. In Russia the word *Vikhr* meaning *whirlwind*, is a title of the ***Zmei Dragons***, sons and daughters of **Zmei-Tiamat**. This confirms that the link between ***Sumaire, Zmei*** or ***Zumei*** and ***Sumeria*** was also known in ***Russia***, once a Viking province.

It also demonstrates that the ***Danish Vikings***, *witch lords*, were ***sons of the Dragon*** and the ***Scandinavian Tuadha d'Anu.*** In *Ireland* the ***Zmei Lord*** or ***Vikhr*** is known as the ***Dark King*** - ***the Whirlwind***, meaning he was *sumaire* or *vampire* and via ***Uber***, a *Witch Lord* or *Wicca.* As the ***Willow*** (*wicker*) bends and yields to the *whirlwind* so the *witch* (*wicca*) yields to the ***Sumaire***, the ancient vampire legacy within him or her, a legacy that is awoken during the ***Mass of the Phoenix***, when the primordial ancestors rise from the dead to take possession of the witch's soul!

Wicca, derived from the same Saxon word as *Willow*, means to "*bend or yield*" ones spirit to that of a daemon (Greek, meaning ***praeter human*** intelligence or inspiration), giving the christian idea of possession, though erroneously. The ***witch*** was indeed possessed by a ***daemon*** and that *daemon* was certainly ***praeter-human*** and not of this world.

Any spirit, including the ***archangels***, conjured by the ***witch*** or ***magician*** (the distinction, like that between pagan and christian, is fallacious), as in ceremonial magic, was actually the ancestor (antecessor) of the witch her or himself. It was a denizen of the ancient dragon itself - but it was carried in the ***witch's blood*** which, the purer it was through unbroken descent from ***the Dragons***, the stronger would be the return of the ancestors within. The Stronger the blood the stronger the invocation and the more complete the possession. With Mixed blood there was weak inspiration and little discernible presence. "*The Blood is the Life*".

The ***witch*** was possessed by this ***daemon***, because the witch by descent and heredity was that daemon itself. It was his or her genetic inheritance and part of his or her racial consciousness, and to that the ***witch*** would yield, when occasion necessitated, placing the witch and the words *wicce* or *wicca* firmly in the tradition of the trance seer (***derkesthai***), a practice rooted in Scythian shamanic culture.

This is confirmed in the word genius, meaning inborn intellect or inspiration. Closely related to this word is genie, meaning a spirit, as in genius loci - 'a spirit of place'. In Arabic ***the jinni*** is a spirit of fire or inspiration. The Latin *genius*, in Greek, is a *daemon* or inspiring intelligence and the root Latin ***gens*** signifies birth, origin and especially blood. The ***daemon*** or ***genius*** of the ***Dragons*** was inherited through the blood. ***Witches*** are born, not made by silly playacting initiation rituals.

A ***seer*** in *Gaelic* was called a ***Merlin*** and in the tripartite Aryan-Scythian caste system which overlaid that of their clients, the deeply religious ***Celts***, the Merlin was a Druid Prince. Either side of the Druidic caste were the castes of the warrior aristocrats and the craftsmen and although they all tended to behave as equals in this king tribe system, the druids were senior in rank.

Each caste attended to their allotted tasks and the study, teaching and practice of shamanism and magic were strictly the province of the ***Druids*** and ***Druidesses***, forming part of a vast storehouse of knowledge and experience in the crafts and sciences, and in statesmanship and lore.

The ***Druids*** were responsible for bringing into being gods for the ***Celts*** to worship and though they themselves were not religious, scholars agree that ***Druidism*** was the "*religion*" of the ***Celtic world***. So we can see that although the ***Celts*** had their own caste system with their own burgh kings or chieftains, above them were the ***Scythian kings***, and above the Scythian kings were the ***Elven Druids***, the Priest Kings who stood above all others, the ***ultimate Overlords of Eurasia***.

In the Scandinavian countries the *craft* or ability to gain *wisdom* or *power* (Sanskrit - ***Siddhi***) by yielding to *daemons* or *intelligences* (ancestral god spirits which were part of the practitioners' own genetic inheritance and make-up) through trance or dream states was considered to be ***shamanic*** and was called ***Siddir***, whilst those who practiced this art were themselves called ***Siddirs***. The ***Siddir*** knotted together the web of dreams and loosened those knots to release power and knowledge.

In other words they brought together and spoke or gesticulated a series of mnemonics that would trigger off precontrived, imprinted states of consciousness that acted as doorways into deeper seats of consciousness. In *Gaelic Scythian* this ability and the name corresponding to it was called the ***Sidhe***, a term used to describe and name the Irish fairies, the ***Tuadha d'Anu*** or ***Tuatha de Danaan*** as they were later called, a race of priest kings or druid princes.

The ***Web of Dreams*** relates to both the *witches'* knotted ball and the ***Web of Wyrd*** or ***Fate*** (*fata-fairy*) and in the Scythian and Celtic cosmology, the power associated with it was thought to reside in the *Otherworld*, the realm of the gods (druidic ancestors) which was entered via trance or dream states, achieved whilst the *druid* or *druidess* occupied the fairy hills, the mortuary raths where the forefathers were buried.

The ***witch***, as a ***seer*** or ***Merlin*** in Scythian culture and society, consequently belonged to an exclusive genome within a distinct holy and royal caste of overlords, which is reflected in the Gaelic word for a *witch* - ***Druidhe*** - which is pronounced ***Drui*** and is related to ***Draoi*** and ***Dracoi***, meaning a dragon. ***Drui*** itself means ***Man*** (or ***Woman***) ***of the Tree*** (not *men of the oaks*, as some have suggested) and is also related to the Sanskrit ***dru***, meaning ***to run***. This is associated with the ritual of running the labyrinth, with which we will deal in due course.

Therefore in ***Galatia***, which had its own druids and was the site of ***the Nemeton***, the largest regular gathering of druids in Europe, the term for a ***witch*** was ***Uber*** meaning ***Overlord***, whilst in the Gaelic west the term for a ***witch*** was ***Druidhe*** which meant the same as ***Uber*** - An ***Overlord***.

In summary ***vampire*** in its earlier form - ***oupire*** - derives ultimately from the *Galatian* ***Uber***, which itself is derived from the *Aryan* ***Upari*** and linguistically and contextually the ***Vampire*** - the ***witch*** or ***druid*** - was a ***Scythian High Queen*** or ***King:*** an Overlord.

It is interesting to note in this context that when he compiled his journals in the 17th century **Calmet**, who had traveled extensively throughout the Austrian empire as an official *vampire investigator* accompanying imperial officers and soldiers, wrote that he had found no evidence whatsoever to support any notion that *vampirism* was either a supernatural phenomenon committed by *praeter-natural beings* - which he utterly refutes - or that it ever occurred in any form, either as a cult or in any isolated incidents, amongst the lower strata of society.

Without exception the enlightened **Abbé** was able to discover perfectly ordinary explanations for the incidents he had investigated, which in his day was quite remarkable, as ***the Church*** in past times had actively promoted vampire paranoia.

As **Professor Margaret Murray** discovered herself, *vampirism* was not the prerogative of the merchant or peasant classes, but was a cultic observance confined to the environs of the nobility, often as an adjunct to rites of the ***Noble and Royal Witch Covens of Scotland***.

We can say with confidence then that real vampirism was indulged in by living beings who, unerringly, were members of the pre-christian and anti-christian high nobility and royalty. The most famous vampire stories, those of **Dracula**, **Bathory** and **de Rais**, support this conclusion. The historical evidence therefore supports the etymological origin of the word '***vampire***' - ***An Overlord***.

Vampirism, up until the early 1700's, by which time it had been in decline for several centuries, was not merely or solely the practice of a few isolated, *high-born opportunists* seeking some form of personal advantage or satisfying private perversions. *Vampirism* took two forms and the ***bloodline descendants*** of the ancient vampire lords had, in ***Britain***, set the practice within an overall, multi-faceted social and cultural framework, stemming from the Iron-Age, that never gets an airing in the Gothic novel.

Vampires weren't just *vampires*, as the penny dreadful would have us believe, they were individuals and families who used the practice to achieve specific aims and thereby fulfill those specific social obligations which, since the ***Scythian-Celtic period*** of the ***High Dragon Kings***, were equated with their rank and position as leaders and overseers.

The Scythians

Throughout this discourse it must be borne in mind that when we speak of the ***Scythians*** as '***fairies***', '***dragons***', '***vampires***' or '***elves***', we are not talking about either the client races of the Scythians, or the ordinary Scythian citizenry, but of '***Royal Scythians***'.

As we have discovered, the ***vampire*** - as a "***witch***" - belonged by genetic inheritance, to a distinct royal caste in ***Scythian-Celtic society***, that of the priest-king or priestess-queen, the prince and princess-druids who had evolved very early on in human social history and who belonged to a Eurasian-wide hereditary priestly community which had originated with the ***Scythian-Aryans.*** The name ***Scythian*** was originally spelt ***Sithian*** in 16th century England, and it is from this tribal name that we obtain the word ***scythe***, denoting a curved bladed agricultural tool, so named because of its similarity in shape to the Scythian sword.

The ***Scythians*** weren't however named after their use of a curved sword. The name ***Sithian*** is related to a group of words that appear in Indo-European languages which are found as far apart as ***Eire*** and ***Northern India***, indicating that they had a common ***Aryan*** origin in ***Scythia***. These include - ***Sithia, Sidhe, Siddir*** and ***Siddhi***.

In *Cymric* '***dd***' is pronounced '***th***', whilst in *Irish* and *Scots* the '***th***' is spelt dialectically '***dh***' whilst the '***s***' beginning a word is pronounced '***sh***'. As we have related, the ***Siddir*** in *Danish society* were ***witches*** who practiced the art of knot tying and loosening.

These ***Siddir*** were directly related to the ***mythic Norns***, the ***Mori*** or ***Fates*** who were said to be responsible for the fate of mankind by the patterns that they wove in the way that they tied and loosened the knots of the ***Web of Wyrd***. The ***Siddirs***, as well as being ***seers***, could control such power as to influence the outcome of human affairs and in this respect their name reflects their abilities which, in ***India***, were called the ***Siddhis***, a word used to describe the powers of the Yogi who had self-realized.

The curious ***Irish*** word - ***Sidhe*** - pronounced '***shee***', '***sheeth***' or '***sheeth-ay***', attributed to the fairies and meaning '*powers*', is therefore identical to ***Siddir*** (*sheeth-eer*) and ***Siddhi*** (*sheeth-ee*) and is derived therefore, from the people of the powers - the ***Scythians*** or ***Sidheans*** (*sheethee-ans*). In ***Scotland*** the royal fairies were called the ***Seelie*** or ***Sheelie*** and their princesses were related to the sculpted ***Sheelagh Na Gigs*** over church doorways, who do NOT depict ancient goddesses of fertility, but were the royal Grail Maidens of the Elven kings and queens.

The ***Sheelagh na Gigs*** were goddesses of sovereignty and transcendence, and their place over the doorways of churches, many of which were built on the sites of ancient sacred groves, indicated that in entering these buildings one was entering through the vulva of the maiden into the otherworld, the ***realm of Elphame*** and the ***Kingdom of Heaven***.

They were permitted above church doorways because the early church itself wanted to be identified with the old ways, firstly because it was in fact, at least in the beginning, part of the old ways and later, when catholicism took over, the ***Sheelaghs*** remained in place - in order to attract and convert "*pagans*".

Along with the *Irish* ***Sidhe***, the ***Seelie*** and the ***Seelie Court of Scotland*** had a distinctly royal origin in the ***Tuadha d'Anu*** who when asked, like their *Pictish* descendants in *Scotland*, said of themselves that they were ***Scythian***, as **Canon Beck** himself has insisted.

Some people tend to think that the word ***sidhe*** means a hill and therefore that the ***Irish Danaan***, as the ***Sidhe***, inherited this name as a consequence of fleeing into the hills after their defeat by the ***Milesians***. As we can see this is not so and the *fairy* "*hills*", where the ***Aes Dan*** or ***Danaan***, the gods of the Irish, were said to live, weren't all *Sidhe hills*.

These - the ***power hills*** - were the sacred temple-mortuary raths and barrows, the *creachaires* or *tomb-sepulchers*, that the ***Danaan priest-kings*** were wont to ritually occupy for millennia before moving to ***Eire***, and centuries before their Iberian kinsmen, the ***Milesians***, came looking for a fight. The ***Sidhe***, the ***Fairies***, were the 'controllers of the fate of mankind' and so named in remembrance of, and in identification with, their ancient ***Anunnaki*** (***Anunnagi***) ***ancestors***.

In pre-christian history, although some practiced agriculture for a while, according to **Murray-Hall M.A.** they abandoned it for their traditional way of life and many of the ***Scythian clans*** remained solitary and insular nomadic pastoralists - horse lords who ranged across large tracts of Europe and Asia for centuries. Others opted late for a more settled existence and mixed settled agriculture with pastorialism, a system that can be found in both ***Takla Makan***, where they built fine cities, and in Ireland, where they became know as the trooping fairies.

In general they were usually tall, pale skinned, with golden red hair and green eyes, unlike the ***Celts***, who were stocky and squat, with ruddy complexions and dark hair, and practiced settled agriculture from a very early period.

The recent and rather unfortunate propagandist depiction of ***the Aryan*** (***Scythian***) as a tall, ruddy complexioned blonde racist yeoman-farmer-warrior-god has no basis in truth. In pre-christian history an ***Aryan*** was a High King, a warrior was a warrior and a farmer was a farmer and ne'er the three e'er met. The real *Aryans* of fact were red haired and green eyed, their hired military help, derived from their
lower ***Ksatriya caste*** who were not Aryan were, sometimes, blonde and blue eyed.

The ***Aryan royal families*** didn't intermarry with other tribes or castes but, with the development by many of their clans of settled city-states such as ***Scythopolis*** (30 AD, on the banks of the *River Jordan* just south of *Galilee*) nevertheless they became urban multi-racialists and appreciated cultural diversity.

The ***Aryan Hittites*** in particular were close allies of ***the Jews*** whose Draconian royal family, the ***House of David***, made the ***Israelites***, in a cultural sense, an early Aryan nation, and the ***Scythians*** and the ***Aryan Scythian Gaels*** had numerous settlements either in or adjacent to ***Israel*** and ***Judea***.

The comparatively early use of the horse and of horse related technology separated the ***Aryans*** from the other tribes that occupied the middle-east and Eurasia.
In ***Mittani***, ***Mesopotamia***, ***Akkad*** and ***Anatolia*** the ***Hurrians*** (whom in the 1920's **B. Hrozny** described as the *earliest Hindus*) were the absolute ***Overlords*** and their supremacy is credited to their early use, like the ***Kurgans***, of horse-drawn chariots.

The *Hur* syllable in *Hurrian* has been asserted by scholars, including **G. Contenau** (*'La Civilisation des Hittites et des Hurrites de Mittani'*) to be ***Har*** or ***Ar***, meaning that the ***Hurrians***, like the ***Scythians*** were Aryans with an Aryan Vedic royal-sacral family of gods.

These they bestowed upon the ***Hittites*** whose culture they dominated, (as the ***Hurrian*** or ***Aryan Mittani*** did in ***Mesopotamia***) and the ***Hittites***, in turn, provided the ***Greeks*** with these red-gold haired gods, including ***Zeus*** or ***Dyas Pater*** - the ***Jewish Jehovah***, whose ancient symbol, shared with the sacred dynasty as a whole was - ironically - the swastika.

The early "***Scythians***", the people of the powers, occupied a region spanning ***The Balkans, Transylvania, Carpathia,*** the ***Ukraine*** and later, ***Siberia*** and ***Takla Makan*** where the ***Tocharians***, as ***the Elves*** were mistakenly called by early linguists, spoke a ritual language which is now called *Tocharian A* but which originated in ***Thrace*** in 1800 BC and thus had connections with the ***Fir Bolg*** and consequently with the ***Tuadha d'Anu*** as a whole, who began migrating from Central Europe to Ireland at that period.

Over the centuries, from 5000 BC onwards, the ***Scythians*** had also migrated into the middle-east and had provided ruling families for many tribes and nations along and beyond the eastern Mediterranean coast.

In the *'Annals of Irish History'* the ***Scythian 'Tuadha d'Anu'*** who had migrated farther still, to the islands of the north, were described as a tribe of deific queens, kings, princes and lords and were noted for having ***druids*** of their own. In ***Japan***'s North islands there lives a shamanic tribe called ***the Ainu*** whose early writing style has been identified as being ***Gaelic Ogham!***

As a noble tribe, a sect of the Aryan peoples who, during various migrations, had also wandered east several centuries before the ***d'Anu*** displacement and their reputed first journey to ***Eire*** in 1500 BC, the *Aryan-Scythian* horse lords, traveling south-east via Persia (Iran) from 1800 BC onwards, had entered the ***Indus Valley*** and intermingled with the Dravidian population.

This migration was to lands already formerly under ***Sumerian*** and consequently ***Ubaid*** control. The westward migration of the ***Scythians*** or ***Sidheans*** also included these very same ***Dravidians*** who, so British traditions state, were the messengers and *summoners* or *'fetches'* of the ***Merlins.***

These curious and delightful beings were also known as *brownies*, for obvious reasons and adopted the habit of body tattooing in emulation of their ***Scythian lords***, who in Britain and Ireland were known as ***the Pixies***, which is a name derived from ***Pict-Sidhes*** or painted fairies.

The confusion which arises when ***the Picts*** are described as being short and brown may be clarified when we remember that the Scythian Caste System consisted of three closely interknit, co-operating races, whose traditions and practices would inevitably become, to a certain extent, common to all within the system by a natural process of social osmosis.

From this encounter arose the eastern branch of the ***Aryan***, ***Vedic "Hindu" religion***, with its *druids* or *magi* - the ***Brahmins*** - and a pantheon of gods who were virtually identical with the Sumerian, the Egyptian, the Hittite, The Irish, the Gaulish, the Danish and the Greek, all of which stem from this early family of ***Elven goddess-queens and god-kings*** whose first home was to be found in ***The***

Balkans*, *Transylvania*, *Carpathia and the ***Caucasus*** regions of Greater and Little Scythia.

Within the ***Brahmin caste*** special Tantric rites were and still are studied and practised. Evidence suggests that these ancient rites were brought to India from ***Sumeria***. This accords with the assertion that ***Qabalah*** itself originated there also and the author has long maintained that ***Tantra***, particularly the Kaula Vama Marg and Esoteric Qabalism are simply variations of each other. The *Tree of Life symbol* and its hidden meanings appears in Druidism and given the evidence to date, we can confidently say that ***Tantra*** and ***Qabalah*** are descended from ancient ***Ubaid Druidic philosophy***.

The ***right hand path*** version of Hindu and Buddhist Tantra concerns itself with studying and practicing sexual rites that one might find associated with the ***Kama Sutra***. This form of ***Tantra*** promotes penetrative intercourse as a method of changing consciousness and has attached to it various commentaries on right-living and right-thinking. This was thought by some Indian scholars to have originated with those who were depicted by one Indian scholar as the animistically minded, sex mad weasels, the ***Dravidians***. The ***left hand path*** however is somewhat different.

This discipline can be found in both *Hinduism* and *Buddhism* and concerns itself with the practice of vampirism. This alone is sufficient evidence to allow one to ascertain that the '***Black***' or ***Left Hand*** or ***Kaula Path*** preceded the later ***right hand path*** which, though joyously tactile and self indulgent to begin with, appears many centuries later to have been somewhat sanitized for public consumption. The yogic disciplines associated with the ***Kaula Path***, originating with ***the Scythians***, are intended to lead the practitioner to what one might call 'union with godhead'.

This psychological condition is manifest in mystical christianity as being the perception by the devotee of 'the kingdom of heaven'. That few christians ever achieve such a state is not to be wondered at, as christianity is also a royal blood tradition, exactly like its brother and sister, ***Druidism*** and ***Witchcraft***.

Many christians haven't got a clue about this aspect of **Jesus**' teaching and are in any case not encouraged to explore its possibilities because such union leads to physical and psychological freedom, the very last thing that the established churches wish to encourage in the masses, even though **Jesus** himself preached it.

Union with *Godhead*, dwelling in *Elphame*, realization of the *Buddha* or whatever one likes to call it is accompanied by a range of powers which were catalogued by the amazing Edwardian lady explorer **Alexandra David Niel**, who witnessed the performance of these remarkable powers or ***Siddhis*** by Buddhist monks in *Nepal* and *Tibet*, whose ritual and philosophy owed much to the indigenous religion ***Bon-Po*** which ethically followed the same path as ***Kaula Vama Marg***.

In the west we call it *magic* but, as we have seen, it was also known as ***the Sidhe. Kaula Tantra*** is dedicated to the ***Goddess Kali*** who is associated with both creation and destruction in the Hindu pantheon. ***Kali*** is a lunar deity who, like ***Tantra*** itself, moved east from ***Sumeria***. As a moon goddess she is associated particularly with moon blood and the essences of the female organs of generation.

So what can we say of the nascence of ***Vampirism*** so far? Principally that it originated, not surprisingly, in ***Transylvania*** and the Central Eurasian region known as ***Scythia*** and that its practitioners were of a distinct race, the ***Elves***, the high goddess-queens and god-kings of the ***Arya*** or ***Aesir***.

Vampirism was the central feature of a philosophy based on endocrinology, rather than occult mumbo-jumbo and used the consumption of female blood and mumae to enhance awareness and lead the practitioner to union with godhead.

The powers accompanying such an elevated state of consciousness were called the ***sidhe*** or ***siddhi*** and were, with *vampirism*, the foundation of the cults of ***Druidism, Tantric Kaula Yoga, Qabalism, Alchemy, Rosicrucianism*** and ***Witchcraft.***

Kali, like all the ***Ubaid Deities*** was a flesh and blood being. She, **Kalimaath** or **Kali Marg**, was a daughter of **Lilith** and **Samael**, son of **Anu**, who appears in the Aryan pantheon as **Ahura Mazda** and in ***Iran*** as the *Medean god* **Zoroaster. Anu** himself was the god who gave his name to the ***Tuatha de Danaan*** and as **Sitchin** has suggested the definition of the word ***god*** itself is '***descended of Anu***'.

Based on the spelling '***Tuatha de Danaan***', some have suggested that these Irish elven folk derived their name from an Irish mother goddess named **Dana**. If they had checked the earlier spelling - ***Tuadha d'Anu*** (***Tribe of Anu***) - they would have discovered that the ***Scythian Sidhe*** were the sons and daughters of **Anu** and the ***Ubaid*** gods and goddesses.

To recap then we have a clear connection between the words ***siddhi*** and ***sidhe*** both of which originate from a ***Scythian*** or earlier proto-Aryan-Ubaid root. The ***Scythians***, as the Aryans of Persia and Asia provided the people then with their religious and social structures and mores and spread their wisdom and overlordship, mostly by invitation from prospective client tribes, throughout Britain and Europe.

The ***Scythian Aryans***, as the '***Danaan***' settled in ***Eire*** and ***Scotland*** whilst in ***Wales*** they were known as the House of Don (*Dan*) or the House of Gwynnedd. This house sired the line of **Llewelyn Princes**, whilst in ***Scandinavia*** the Danaan became the Danes or Vikings and produced a junior cousin line - the ***Svei*** or ***Swedes*** - from which descended the ***Ruotsi clan*** who founded ***Russia***. In ***Denmark*** the ***Sidhe*** was present as the ***Siddir***, a class of seer or witch who were later separated from the ***Godthi*** or ***Gothi***, the Danish Druids.

The ***Scythian Danaan*** in ***Eire***, as in the rest of Europe, were a race apart, a ruling caste within which, like the original race of the Gods from whom they descended, there were further caste classifications.

In ***Denmark*** these were later named the ***Jarl***, ***Carl*** and ***Thrall*** castes whilst in Eire they were broadly speaking the Druids, the Kings and the Warrior Smiths. In ***India*** they are still defined as the Brahmins, the Ksatriyas and the Sudras.

The original castes of the Gods were:

a) **The common gods – the gods of Earth**
The first class were what we might call "jobbing gods," the powers of field, forest and hearth who in time became the *genii loci* or pagan spirits, the local deities of place and craft.

b) **The gods of Heaven and Earth**
The second class were the great intermediaries — the Titans, the Repha'im, the Morrígna, the Angels and the Valkyries — who moved between the mortal and the divine, interceding between man and the transcendent powers. They were the messengers and battle-hosts, those who stood at the threshold of Heaven and Earth.

c) **The transcendent gods – the gods of Heaven**

The third class were the divine ancestors themselves, the sovereign and eternal ones, the true gods of Heaven. These were the All-Fathers and Sky-Mothers, the primeval creators, worshipped not as jobbing nature spirits but as the ultimate sources of law, sovereignty and order, from whom the ruling caste of kings and priests claimed descent.

The first class were what we might call jobbing gods who became the ***genii locus*** or ***pagan spirits***. The second class - the ***gods of Heaven and Earth*** - were the *Titans*, the *Repha'im* and *Morrighans*, the *Angels* and *Valkyries* who interceded between the transcended gods, the divine ancestors - the gods of Heaven - and man.

Heaven was the otherworld, not a place up in the stars, but a ***state of being*** which was adjacent to our own dimension - called sometimes the mirror-world, most competently described, more than once, in the *Mabinogion* - which could be freely entered and left by the gods of Heaven and Earth, the Portal Guardians. In this place, also known as *Elphame, Hades, Hel, Caer Glas* and *Tir Na n'og* there dwelt the essences of the previous gods of Heaven and Earth who had passed on to become the transcended ones, the '*antecessors*' or ancestors of the later ***witches***.

By dwelling in tombs the gods of Heaven and Earth, the ***Danaan Queens*** and ***Kings***, made contact with their ancestor Gods and passed their wisdom and edicts on to mankind. Today we might call this process invocation.

These gods are carried in the blood and by invocation, we bring their qualities and identities to the forefront of conscious being and give them voice. These druidic gods and goddesses of

Heaven and Earth were effectively the highest overlords on Earth, the ***elven*** rulers of the human kings and queens who ruled beneath them.

Often we find mention of the fairy blood in the medieval era in connection with the ruling nobility of the time. We might then be tempted to come to the logical conclusion that *all nobility and royalty* was thus of Fairy origin. However this is simply ***not the case***. Despite the usurpation of the original fairy families by the church sponsored new nobility, the previous kingly and noble dynasties were essentially human anyway.

The ***fairy blood*** at that time, the dark ages and the medieval period, was carried by the descendants of the ***Archdruidic dynasties*** who formerly ruled over the contemporary Celtic and Eurasian kings and lords, it was not carried by any or all of the royal or noble families of the time simply because they were the heads of their castes, because over such class distinctions were positioned additionally, the castes of ***the elven god-kings*** themselves.

The gods of Heaven and Earth - the ***Archdruidic caste*** - dwelt in ***Barrows*** and ***Bergs*** which in Eire were called ***Raths***, meaning a '*royal seat*'. These ***Raths*** were the holy shrines and sepulchres built by the ***Danaan*** - the original *Gods of Ireland* according to the '*Annals of Irish History*' - to house the mortal remains of their ancestors and act as royal palaces for the Portal Guardians. In specific cases these Gods are named, and we learn, for instance, that ***Newgrange*** was the shrine occupied by Nuadha and later Oengus.

The devotional and holy nature of these places has led some scholars and commentators to believe that, because they were tombs and temples, then those said to occupy them must be purely spiritual entities, gods of an ethereal nature. Originally nothing could have been farther from the truth.

Both ***Nuadha*** and ***Oengus*** were kings of the Danaan and contemporary descriptions of them and their kin leave us with the picture of the ***Danaan*** as a race of people with prodigious and very earthly appetites.

From their kinsmen in ***Siberia*** we know that, by our dubious standards, they were complete junkies and imbibed any form of drug they could get hold of. These would have included cannabis and cocaine, prevalent in ***Egypt*** and the ***Levant*** at the time, as well as the drugs classically associated with the ***druids*** and the ***elves*** such as *Amanita Muscaria* and *Psylocybin*, the fairy mushrooms of children's picture books everywhere.

The ***Danaan*** were hardened drinkers and unscrupulous womanizers, whilst accounts of their princesses relate that they often mated in public with the highest nobles of their clan, to prove or reiterate their social standing to onlookers. (**Heroditus**: *The Histories*).

Counterbalancing this view of them, born of our own hypocritical conditioning, the ***Danaan***, whether in ***Eire*** or mainland ***Europe*** or ***Asia***, were the finest smiths, jewellers, poets and musicians of their time, they were the Lords of fearless warriors and gifted horsemen and, despite what we might think of the foregoing, they were a righteous, meticulous people who maintained standards of conduct in areas of their social life where such standards were considered essential for the harmonious order of society.

Great emphasis was laid upon honesty and truth in one's words and one's dealings, the maintenance and conservation of the natural environment was paramount, and infractions, such as the cutting of trees, could mean death. Emphasis was also laid on hospitality and courtly behavior to one's peers or guests, the honoring of one's ancestors and heroes, and the maintenance of extended family ties through fostering.

They weren't bothered about the petty morality we imbue our sexual behavior with but would kill a man for breaking his word or lying. They were an heroic people and, compared with us today, a far more moral race whose standards of conduct, not invested or centered on our kind of childish taboos - but placed where it matters - puts us to shame.

They were a race centered on their spirituality which itself was centered on gnosis and transcendent consciousness. This made them, like their later ***royal Viking*** cousins, a fearless people much loved and also much feared in turns, by all who knew them, whether in Eurasia or the British islands.

In about 500bc the ***Milesians*** entered ***Ireland*** from ***Iberia***. Having defeated the ***Danaan*** tribes they put many of them to flight. It was during this period that the ***Danaan*** became known as the Daouine Sidhe - the people of the hills - an erroneous use of the word *sidhe*.

One group, the tribe of the Danaan king of Ulster, ***Bruidhne*** (mistakenly called *Cruithne* by the Romans), fled to ***Caledonia*** where they became known as the remnant of ***Cruithne*** or the '*Cruithainn*'.

Other ***Danaan*** clans fled to ***Wales*** and the south west of mainland ***Britain***. Several centuries later, when the Romans were unfortunate enough to encounter them in ***Scotland***, they referred to these *Danaan* as '***Picts***' and it is this word that has adapted itself to become one of the names we use to describe the elven peoples - the ***pixies*** - or properly the ***Pict-Sidhes*** as we have already seen.

These being also came to be known as the ***Leprachauns*** and the etymology of this word, though thought to mean '*small-*

bodied' actually means '***scaly-bodied'*** from the Latin word *lepra* as in *leprosy* - scaly skinned.

The scaliness referred to was derived from the ***fish*** -scale style of armour which was common to the ***draconian Dacians***, the ***Zmei***, the ***Danes*** and the ***Danaan***, all of whom originated in the region now known as *Greater Scythia.*

The scaly, twin-pronged tail of the wouivre or mermaid was also derived from the use, by ***grail maidens***, of ***fish-scale plated leggings***. When worn with the swan's or raven's feather cloaks, we have the classical image of the ***Harpie***, reproduced in medieval depictions of Melusine.

Pict or ***Pictish*** means '***painted'*** and the ***Danaan*** earned this appellation by virtue of their use of tattoos or woad to decorate their bodies with totemic or magical markings, the favorite being the labyrinth or spiral whorl.

The ancestors of the ***Irish Danaan*** - the ***Ubaid Danaan*** - had been using tattoos and woad since 4000 BC and examples of it can also be found in depictions of the Egyptian god ***Osiris*** or ***Asher*** as he is also known, and in the depictions of the Hindu gods ***Vishnu*** and ***Siva***. ***Kali*** herself was also known as ***Kali Azura*** - the Blue Kali.

The spiral or whorl - the labyrinth - is the subject of a later essay in which it and its painted or carved symbol, lie at the centre of ***vampire*** and ***elven tradition***. The spiral can be found carved into the rock at ***Newgrange*** in ***Ireland*** and also featured as a sacred design associated with the dwellings of the related ***Kassite Danaan*** clans who migrated to Britain.

In the Gaelic language we find two words specifically defining '***vampires'***. The first - ***Creachaire*** - means a sepulchre, a tomb, a shrine and a temple, indicating that the character we later become familiar with as the "***vampire***" of Gothic legend was in fact a "dweller in the tombs", a druidic priest-king or priestess-queen - an ***Uber*** or ***Witch Overlord.***

In Eurasia, particularly in the permafrost of ***Siberia*** and the arid wastes of ***Takla Makan*** in ***China***, the mummified bodies of ***Scythian Chieftains*** and ***Shamankas*** or ***Priestess queens*** have been found. In ***Siberia*** the frozen remains of a male were unearthed. He had been tattooed with animal designs reminiscent of the totem ***Pictish*** salmon often found carved on stones in ***Scotland.***

In the same region a ***shamanka*** had been unearthed who had been tattooed with the spiral labyrinth design. She, like her counterpart in ***Takla Makan***, wore the conical headress of ***the Anunnaki*** gods of ***Sumeria*** that is also associated with medieval witchcraft. This same headress is depicted in bas-relief on the walls of the palace of Darius as being worn by those ***Scythians*** who brought him gifts in 500 BC.

The ***Takla Makan*** mummy, excavated by the Chinese in the 1960's had red-gold hair and was buried adjacent to a cache of tartan plaid cloth and spiral painted pottery, similar to that found at ***Al'Ubaid*** in ***Syria.*** In the same region caves have been discovered where the walls are painted with devotional Buddhist pictures featuring the ***Tocharians***, as they are known, conversing with **Buddha**.

Geoffrey Ashe states that the western ***Druids*** were interviewed by **Buddha** who claimed that they, the ***Druids***, had established ***Shangri-La*** in the west. This should give the reader some hint as to the general thrust of druidic philosophy and of the hidden nature of that promoted by **Jesus**, whom **St Columbus** clearly stated was also a druid and magus himself.

Chapter Three

The Thousand Year Elven Holocaust

Part 1

The study of history is as much the study of etymology as it is the study and interpretation of actual events. Both are often a daunting task because ultimately history is always written by the victors and the meaning of language and the significance of historical events are invariably decided by those whose hands have taken a firm hold of the tiller that steers society's ship.

The word '***fairy***' as we have come to understand it from our educators (or deceivers) suggests one of a variety of mythic or imaginary beings whose shape, size, habitat and customs differ according to geography and ethnic or aboriginal folk tradition. Lately a ***fairy*** has come to mean a homosexual as well.

A ***real fairy***, who couldn't give a toss about anyone's sexual orientation, "it's all bread and bread after all", whilst dismissing the latter definition entirely, would nevertheless take extreme exception to the former definition for the following reason. Next to the Jews, no race in history has suffered more brutality and racial prejudice than ***the Elves***.

For over a thousand years the church initiated a consistent policy of genocide that was and still is unrivalled in human history in terms of its relentlessness, violence and hatred. The author uses the word genocide and in 1944 **Raphael Lemkin** formulated the term to define,

> "an attempt at the destruction of the national group as an entity, and the actions involved are directed at individuals, not in their individual capacity but as members of a national group".

The *United Nations* elaborate by saying that genocide includes "the systematic moral debasement of a group, people or nation". The Jews have suffered just this except in one particular respect. If you were asked your race or nationality today and you replied "Jewish" no one would think twice about it.

However, **Mr Green** or **Miss Leibowitz** if instead, after replying "*Jewish*", the listener burst into fits of laughter and replied "Don't be such a lunatic, Jews don't exist, they're just a myth", how would you feel then? Isn't that what genocide or ethnic cleansing is all about, eradicating all trace of a culture from the human consciousness? This is what has happened to ***the Fairy Race***.

Certainly the Germans tried it with the Jews and if they had been given the time the Church has had to achieve what they have achieved, no doubt in a thousand years from now the Jews would have also become a myth. But this has already happened to the Fairies. Little trace of their culture or identity exists outside a handful of the old families or beyond the covers of sanitized story books for children, or tomes on rustic folk tradition, in which hints of the old lore still remain hidden.

Mr Green and **Miss Leibowitz** can go about their business in relative freedom and can be openly proud of their nationality and their cultural heritage. For a thousand years ***the fairies*** have had to conceal their identities and live in hiding for fear of being torn to shreds or burnt alive. For a thousand years it has been a crime to be of the elven race, and you may be surprised to learn that it still is.

Today, whilst the Jews, by the Grace of God, enjoy the acceptance of their race won through the backlash of public opinion against the Nazi Holocaust, the ***Thousand Year Elven Holocaust*** has been forgotten and still the fairies have to remain in hiding contemporarily for fear of ridicule and ostracisation.

In 1736 the Witchcraft Act was repealed. However, it was replaced by the Fraudulent Mediums Act which ***is still in force*** and simply says in one way what the Witchcraft Act said in another.

According to *Christian doctrine* no one can contact departed spirits and if this is admitted, then perforce all *Mediums* are fraudulent because the English language defines a medium as being a person who has commerce with the souls of the dead.

By ***Dragon definition*** a ***witch***, meaning a ***Fairy***, is a Medium and the law wouldn't lay a fine distinction upon exactly what the witch mediates with or how, if they decided they wanted to win an argument. It will be noticed at this juncture that by definition, in their prayers to - and visions of - Christ, the Virgin Mary and the departed Saints, all those who currently call themselves Christians are in fact ***indulging in***

mediumship, the very act which *the church* says is impossible and by which edict they render their entire following heretical. This has always been the case and during the witch craze, all things considered, it was actually the heretics who were burning the orthodox Christians.

If the ***witch*** mediates with ancestors, she claims to be able to contact the dead. As the *church* says this is impossible, the witch is a fraud and is breaking the law. Ergo to be, or claim to be a ***witch***, and consequently a ***fairy***, on that count alone, is illegal. The witchcraft laws are alive and well and living in a statute book near you. Further by implication, it is possible for a ***fairy*** to be tried under the treason act as well, on two counts.

Firstly **Her Majesty the Queen** is a Christian and head of the *Church of England.* No ***fairy*** aware of his or her history and the atrocities committed against their people could ever be what is contemporarily thought of as an orthodox Christian and in this sense they run the risk of committing an act of Treason by denying the Christian faith, because in doing so, like others following different paths, they refute and insult the faith of the **Her Majesty**.

Secondly, the ***fairy families*** stood in absolute opposition to the ***Donation of Constantine***, this being the document that was used to usurp them and initiate the ***Elven Holocaust*** itself in the first place.

The Donation of Constantine (***Latin Version:*** HERE - ***English Version:*** HERE)

The ***Donation of Constantine*** first appeared during the 8th century and was a document which purported to recognize the Roman popes as Christ's representatives on Earth and to donate to **Pope Sylvester** and the ***Roman Church*** all those Imperial powers formerly invested in the ***Throne of Byzantium***.

The '***Donation***', the Church claimed, was written in the 4th century at the insistence of the **emperor Constantine** who, the Church said, was so grateful for having been cured of leprosy by **Pope Sylvester**, that he gave into the Church's hand, the entire power and wealth of the unified Roman Empire, including the right to crown and dethrone kings. Now that is what you call *expensive medical insurance.*

Supposedly written before 337 - the year of **Constantine**'s death - the *Donation of Constantine* actually didn't make an appearance on the stage of European history until four hundred years later. So far-reaching are the powers bestowed upon the Church by this document, one would have thought that it would have been made public at the time of its bestowal and not centuries later.

The provisions of *the Donation* were enforced in 751 AD. following which the ***Merovingians*** were deposed by the Church and replaced by their *lackies*, the *Mayors of the Palace* who later became known as ***the Carolingians***. The Church had made a compact with *the Mayors* and offered to 'recognize' their legitimacy as rulers if they would dispense with the true ***Dragon Kings***. The deal was done and ***the Carolingians*** were made the puppet rulers under the Roman Church.

The Donation, because it was made by a ***Dragon King*** - **Constantine** - legitimized the Church's right to take this action because, to all intents and purposes they had the authority of ***Dragon Kingship*** given up to them by this Charter, which no doubt the ***Merovingians*** knew to be a fraud, which is why they refused to recognize the authority of the Church to meddle in affairs of state. What do we learn from this?

We can see from the Church's choice of '*benefactor*' that the Church was well aware that universally, only the ***Dragon Blood*** would be recognized as true kings and so they chose **Constantine** because he was known to have been descended from both the ***Brittanic Pendragon House*** and the ***Dragon House of David***. Furthermore as a member of the *desposyni* - the heirs of the Lord - the blood descendants and legitimate representatives of **Jesus Christ**, in *the Donation*, it appeared as if **Constantine** had relinquished his hereditary spiritual position as a *Messiah* and invested it in *the Papacy*.

By suggesting they were the *representatives of Christ*, the ***popes*** were claiming Dragon descent for themselves, because it was well known that **Jesus** had descendants and that those were part of the only Eurasian dynasty which was authorized to be kings - the ***Elven Overlords or Dragons***. It would have appeared to the public then, that in the displacement of the ***Merovingians***, one ***Dragon*** dynasty was being replaced by another, albeit a paper one.

This would reduce any danger of mass unrest. As time passed however, it became uncomfortably clear that the function of kingship under the ***Merovingians*** had been entirely different to that under the ***Carolingians***. Whilst the ***Merovingians*** had formerly assumed the role of overseers, sages and wise counsellors, the ***Carolingians*** and their successors, prompted by ***the Church***, became deliberately poorly educated, pig ignorant, insensitive tyrants and territorial tradesmen.

Dragon Kingship and the ***Grail Code*** had died to be replaced by a corrupted form of feudal totalitarianism and brutal, economic slavery as ***the Church*** carefully and strategically replaced the old dynasties with its own merchant-class client families who, from that day forth, became vassals of ***the Vatican***.

Lastly we learn that from 751 AD ***the true Dark Age*** began in earnest and the ***Elven Holocaust*** was initiated and would run its course for another thousand years until, in ***England*** at least, the ***witchcraft laws*** were repealed in 1736. North of the border in ***Scotland***, however, the persecution of witches in the 1700's was at its fiercest until the end of the century.

During this time history has witnessed the rise of the ***Church of Rome*** and its successful struggle for power. In time no dynasty ruled in Europe or remained in power unless the Church sanctioned their reign. The Church chose the royal families, it crowned kings and it deposed its detractors. In short, ***the Church***, under the auspices of the ***Donation of Constantine*** was the sole and supreme temporal power in Europe and the known world. Without this purported imperial benefice however, the Church would have remained a marginalized mediterranean cult contesting for patronage along with a host of other *gnostic Christian* denominations.

The royal dynasties sponsored by the *Church* and crowned by its *Divine Right* instituted their courts and parliaments, passed laws and employed agents to act on their behalf. To all intents and purposes it seemed as if ***the Church*** had the absolute right of ***Dragons*** and wielded power by the very sanction of Jesus Christ and God.

No monarch reigning today and no government under the monarch or instituted in their name would enjoy their position if the Church, empowered by *the Donation*, had not given them permission to rule in the first place. Without ***the Donation of Constantine***, European history today would be totally different and none of the dynasties past or present would have had the right to have reigned and nor would they reign now and none of their governments or agencies would have exercised power.

One wee hiccup though, one slight problem. Not much the

author grants, but worth a passing mention all the same. The ***Donation of Constantine*** is a complete and utter fraud and the Church was never given any temporal powers at all, let alone the right to found dynasties, crown kings or institute governments. The whole document was a lie from beginning to end and was known to be a fake since **Lorenzo Valla** applied the methods of historical criticism to it during the *Renaissance* and found the thing to be a worthless sham.

How do we know **Valla** was correct? The *New Testament* references incorporated into the wording of *the Donation* were taken from the Latin Vulgate version of the Bible. The ***Vulgate Bible*** was compiled by **St. Jerome** who was born more than two decades after **Constantine** was supposed to have signed *the Donation!* The actual Vulgate Bible wording that appears in ***the Donation*** didn't exist until **St Jerome** invented it, fifty years after the document had supposedly been dated and signed by the emperor, by which time **Constantine** had been dead for decades and couldn't have signed the ***Dragon***'s rights away anyway.

The language of ***the Donation*** is eighth century clerical or dog Latin, whilst the Latin used in the 4th century Empire was late classical Roman. The Imperial and Papal ceremonials described in *the Donation* didn't exist in **Constantine**'s time but were developed some centuries later and because of all this, every historical scholar on the entire Planet acknowledges the fact that the ***Donation of Constantine*** is an utter fake.

Several documentary instances of the Church's use of *the Donation* to assert their authority in the medieval period still exist, including the letter of **Pope Gregory IX** entitled '*Si Memoriam Beneficiorum*' dated October 23rd 1236 and addressed to the **Emperor Frederick II. Pope Gregory** writes:

> ".......that as the Vicar of the Prince of Apostles (the ***Roman Pope***) governed the empire of

> priesthood and of souls in the whole world so he should also reign over things and bodies throughout the whole world; and considering that he should rule over earthly matters by the reins of justice to whom - as it is known - God had committed on earth the charge over spiritual things, the **Emperor Constantine** humbled himself by his own vow and handed over the empire to the perpetual care of the ***Roman Pontiff*** with the Imperial Insignia and sceptres and the City and Duchy of Rome........".

People in the medieval and *Renaissance* period, confronted with this document, didn't generally criticize *the Donation* on the grounds of its veracity, they just exclaimed aghast that they couldn't believe that **Constantine** would have been stupid enough to have given the Roman Church everything.

From *the Donation* we understand that **Constantine** offered ***the Pope*** all the robes and Crowns of office but the Pope, being such a humble man, gave them back to the Emperor. Which sort of lets the Church off the hook should some malcontent turn up and say "show us the geologically encrusted tin hat and flash threads that Connie gave you then, tosh". If the readers peruse *the Donation* for themselves they will be appalled at the pretentious egotism, the arrogance and the sheer material greed of ***the Church***, as authors of the document.

The ***fraudulent imperial power of the Vatican*** to create kings by 'coronation' - derived from this *faked 8th century* '***Donation of Constantine***' (english version) - was later adopted by the Archbishops of the Church of England with the complicity of the ***Tudors***, who were Catholics themselves.

When he split with Rome, **Henry VIII** still retained and later ratified and re-established in the *Anglo-Catholic Church of*

England the fraudulent right of the Church's clergy to create by coronation, a succession of British monarchs. Because this was an illegal act, the '***Donation of Constantine***' being proved to be a completely fake document, no ***Royal Elven House*** that 'knew its Onions' and cared about social justice could possibly bring itself to recognize a Christian British Monarchy or any of their Church sponsored, Church crowned predecessors or any of their regnant or formerly regnant, European cousin Houses.

Because *the Donation* was a fraud and no subsequent priest of any Catholic derived denomination ever had the right to crown kings, ***Britain*** has had no legally reigning Monarchs for 900 years. As a consequence of this, ALL the laws passed by these monarchs were and are illegal and worthless and ALL the governmental agencies set up by or derived from these monarchs or their laws are also illegal and worthless up to the present day.

When considering this, the reader might like to think of the fact that all the arrests ever made by the Police in Britain and Europe are acts of kidnap and *Habeus Corpus*, whilst any man who took up arms for the Crown and killed for his country is unprotected by law and guilty therefore of murder.

However, paradoxically, as the entire British legal system is illegal, there are no laws, and so the crimes of *Habeus Corpus and Murder* as we define them today, simply don't exist. Subconsciously people know that their politicians and monarchs have no legitimate authority to rule over them and they manifest this knowledge in an increasing disrespect for these optional, arbitrary and illusory social conventions, which is yet another reason why social order is breaking down. If the ***UN*** is right, we may face chaos in the near future; and all because of a stupid fraud, perpetrated by a bunch of myopically greedy, maniacal peddlars of false religion who are now long dead.

Again, for asserting this kind of view the ***fairies*** are implicitly guilty of Treason, even though all British laws are constitutionally illegal and the act of treason itself is a non sequitur. Think of the implications of this.

Any nation state in the Christian world today which is still a monarchy or which has evolved as part of a successive, developing political process originating from a monarchy, by virtue of its continuing sanction from, or sponsorship by, ***the Church*** of whatever denomination, it is unauthorized by any temporal or divine power to coerce anyone to obey any law originating at any stage of that government's evolution.

In effect ***Britain, Europe*** and ***America*** are ruled by the sword and that sword is being wielded by people who are no more than short sighted, self seeking robber barons. They have no constitutional right to rule even in America, where in the 19th century the libertarian commentator, **Lysander Spooner**, demonstrated that the consensual nature of the original document, upon which the subsequent, consecutive clauses are founded, was being flouted, thereby making the entire Constitution illegal. **Pierre Proud'hon** called them all "*Tyrants and Usurpers*". Next time you are tempted to eulogize Western Democracy, bite your tongue and let your brain select first gear before you open your mouth. Flawed or otherwise, the idea that the English speaking world has any democracy at all is a joke.

At the beginning of this work the author stated that the people have been conned enough. He now hopes that the readers might appreciate for themselves the precise extent to which the people have actually been deceived and have accepted a state of affairs where they and their ancestors have been enslaved by a <u>Chameleon-like corporate body</u> that has destroyed their creativity and robbed them of their psychological liberty and their freedom of conscience for over a thousand years.

The entire moral basis of our society is founded upon a massive historical lie which has twisted the minds of generations of individuals until they have become terrified of the natural drives of their own bodies and souls.

The resultant taboos that have been created by the sick, manipulative moral standards of a usurping bunch of egomaniacs have been used to divide the minds of the people and make them dependant on the Church-State for solutions to the problems of resisting *Satan* and fighting temptation and sin, when these contrived, nonsensical whimsies never existed in the first place.

As a result, *western Christian society* was turned into an open air lunatic asylum packed full of lost souls who weren't lost at all and had no need of a cure for diseases of the soul they weren't actually suffering from in the first place.

The Church created the confusion and the division and then offered the solution. In fear the population invested its trust in the perfidious Church and in return for their confidence ***the Church*** turned the people into slaves and an entire civilization into a manufacturing plant to service their own greed for luxury and power.

For a thousand years ***the fairies*** have remained silent about their identities - formerly for fear of their lives - latterly for fear of becoming social outcasts and objects of mirth and derision. Still however, a shadow of menace lies over the ancient families. Greed will go to any length to ensure the continuity of its satisfaction and the same motives that prompted the Church to murder and lie in the past, still prompt their merchant-class puppets to kill and deceive today.

Whilst people therefore now understand ***the fairy*** to be either a gossamer winged sprite or an effeminate male - both are considered harmless jokes - such a contemporary opinion flies in the face of the facts where the fairy of history is concerned.

In studying the fairy in the context of both ***Celtic*** and medieval history it must be remembered that the tribes to whom the *Victorians* ascribed the appellation '*Celtic*' were not a homogenous or integrated racial group and ***the Celts themselves*** never saw themselves as a cohesive, pan-European nation of peoples.

Furthermore, like their medieval descendants, they had, within an indistinct collection of tribes, a patriarchal, misogynistic culture, which stands in complete opposition to the popular view that the matriarchal 'Celts' promoted a policy of sexual equality. (Green: 'Celtic World')

The modern myth concerning the *Celts*, promoted by '*New Age*' racketeers who are rehashing earlier popular trends, tends to set these rather ordinary people into some kind of '*Golden Era*' of cultural expression and heroism, punctuated by the achievement of a state of high spiritual awareness, when in fact they were average, workaday farming folk who treated their women like dirt.

Nymphs and Shepherds....Go Away!

The ***Georgians*** and ***Victorians***, for socio-political propaganda purposes, had various revivals and retrospectives that were intended to celebrate the merchant-class era of industrial prosperity and the ***British Imperial*** oppression and destruction of the cultures of other peoples, by having the audacity to equate such dubious ventures with various '*Golden Ages*' of the past. (para Gombrich).

Principally it was these individuals who patronized the artistic movements whose *Svengalis*, seeing that the parvenus were only too willing to advance and buy the lie, produced the kind of sentimental, heroic nonsense that plugged the gap in the nostalgia market which was created by the desire of the newly rich to feel that they were justified by history in the exploitation of the poor in the mills and the mines.

They wished to equate their 'victories' in the market places with those of the 'warrior king' or 'noble savage' on the battle fields of classical antiquity and, by sponsoring kitsch daubers, they felt they could become identified with the highest artistic and cultural achievements of the various ages whose ***elan*** flattered these imperialists' and industrialists' egotism and furthered their exploitative, propagandist aims.

However, in Newtonian terms, where every action engenders an equal and opposite reaction, the patronage afforded these malodorous pigment shufflers and pebble shavers, by magnates whose cultural tastes, nevertheless, only ran to the kind of jingoistic or sentimental - one hesitates to say pictorial or sculptural - effluent that would have us pseudo-intellectual, epicurean types running to **Thomas Crapper**'s *Patent Water Closet* to be sick; led to a calamitous pass where the aesthetically ambivalent skill these pallet-knife and chisel-wielding cultural assassins lent to the rectally retentive rendition of what they had the temerity to call "*Their Art*", set a trend where utter shite became the highest and the most prevalent expression of Victorian middle-class and pseudo-aristocratic cultural sensibilities.

In the words of the art historian **Sir Ernst Gombrich** "There is no such thing as 'Art'......there are only artists". And by God: By their fruits ye shall know them well enough.

For instance:

William Colman Hunt

Now there's a name to conjure with. And if you did you would arrive at an adequate approximation of what his art was like, without actually having to go through the unnerving experience of having to look at - or even be in the same room as - one of his paintings.

Indeed, if you juggled with his name for long enough, you wouldn't even have to risk being on the same continental land-mass as one of his venomous vignettes, but you would still be able to intuitively apprehend the full extent of the bilious upwelling of horror and revulsion engendered in those who, by hap-chance, have stumbled unawares upon one of his smug abominations. Particularly distressing, although possessed of an almost imperceptible, indefinably reassuring quality nevertheless, is his *Swansong* which he poignantly entitled: *'Portrait of the Artist as a Diseased Badger'*.

'Portrait of the Artist as a Diseased Badger'

Although this is a little known, difficult and obscure work, it is thought by some to be a fitting obituary for a man who is described as "a crude and rudimentary colourist with little taste or sensibility... whose works are now regarded as failures" (**Osbourne**). The Victorians loved him.

In their gaudy, nouveau-riche Georgian-Classical or Victorian Neo-Tudor demesnes, which they mercilessly and relentlessly adorned with inane moral and social re-affirmations, revivalist Gaelic gauche and pseudo-Medieval Art and Arms; culturally vacuous steel barons and cotton magnates would often display framed family charts - tracing the kinds of instant, purchased ancestry purchased by an ancestor - that any genuine self respecting nobleman would run screaming from in horror.

Their '*miladies*' would hold soirees, for the local cognoscenti and well-to-do, where the cultural á la carte invariably offered copious helpings of moronic, Byronic neo-classical claptrap garnished lavishly with choruses of criminally insane, musical atrocities like "Nymphs and shepherds come away" sung by fat falsetto aunts who hadn't a clue what Nymphs were customarily renowned for getting up to when they actually did 'come away' with or without the rustic parties of the second part.

And these arachnid recreational activities were namely: ***Cannibalism*** ("fancy another helping of Shepherd's Pie, Myrtle?") and - as their name unavoidably suggests - ***Nymphomania***; which found the outworking of the expression of its inner, emotive rage and lust to be manifest in such acts as oral sex, buggery, simultaneous multiple penetration and bestiality; with a wide variety of domestic livestock, and an equally varied selection of naturally occurring regional fauna - including wolves, dogs, donkeys, wild goats, rams, horses, snakes and - purely for betting purposes - ferrets.

Such sexually epicurean piquancies were practiced with gay abandon alongside rampant homosexuality (amongst the shepherds who'd managed to survive lunch), ***Sapphism***, drug abuse, alcoholic debauchery, Travel Scrabble, and a range of other delightfully civilized, lubricious distractions. (**Riley-Scott**: '*Phallic Worship*')

At that time the true nature of ***Celtic culture*** was censored, sanitized and idealized so much that the view we have had of it up until recently reflected more our predecessors confusion, chauvinism and wishful thinking concerning the period than it did the reality of the era they lauded.

Modern archaeology coupled with a realistic interpretation of the information, less colored by the concern for moral rectitude, has uncovered a picture of '*Celtic*' society that is clearer than it was in our great-great grandma's day. Indeed with the wealth of new knowledge we find it difficult to apply so liberally the generic term '*Celt*' in the same way our forebears were wont to do.

Scholarship concerning what previously we might have thought of as the '*heroic era*' of *Celtic civilization*, conveyed in modern popular works that owe much of their sentimentality to the erroneous and prim historical view of yesteryear, is garbled and confused.

The images of the *Noble Celt:* the tall blonde warrior chieftain, or the flaxen-haired *Swan Maidens of Lyr* are not Celtic at all. We still seem to think of all ***Celts*** in that way though because we are sold the image by people who, in accepting as fact the *Victorian delusion*, think that this distinct caste was representative of the ***Celts*** as a whole, when in fact they represented a tiny minority of individuals who were foreign to and essentially divorced in racial and cultural terms from the people we now know were the ***real Celts*** living in that era.

When we looked at the stories contained in the '*Annals of Irish History*', the ***Irish*** '*Book of Invasions*' or the ***Welsh*** '*Mabinogian*' we would have been inclined to think that these documents were about the ***Celts*** when in fact they were about a strange race of foreigners who reigned alongside these dark-haired, swarthy, stocky little farmers for nearly two thousand years. From these stories we obtain our idea of what the 'Celts' were like, when in fact they weren't Celts at all, they were ***Scythians***, ***the Elves***, ***the Fairies***, ***The Aryans***.

These ***Scythians*** were a tightly knit, insular group who practiced ***Phoenician*** and ***Pharaonic marriage*** customs to keep the blood pure and in all other respects they also tended to remain detached from the common swell of humanity.

Differing greatly from the customs of the *patriarchal Celtic peoples* they reigned over, theirs was a society that appreciated the position and the power of its women and correspondingly favored the idea of matrilinear descent.

The ***Scythians*** came to reign across ***Eurasia*** and normally we find them attached to various indigenous populations, but occasionally they were an indigenous population in themselves, such as the ***Danaan of Eire*** and the ***Ainu of Hokkaido***. Unlike their ***Celtic*** clients, whose caste system, based on kinship, was male dominated and hierarchical,
the ***Scythian*** caste system which operated amongst their own people was egalitarian.

Though individual's functions and tasks varied, all nevertheless were ***Royal*** and therefore equal. Proof of this is to be found in the *Brehon Law* concerning inheritance. This social structure became superimposed onto the ***Celtic system*** and produced the sort of divisions we find in ***Hinduism*** where the people are separated into three distinct classes:

Brahmins or Priests.

Ksatriyas or Warriors.

Sudras or Smiths.

beneath these are settled the untouchables or slaves.

The Scythian system had the same three divisions but these were arranged on the horizontal plane and did not proffer any superior status in relation to the other castes. If one overlaid the Elven, Scythian system onto that of the Celtic, which is virtually identical with the present Hindu system, we would have the following social configuration:

Scythians: Gods of Heaven

Gods of Heaven and Earth

Gods of Earth

or

Druidic Royal Ancestors, the transcended ones

Royal Archdruids, Druidesses and Pendragons (vampires)

War Kings, War Lords, Craftsmen, Metalworkers etc.

Caucasian footsoldiers and Dravidian 'Brownies'

- 0 -

Celts: Burgh Chiefs

Men-at-Arms

Farmers: Tinkers: Traders

Women

Slaves

(Celtic source - Miranda Green 'Celtic World' Routledge, London 1995)

It will be noticed that, contrary to contemporary misconceptions, ***Celtic women*** were in fact just above slaves in terms of their rank and were regularly bought and sold or exchanged by their men for cattle, along with the slaves.

It is not a popular view but sadly - given the contemporary academic discoveries concerning the real nature of ***Celtic society*** - it is an accurate one and, although we would love to blame ***the Church*** for everything, including the oppressive patriarchy that subdued women - the fact is that the ***Celts*** were already treating their women like chattels before the Church reared its ugly head above the blood-stained meniscus line of history.

The conversations or entreaties of love we see recorded in the *'Celtic' Sagas* between *'Celtic' lords* and *ladies*, were in fact the exchanges between ***Scythian men and women***. That which is reported as being the love poetry of the *'Celts'* was instead the love poetry of ***the Elves*** - the ***Royal Scythians*** - not that of a brutal farming folk who had neither lords nor ladies.

Who in history, if he had the rare gift of writing, would bother wasting such a talent, do you think, by eulogizing the sexual peccadilloes or romantic longings of a bunch of turnip farmers who wouldn't have spoken to women on such equal terms anyway? Romance in any case didn't come into it, the Celtic woman shut her mouth and opened her legs - period.

The art of male wooing and flattery arises when the woman has the freedom to choose to say no, and the only women who had that choice then were ***Scythian Princesses*** who, because of the mysterious composition of their blood and its consequent magical powers, had a lot more to offer their ***Elven menfolk*** than the occasional *legover*, which is all that nondescript Celtic women could hope to have in their favor.

The beauty and exquisiteness of the magic that a ***Scythian Princess*** had to offer could not be taken by force, she had to give it willingly, otherwise in the act of coercion, her magic would be tainted and become either useless or poisonous.

Occupying a position higher than the ***Elven male*** as Goddesses incarnate, ***Elven men*** were pleased therefore to treat her with deference and honor and to offer her court in a manner that would secure her voluntary participation in their sacred congress.

From this obligation of service to such ***Earthly Goddesses*** arose the medieval tradition of Courtly Love which, by no means and under no circumstances, was ever intended to be offered to the female descendants of either ***Celt, Norman*** or ***Saxon.***

Today, after hundreds of years of oppression, the female descendants of these poor, downtrodden ***Celtic*** and later ***Anglo-Norman*** women have managed, during the closing years of the millennium, to wrest from their men the equality that evaded their mothers for centuries and now they demand to stand on an equal footing with their menfolk but - like their sisterly ancestors, when push comes to shove - they have nothing more dynamic or magical to offer than a leg over.

However, as the male descendants of the ***Celts*** and the later ***Anglo-Normans*** - the examples of manhood living today - have nothing better or more magical to offer their women either and never have had, equality between the sexes seems to be quite an equitable and logical arrangement whereby the mediocre do not differentiate between, nor discriminate against, each other's mediocrity on the basis of gender.

Passing on from the politics of sex originating in the caste system, we now return to addressing the system as a whole and notice that the figure above is a generalization which encapsulates the main divisions between each social level.

As time passed and the population increased, technology developed and diversified and the main castes became subdivided into classes within classes. At length the castes themselves eventually became overturned and the *Warrior Class* gained the ascendant, later to be upturned, in the last 1200 years, by the *Merchant Class*, whom the Hindus call the *Vaisha*.

In the twentieth century we also saw situations where the untouchables became the rulers, as in ***China*** and ***Soviet Russia***. Presently we have a situation where the ***Elven Race***, at the bottom of the pile have become the untouchables, whilst the increasingly and frighteningly acquisitive *Peasants* and the *Merchants* are at the top, having wrested their positions from the block-headed *Warriors*. The end product of this fiasco over the last millennium and a half can be smelled in the air, tasted in the water supply and seen in the eyes of diseased, starving, third world children.

Its results can be heard in the screams of animals gratuitously tortured in experiments aimed at testing the toxicity of vanity products or of medicines intended to make money for these gauche extortionists whose worthless over-inflated products titillate, save or prolong the vacuous lives of a race of glorified peasants whose continued existence has become an abomination to nature and a threat to Life itself.

At its inception the caste system was not an arbitrary set of divisions or inequalities established through main force by a varying collection of sequential oppressors, but a ***reflection of the fact*** that there were differences in the capabilities and capacities of the different types of human beings alive at the time.

Some were ingenious artists, builders and artisans, some were naturally gifted traders and negotiators, some had been bred to have an overview and some were fearless, heroic soldiers. Each group had its part to play in the functioning of society.

Whilst some peoples - like the ***Celts*** - had green fingers and could make carrots grow rose blossoms in Hell, most ***Scythians*** couldn't even grow an *Infants School size* tray of mustard and cress. However, the ***Celts*** were useless at organizing complex societies and depended on the ***Scythians*** for foresight, guidance and protection.

Centuries earlier similar arrangements developed in the east where the ***Aryans*** and the ***Dravidians***, having bashed nine barrel loads of horse feathers out of each other, finally came to an amicable social arrangement whereby all parties ultimately benefited. Like the ***Celts***, the ***Dravidians*** could get dinner from dust and their expertise and practicality was the backbone of the Aryo-Dravidian symbiotic culture.

Such relationships are also commonly to be observed amongst different species in the natural world and work brilliantly within what must be admitted is a hierarchical natural order which, nevertheless is not a system of inequality or self conscious elitism, but one of necessity.

From about 1800 BC onwards, with the increase in Eurasian populations, the occurrence of a variety of natural disasters and the diminishing of range territory through foreign conquests, the ***Scythians*** and the ***Aryans*** were forced to seek more settled lives but, being mainly predators and rangers, they lacked the skills to make farming work.

They needed the Hobbit-like peoples of the ***Celtic*** and ***Dravidian*** cultures to tend the land and in times that were becoming increasingly more violent, these cultures needed the ***Aryans*** and ***Scythians*** to protect them.

This tolerance and co-operation continued until the emergence of the warrior lords, literally the *middle class* of their day, whose elitist, hierarchical governmental structures - based on the right of might - became entrenched in western civilization as the ***feudal system*** during the years of the ***Roman Church***'s ascendancy and totalitarianism.

From this point onwards the exploitation of the caste system as an ideal tool for *breeding elitism*, division and inequality became rife as the Roman church, comprising mainly *vaishas* and *peasants*, seeing a chance to claw their way to power, upturned the original caste system by ninety degrees and turned it into a ladder to enable them to climb to what they conceived to be the top of the pile and the easy life.

Only humans would seek to differentiate and assert their superiority based on their position within a social structure that, based on natural law, was originally intended in contrast to be for the benefit of all and to function through cooperation. In their egotism humans abused a natural and beneficial order to the detriment of all those subscribing to it.

In the 20th century the audacity of usurpation continues when the ignorant middle-classes, shopkeepers and their ignorant shopkeeper sons, join groups of white supremists who idolize the image of the blond haired, blue eyed Aryan.

This particular genotype, ***the warrior***, who also occupied the middle class or caste, seems naturally to appeal to this middle class today, who unaware of the fact that ***Aryans*** had red hair and green eyes, as a result of their lack of education and intelligence, have elevated the usurping warrior to the status of a *true Aryan king* when in reality the blond haired blue eyed ideal, so beloved of the Germans and for good reason, was bred, like your average white racist today, to be as thick as a plank.

A ***warrior*** could never have manifest the attributes of *Aryan kingship* in a million years. ***Kingship*** took spirit, wisdom and brains. The blonde warrior had none of these qualities and wasn't bred to have. In the feudal period the warrior was called a baron which stemmed from the earlier Latin word *baro* which was in circulation at a time which was contemporary with the rise of the warrior classes. *Baro* literally means '*thickhead*'.

It is typical of the racist working and middle classes that they would pick such a figure to
emulate. ***Aryan*** means ***wise king***, not dumb blonde. The adoration by the *German National Socialists* of the blonde warrior god-king and the assumption ever since by successive generations that he is an *Aryan*, must have been heavily influenced by the 13th century **Royal Poet Snorri Sturleson**.

In his '*Sayings of Har*' he defines a
corrupted ***Scandinavian*** caste system consisting of *Jarls, Carls* and *Thralls*. The ***Jarls*** says **Snorri** were blonde haired, the ***Carls*** were red haired and the ***Thralls*** were black haired.

Everywhere else the royal colouring is red and this tradition goes back in the ***Aryans*** to **Radamanthus,**
Ariadne and **Minos**, and through them to **Lilith** herself. Even **Jesus** and **Magdalene** are regularly and invariably portrayed with red hair in the Renaissance masterpieces. A reversal has taken place here where warriors usurped or replaced kings as leaders of the people.

The ***warriors*** were hired Caucasians not bloodline Aryans. The upheaval and resultant inequity and iniquity within the caste system occurred when many ***Aryan queens*** and ***kings*** were legitimately displaced by their society's ***War Kings*** in times of trouble, but were never to return to their thrones because the conflicts often carried on for decades.

Sometimes however, having had a taste of power, treacherous and greedy *warrior Captains* decided they would either go it alone or take over permanently by force of arms. Following this however, an even more stupid class of people managed to trade and poison their way to the top.

And who were they? that's right, the settled warehouse tinkers - the cheating peasants with money who were the ancestors of the upper and middle classes of today. Mind you, some of them were sneaky and one wouldn't realize that they were and still are middle-class peasants even today.

Part 2

You might think that they were genuine aristocracy because they have inherited titles like *Earl* or *Duke* or *Lord.* What you wouldn't realize was that they only inherited these titles because their ancestors were traders who had had enough money to buy them from *christian kings* who were also elevated peasants. And you wonder why the Earth is in such a state? What are you, stupid?

When the world is run by tinkers, as it is now, then the tinker mentality sees everything as having a price tag attached to it and everything then becomes a 'marketable commodity' and its significance or importance becomes linked to its 'marketing potential'.

We have become so used to such values and the buzz words that accompany them that we no longer see the inherent immorality or dangers implied therein. It has got so bad now that profiteers calling themselves 'doctors' can visit indigenous peoples, take blood samples and patent those individuals' genes.

In effect it would then be possible for the doctors of the *Human Genes* 'R' *Us Corporation* to file a complaint in an international court and prosecute those same indigenous populations for the theft of the doctors' patented property.

Essentially this is slavery under a different guise, where various ethnic peoples belong to an *American Medical Corporation*, run by a government backed elite who are, worst of all - Americans - a nation whose leaders are singularly the most vacuous, morally twisted and hence dangerous social group on Earth.

The ancient, egalitarianism of the ***Scythian***'s own social order manifested itself in such concepts as the democratic system of voting for ***Archdruids*** and ***Pendragons***, where the 'family', comprising of the regional divines and princes, would elect both chief priests and high kings - sometimes one and the same person - for priests and kings were interchangeable. In many ways this system was replicated in the *Saxon Atheling Pool*, where prospective rulers were chosen from the most suitable candidates available. (**Dufton**).

This royal reserve, from whence were chosen kings from a race of kings, also extended itself to mediate in matters of marriage. Where election to high-priest or priestess-hood and kingship were concerned, only the very best and the most qualified would be picked. In the case of a king he must be without physical or spiritual blemish. The successful candidate was the most spiritually powerful, learned and gracious of manners. (Annals of Irish History).

Such criteria were also applied when princesses or princes were selected for marriage to each other. These were arranged by the ***druids*** between the very best families within the various *tuadhes* in the kingdoms.

This ensured that the fruit of any such royal union would

represent an enhancement of all the most admired and required attributes necessary for a royal dynasty, thus reinforcing the perfection of the royal race itself. Both *Hindu* and *medieval marriage customs* were derived from this ***Scythain*** practice. (**Hall**).

For the ***Scythians*** the ability to perform magic - to manifest the ***Sidhe*** - was innate and hereditary in very much the same way as we view others skills as being today, such as Art, for instance. Selective unions gave the race the opportunity to breed outstanding magicians whose gifts of natural perception and understanding: and whose ability to access the '***Otherworld***', helped to produce and guide brilliant kings who reigned with elegant aplomb.

The ability to perform magic was carried in the blood and if that blood became watered down by marriages entered into with outsiders, the genetic strain was weakened and so was the ability to perform magic.

The ***Aryan-Scythians*** weren't color prejudiced because, although they were white themselves, they didn't even marry other whites. The ***Elves*** were relied upon by their client races to be able to see things and perform feats that these client races couldn't.

The purity of the ***Elven blood*** was absolutely necessary in order to enable the ***Dragon Kings*** and ***Queens*** to maintain their magical abilities and the quality and depth of their perception and thereby fulfill their obligatory roles as the ***Seers*** and ***Guides*** that their clients had wanted them for in the first place.

These clients acknowledged that they were naturally unable to have an overview or to perform higher magic and so it was not in their best interest to allow the ***Elves*** to water down the ***Elven blood*** by intermarriage with members of that client race. This wasn't racism but a mutually acknowledged understanding that the ***Elves*** were originally of an entirely different sub-species, rather than just being of a different race.

This separatist custom was still vigorously upheld by the ***British*** rural working classes up until the first half of the 20th century when they themselves still considered intermarriage between the castes to be an outrage and a danger to social order.

Though somewhat of a misguided view, given the arriviste backgrounds of most of the contemporary aristocracy then, it is a clear example of they way in which custom, however inappropriately applied, arises from ancient racial memory.

If a white person refused to mate with black people, you might be tempted to call the individual a racist. If anyone of any color refused to mate with other primates though, you wouldn't for one moment think of accusing them of racism, whatever their color.

The *Holy Bible* refers to the sons of **Samael** as *goats* and the sons of **Jehovah** as *sheep* and here then we have a classical acknowledgement that it was understood from ancient times that there was in fact a difference between ***Elves*** and ***Men***.

This difference is also recorded in the ***Sumerian cylinder rolls*** from whence the biblical material was extracted. These same cylinder rolls record the assertion that the ***Elves*** made man by a series of processes that resulted in the ***Elves*** being only a quarter related to man at the time.

Whilst it is known that in antiquity the ***Nephilim***, the ***Elven sons of the Anunnagi*** interbred with human women who were the result of this experiment and who in their turn produced the ***Naphidim***, it is recorded that these half breeds were destroyed long before the ***Black Sea Flood*** and the slate was wiped clean.

The next experiment produced a lineage of ***pure bred Elven queens*** and ***kings*** who were to supervise a *race of quarter breeds* who were originally created for manual labour. The *quarter breeds*, nevertheless, were eventually to gain their freedom and elect their own chieftains, helped by the ***Elven dynasty*** whom Christians now think of as the spawn of *Satan*. This kind of attitude goes a long way in determining exactly what ***the Church*** feels about human emancipation.

These people interbred with anyone and we know them now as the ***biblical race of Adam*** whose ***elven blood*** today is so diluted as to be infinitesimal. The ***pure Elven Queens*** and ***Kings*** however bred with no-one but themselves and so throughout the past five or six millennia, the blood has been kept *more or less pure* in several unbroken lines of descent until as late as the 8th century AD.

From thence however, only one bloodline descent is recorded as being pure and unbroken and only that one single named dynasty driving from an historical ***Elven Royal House*** contemporarily described as such, still exists today.

As human blood diluted however, the need for ***Elven Overlords*** increased and from the second millennium BC the ***Scythians***, as they came to be known, were in great demand as *Queens* and *Kings, Seers* and *Magi.*

This continued up until about 751 AD, when the ***Elven Holocaust*** began in earnest. During the decline of the increasingly insular ***Elven*** population in Europe, from 500 BC it was not the case that they, at that time were 'higher' than the other species as they had been previously, but that they were simply different from them.

In a world that was becoming increasingly more structured, the ***Elves*** needed man as much as man needed the ***Elves*** and one should understand that during the various later periods in history when these social arrangements were entered into, they were seen as being complementary, not competitive or hierarchical.

Such separatism then was born of pragmatism and necessity. In those days it was known that hormonal levels were influenced by genetic inheritance and that hormones affected the *individual's perceptions*, *psychological unicameralism* and the subsequent ***ability to transcend*** and perceive the intricacies of the workings of the cosmos. ***Elven blood*** was rich in these substances.

Maintaining the purity of the blood therefore was of paramount importance and intermarriage between the ***Scythian*** reigning houses and members of the ***Celtic*** or any other race was strictly forbidden and greatly lamented if it did occur. However on occasion we read in folktales or histories the stories of the mutual theft of brides from each camp by both ***Celtic*** chieftains and ***Scythian*** kings.

Many of these stories are suspect and were written during the period of the *Roman Church's ascendancy*. The motive for these stories was to propagate the myth that the fairy blood was being watered down.

The church, by spreading this rumor, hoped to persuade the peasants that their traditional friends and protectors, the ***Elven Queens*** and ***Kings***, were losing their power along with the purity of their blood and were thereby becoming ineffectual and thus redundant.

If the people could be convinced of this, then they would believe that the age of magic was dying and invest their support in the church instead. A clever lie. In most instances, if not all however, these so-called ***Celtic*** chieftains were not in fact '*Celtic*' at all but ***Milesian Scythians***. Such misrepresentations occur throughout the monkish reworkings of Gaelic history and an apt example of this is in the christianized story of **Lugh** and the ***Queen*** of sovereignty where **Lugh** admits to once being a mortal king, which is rubbish.

Sometimes too we read the stories of the love between fairies and humans, representing the marriages between ***Scythians*** and indigenous families. In later times far more unpleasant tales emerged concerning the decline of the ***Elven families*** who had had to go into hiding from, the *Church fathers* said, the *Celtic Milesians.*

At this point, in ***Eire***, the ***Danaan*** became the *daouine sidhe*, the people of the hills. This would have occurred from about 500 BC onwards. This didn't actually happen with the ubiquity, rapidity or finality that the Church reports. ***Scythian*** princes and princesses of the ***Tuadha d'Anu*** or ***Danaan*** were still walking around at large up until the B*attle of Clontarf.* Why did the *Church* bother with the weak blood yarn if they had all been wiped out, unless they were adopting a Belt and Braces policy?

If anyone drove the ***Elves*** into hiding and instigated their 'final' (?) decay it was not the ***Milesians***, but the church itself. From this period in time arose the tale of the fairy changeling. It is asserted that after waves of invasions and the decline in ***Fairy*** numbers following wars with people such as the ***Milesians***, though now living in virtual isolation in the forests, the fairies still maintained their taboos concerning marriage between the races.

The result of this, said the *Church chroniclers*, was continuous inbreeding resulting in deformed and sickly offspring. When an enclave of ***elves*** had become that inbred, they reported, it was often their custom to steal local children and raise them for breeding purposes in order to inject some fresh ***DNA*** into the ***fairy*** gene pool. Though that apparently, wasn't the only reason for such thefts, it was intimated darkly.

As has already been pointed out,
the ***fairies*** practiced ***Phoenician*** and ***Pharaonic marriage***. The former is the union of father and daughter, which in the horse-breeding world is acclaimed for producing the finest, healthiest thoroughbreds, and the second is union between brother and sister, an arrangement that, according to geneticists at Cambridge University, can continue for up to three hundred years - *ten generations* - before any genetic problems are made apparent.

As they didn't suffer from the moral stupidity encouraged by *the Church*, they had ample scope to vary the types of alliances they made in-caste, and thereby prevent hereditary problems from occurring too often.

However, leaving that to one side, if you allow for the probability that at least a thousand ***elves*** survived the various calamities reported to have befallen them, prior to and following the first millennium AD, and that those thousand ***elves*** came perhaps from six loosely related clans, you have at least six varying gene pools from which to choose partners, before resorting to intense incest in any case.

From the time of the *Milesian victory* and the flight of the fairies into the hills in 500 BC and the emergence of these church sponsored stories of child kidnap and incestuous deformity, there must have lapsed about a thousand years, this form of ecclesiastical propaganda having begun in earnest after 751 AD.

Given that the ***Milesians*** and the ***Danaan*** had settled their differences some time before and were interbreeding, they both being ***Scythian Tribes***, the occurrence of deformity and the consequent necessity to steal peasant children either to breed from as the church hinted, was negligible. As far as the accusations of willful and unnecessary perversity are concerned, where *the Church* accused the ***elves*** of stealing human children to eat, this is misinformation.

Nevertheless, during times of hardship, such as the medieval period, when disease and death were rife, necessity sometimes forced human communities to resort to cannibalism simply in order to survive, and instances of peasants being driven by circumstance to eat the flesh of condemned criminals are unequivocally recorded.

The ***Elves*** did maintain the cult of the sacrificial king amongst their own adult population but the stealing of human children for these ritual purposes never occurred because they were of a different race.

Nevertheless, here we have an example of the kind of ecclesiastical deception that, in order to further brainwash simple folk whom it had already conditioned by deception and terror to be gullible, priests would use the idea of evil beings preying on children because during any period of history it seems that the "send five dollars and we'll stop this man from shooting the puppy" approach to such a concept is always guaranteed to elicit a highly-charged, emotional, socially cohering knee-jerk response from a poorly culturally developed and badly educated public, who in sheer terror would close ranks, toe the party line and reaffirm their loyalty to the establishment and its glib, self satisfied, easily digested, chintzy morality.

"<u>In Some Enchanted Cliché, You Will Meet a Stranger</u>..."
And what was the purpose of this kind of *scapegoatism*? To ratify social identity under a specific ethical, cultural banner and thereby keep the transvestite peddlars of religious quackery in full and gainful employment by using psychological terrorism to ensure that they and their gravy train kept on rolling.

The fascinating aspect to this kind of propaganda is that today it still works just as insidiously and effectively on people who like to think of themselves as modern, intelligent sophisticates living in an enlightened and educated society, as it did on a medieval population whom these suckers are taught to regard with a patronizing demeanor as being little more than gauche, priest-ridden, superstitious ignoramuses.

To all intents and purposes this kind of indoctrination is *fascism*. Those familiar with the work of **E. A. Blair** will remember the scenario he presented in his novel '1984' where a totalitarian regime maintained social cohesion by pitting one social group against another.

This trick was used by the *National Socialists* in Germany, who also accused the *Jews* of molesting and eating children, and it is now being utilized with roaring success across the world by drawing a clear demarcation line between the inhabitants of Middle-America and Middle-England and a new group of evil social saboteurs who are trying to undermine the very fabric of our *Great Western* democratic society whom the ***FBI*** and the ***CID*** - in cahoots with the gutter rags - call *Paedophiles* and *Satanic* child sex abusers.

In the **Macarthy** era there were '*Reds*' under every bed. Today, living in a shabby bed-sit apartment next door to you and every other respectable working or middle-class family across the entire planet, there is an evil, filthy MAN (rarely a woman, one notes) who is just waiting for the opportunity to rape and murder your kids. You must be ready to inform on anyone. It is your duty as a citizen and if you don't, people will believe that you are a *Paedophile* as well and you will end up on the "*Suspected Paedophile Register*", without ever having been formally accused.

CONFESS, CONFESS!
Burn the Witch, Burn the Witch!

The really amazing, but hardly original, aspect of this latest manifestation of the ***witch hunt mentality*** being used in the service of political propaganda, is that THIS TIME you can't tell who these unspeakable Spawn of Satan are. "They could be a member of your family", says the social worker with the fixed, glassy stare; who is called into the studio for his or her professional opinion.

"They could be the children's grandparents" says the gravely concerned and sincere-looking police inspector who "has witnessed many cases like these" in his career. They could be YOU. The enemy of social order is everywhere and only by being constantly vigilant will we have any chance of saving our children from what?

<u>What is 'abuse' and how prevalent is it</u>?
The answer to this will be known by ***British*** readers who remember the *Rochdale, Orkney* and *Cleveland child abuse fiascos.* In these cases, families were split up and psychologically tortured, and whole communities were destroyed by the maniacal obsession of a group of over zealous social workers who systematically interrogated children for weeks on end, using methods reminiscent of those adopted by **Matthew Hopkin**, the self appointed 17th century 'Witc*hfinder General*'.

The interviewing techniques used were structured in such a manner as to gain exactly the kind of responses required. In the Cleveland cases the children were actually told by the social workers interviewing them that they had been abused and were thereafter subliminally tutored in the kind of response they should make in the Law Courts. The S.S. officials conducting the investigations actually told the children where they had been touched and how they had been violated. The evidence of the *Social Service*'s techniques were videotaped.

Were the children abused before the government intervened? No they weren't. All the *Cleveland cases* were abandoned, as were the *Rochdale* and *Orkneys* satanic abuse accusations. Were the children suffering from sexual and mental abuse after the government had sent in its shock troops? Yes they were (like therapists and so-called *Counselors*, many social workers enter the government *Social Services* in order to find some cure for, or to be near to or punish people for, the kind of abuse or deprivation they themselves have suffered in the past, which is both pathetic and dangerous by degrees. In 1999 dozens of Social Services officers were arrested en masse in Wales and imprisoned for committing hundreds of acts of sexual abuse against children in their care over a period of thirty years).

It would be interesting to discover how many survivors of this particular period of officially sanctioned persecution now have acquired memories of being sexually abused or of being abusers themselves. Elsewhere in the world adults, whose families, personal lives and sense of personal self worth and self respect were destroyed by these *Sicherhietspolezei*, actually killed themselves after suffering this particular kind of unpleasant and unfounded, exploitative state attention.

These horrendous social crimes were perpetrated by an establishment which uses sexual abuse propaganda as a tool for social control. Ordinary, decent families were cynically and deliberately turned against each other in a planned attempt to manufacture a social crisis as part of a progressive propaganda formula intended to rally public support against an illusory enemy within our midst.

Exactly the same techniques had been employed throughout the previous seven centuries, where the priesthood warned the population that ***witches*** and ***vampires*** existed in every family and that the unseen spirit of evil was everywhere.

Children are now growing up in a society where the first thing that they learn is to fear and suspect everyone. Divide and Conquer. Divide the individual against themselves and divide communities and groups against each other. The establishment is playing a very dangerous game which could blow up in their faces.

Countering the so-called enlightened literature accompanying the teaching of child sex education in schools are the seemingly contradictory messages being spouted by both the government mouthpieces and the tabloids in the public arena.

Though not saying as much in their cautionary moral tales and warnings about the dangers lurking in society, the intention snugly nestled between the lines:

> "Abusers are everywhere..... and they want you to do that nasty thing with them..... you will get AIDS..... you will get pregnant" - is to lead any sexually healthy child with a reasonable imagination to infer that they should "fear sex.... sex is painful...... sex is dirty... sex is original sin..... sex is evil".

The establishment can't actually say this with impunity anymore, but by highlighting the dangers of sex and leading the child to make the connections for themselves, helped ably in the home environment by parents who can't completely free themselves of their grandparents' Victorian conditioned sexual prejudices, the modern State can achieve the same prohibitive result as those '*Guardians of Public Morality*' who preceded them in former generations and thereby recreate the same socially essential sexual taboos but on new, pragmatic seeming foundations.

Perhaps the reader has noticed that the burgeoning use of sex to sell nearly everything from cars to coffee to washing powder has increased in tandem with the increase in sexual oppression manifest in concepts like *Political Correctness*, which emerged from the post-boiler suit-feminist attitude that any form of sexual expression whatsoever was an exploitative male fantasy.

Two equally exciting options are then open to the establishment with regard to manipulating the repressed child. Firstly they can rely upon sexual fear to work in conflict with the child's naturally developing sexual appetites and create a behavioral dichotomy which will result in mental confusion, self doubt and guilt.

A natural reaction when a human feels guilty is to find someone in a position of moral superiority to forgive and reassure them. In such a relationship one party inevitably becomes inferior to the other and thus dependant and biddable, a form of conditioning which invariably starts in the home.

Whilst the child is in this receptive state, the establishment's agents will fill her or him full of crap. This will result in the child conforming to the moral and social mores that have also been instilled into their parents and their peer group using exactly the same methods of subliminal indoctrination that have worked so well over the years.

This achieves en masse, from the establishment's point of view, a behavioral status quo that will, on average, work to the establishment's advantage by ensuring that the child is sufficiently psychologically repressed, confused and fearful, that he or she will only fit into and become dependant upon a docile, manipulable social structure where they don't have to think for themselves.

Secondly, by recreating new sexual taboos, the establishment represses the most powerful emotive force on earth and makes it into some sort of exotic forbidden fruit. Human nature being what it is, and suffering from the rebellious and rather stupid conviction that exotic, forbidden fruits taste the sweetest, the child who is subjected to media indoctrination will see that this exotic, forbidden fruit is relentlessly being associated with an endless barrage of products that manufacturers are ramming down peoples' throats at every opportunity and in every social environment they visit.

In due course the forbidden, tantalizing quality associated with sex becomes associated with the range of products to the extent that they too become as forbidden, as tantalizing and as desirable as sex itself. The emotive power of sexual desire is then redirected into becoming the <u>insatiable drive to shop</u>. This is economically motivated child sex abuse which is sanctioned and encouraged by the government. With the shopping disease comes the need for credit and to get credit and then pay it off, which is not encouraged, one needs money et Voila!
The <u>individual is a captive comsumer-producer</u>.

In the last thirty years sex had begun to become normalized, which was a bit of a problem for the manufacturers who relied on the testosterone monkey to ride on the back of taboo and goad simpletons into buying their stupid crap from them. When people began to break down the taboos, sex became ordinary and the market appeal that was to be had by linking products with sex was in danger of waning.

Fortunately however, we are now breeding a whole new generation of consumers who have been brought up, from their early youth, to be sexually constipated; a policy which in the future, other than actually breeding more of the same sexually regressive child abusers sponsored and trained by the government; will also breed the kind of people who are good for the economy, solid citizens who are titillated by taboo and will respond to sex-related marketing images with the same twisted and immature enthusiasm as their grandparents did.

The silliest aspect of the current *Paedophile Witch Hunt* is that, like a really good, messy *'Road Traffic Accident'*, people are fascinated by the gory details and gain a double helping of entertainment from reading about and viewing the news concerning child sexual abuse.

Firstly, whether they admit it or not, the dormant, retrospective parasexual child-pervert, trapped in a parentally suppressed sexual past, is still lurking there inside men and women and it obtains an infantile, salacious and vicarious pleasure from imagining the sexual details. Secondly they can enjoy this whilst the respectable adult aspect of their personas re-affirms their own moral self image in the fact that it wasn't them that did it. It's almost like the deflection of responsibility - for feeling sexual pleasure - that is obtained by indulging in bondage.

The righteous can congratulate themselves that they are not the sort of people who would do this kind of thing and in so doing they can assure themselves that *Big Brother* loves them and will care for them because theirs is the acceptable face of society. Wrong again.

This disgusting type of rubber-necking voyeurism is actually encouraged by the State, along with an obsession for fashion, football and money, because it deflects the observer's attention from the real problems of society (**Chomsky**).

It further prevents them from realizing that the real sexual abusers, the real evil enemies of democracy who are undermining the fabric of society are the manipulative, megalomaniacal but myopic establishment Mandarins who kowtow to the greed of the corporate elites and engineer the numerous social crises in the first place, including the current paedophile scare.

And why do they do it, what higher purpose does the suffering they inflict on innocent children and adults serve? They do it in order to maintain their power and it serves to vouchsafe to them an endless supply of Sullivan's Private Stock ciggies, Caviar and Cavalry Club Champagne; life membership of Whites Club and a permanent invitation to the Royal Enclosure at Ascot.

"Cause enough damage and there could even be a knighthood in it for you, Rupert"

Accounts given by parents who were subjected to this kind of vicious, callous intervention in their lives relate that it felt as if they were the victims of a relentless and interminable act of rape which left them feeling like dirty, worthless outcasts.

No part of their lives was left private and what they assumed were their basic human rights were flouted as the S.S. attempted, day after day, week after week, to wrest from them a confession of their guilt. In the end some actually began to believe that they were paedophiles.

Their subconscious conclusion being that if they weren't guilty, why were they being subjected to so much punishment by people in authority over them?. The mind's grasp of reality is a lot more fragile than people would like to acknowledge and chronically adverse circumstances brought to bear upon them by figures of authority can engender a regressive, almost childlike response, where the individual becomes ingenuous and relinquishes their sense of sound judgment, investing it instead in the figure who is persecuting them.

The Dirty Tricks Brigade

This conditioned response to authority figures is at the heart of the *Christian conversion experience* and can be observed in action under intense police interrogation. In ***Auschwitz*** even, many Jews began to feel that it was their fault that they were there in the first place and that they were guilty and consequently they deserved to die.

Many people become convinced that they are guilty because someone higher than themselves in the social order, whom they have been conditioned from childhood to respect, repeatedly tells them so and consequently, having been brainwashed by their parents and teachers to respect authority figures such as the police or the *Social Services*, in the end they believe they are as guilty as the nice policeman says they are.

Case Scenario

After repeated, joint and individual visits to the house by the *Police* and *Social Services*, the children are removed to a place of safety, the newspapers have been deliberately tipped off and the man is taken into custody.

His neighbors now know what he's been accused of and in the police cells this plays on his mind, along with all the other horrendous implications of the situation he now finds himself in. Whether he is found guilty or not, his life is already collapsing around him like a pack of cards and the worst part is yet to come.

He's in a state of severe psychological trauma within the first hour of detention. He is then subjected to an interim 78 hour period of interrogation which, because of the nature of the charges, could attract a series of extensions which could run into days.

Sophisticated and persistent police interrogation techniques are employed by skilled officers who eventually convince him - in a highly pressured, frightening, inquisitorial environment - that he is capable of paedophilia "under given circumstances".

In cases involving female children, the officers might ask the suspect/victim if they think that, purely scientifically speaking, the onset of menstruation is indicative of the female's biological preparedness to have reproductive sexual intercourse.

The scientific answer to that question is a definite yes. However the average age of the onset of puberty in Caucasian females falls well under the statutory age of consent in British and most American Law. Legally speaking, ready or not, the menstruating female is still a child.

If the suspect/victim answers the question honestly then they are saying that, despite the fact that a female who has reached puberty is still a child, she is ready to have sex. The police record might then show that even though they may be legally under age, the suspect/victim clearly asserted that it was his opinion that children made legitimate sexual partners.

If the suspect/victim mentally concedes the possibility of one of the interrogator's very clever, suggested borderline scenarios, the victim might then admit to himself that technically he is morally capable of having sex with a child. At this point, in admitting the capability of committing the crime, if only to himself, he steps over the line and in his own mind he becomes a paedophile and consequently, in his own mind, he is guilty.

What does it matter whether he's actually abused a child or not, he has now been led to believe that he is capable of doing it, and that is as bad as having done it already, so perhaps he needs locking up after all. Tired and hungry, and having had no time or space in which to marshal his thoughts, and feeling disgusted with himself he wants to get it all over with, and the only way this is going to stop is if he confesses.

Bingo: one oven-ready paedophile to go: heavy on the condemnation, over easy on the truth.

Having been convinced of his capability and thus his culpability, the suspect/victim's self-image and consequently his life would lie in ruins whether he confessed to the trumped-up charge or not. Many lost their jobs or were afraid to return to the workplace for fear of persecution whilst others were forced to flee their communities and move elsewhere. Can you, the reader, imagine what it must feel like to be accused of what has now become singularly the most repugnant and unforgivable crime in modern society?

The innocent victim is made to feel evil, they are a pervert, a psycho, a nonce. Once the S.S. and the police have uncovered and scrutinized in minute detail every aspect of their life, the neurosis sets in and they begin to feel that everybody can see into them and that everybody knows that they have been accused of child abuse.

It's written on their face, it shines out from their eyes. They are the scum of the earth. They deserve to die. This is the psychological effect that these kind of stupid witch hunts had on the individuals whom the establishment targeted and committed so much resources to in hounding, simply in order to win political points.

Without doubt child sex abuse is an abhorrent socially manufactured disease and so it's a pity they didn't invest the amount of energy, money, enthusiasm and publicity that they wasted in *Cleveland*, *Orkney* and *Rochdale* in dismantling the socially and religiously sanctioned causes of abuse in the first place. If they had, then all the children that have died since those fiascos, might still be alive today and the State wouldn't have come out of it looking quite like the complete arseholes that they actually are.

But that's not the way to engineer the required social responses, is it? Those are only obtained by encouraging the continuation - and careful media management - of paranoia, because such lies at the very foundations of a society whose power is traditionally rooted in the manipulative abuse of the individual from the cradle to the grave and beyond.

The public delights in the shivers of revulsion they feel as they ogle the papers and extract every ounce of infotainment out of the victim's predicament and the predicament of their family. Child abuse cases are trumpeted throughout the national gutter press, who pay top money if so-called victims of abuse sell their stories, whilst the public who consume this particular 'media product' find the victims guilty as charged on the no smoke without fire ticket.

In one recent case involving a public figure the victim was promised a bonus by the newspaper if her supposed attacker was found guilty. What incentive to ensure justice is that? Again, the official, public reaction to purported abuse is as foul, abusive and as obscene as the act itself, if it ever occurred in the first place.

Now transpose this entire situation back to the Middle Ages and imagine how it must have felt for the elves who suffered exactly the same kinds of accusations, abuse and persecution for identical political aims. And now add to that the inevitable institutionalized rape and physical torture, and top the whole lot off with a mandatory death penalty.

The Church had instigated just such a relentless and insidious programme of militant, psychotically hateful propaganda and persecution against the elves, a rabid war of lies that attacked every level of their presumed behavior and twisted every fairy custom into an act of abomination ordered by their master Satan himself.

All the efforts of the elves, *the Church bleated*, were ranged against the poor peasant who, because of the abominable traditions of these evil and wicked fairies, the peasant's former friends and protectors, meant that the poor peasant living in fear for his very life and soul, could only rely on comforting, forgiving *Mother Church* for his physical protection and spiritual salvation.

And what little recompense, what mere trifling consideration did the church expect for so great a favor? Merely that the peasant should:

> **a)** Manifest an appropriate amount of gratitude - and an appropriate amount of guilt - for having the audacity to exist on a planet that, in belonging to *'their' God*, was therefore by association also the <u>property of the church</u>
>
> **b)** That he be ravaged by the fear of his own natural inclinations which, the priests instilled into him, were dirty and sinful

Lastly that he work a fifteen hour day, six and a half days a week, allowing time off to go to church, fifty two weeks a year and give what little he had, in tithes, taxes and portable goods; to these corrupt, lying, murderers who, though mere ignorant, jumped-up peasants themselves, were in fact making the peasants' life more hell than any fairy could. If Jesus could have seen the atrocities and social injustices that these blood-soaked carrion were perpetrating in his name, he would have turned in his grave.

The ***Scythians*** didn't prey on peasants, merchants, human nobility or so-called 'royalty' for reasons intimated previously, namely that in comparison, those not of the fairy race had dead blood trickling through their veins.

In their heyday the fairies practiced familial vampirism which, in tandem with their tradition of living with the remains of their ancestors in tomb or ***temple Raths***, established the folk tradition which tells that the *vampires* returned from the dead - rose from the tombs - to feed from the blood and life force of their living relatives.

During the *Medieval and Reformation Periods* this tradition was gleefully expanded upon and misreported by both the ***Roman*** and ***Protestant churches*** (who are both *Catholic*, *lunatic* and just as *evil as one another*) to give the erroneous impression that *vampires*, or indeed werewolves, could occur in any family, peasant, merchant or otherwise, and that those families therefore were constantly in danger from their own departed.

What kind of twisted pieces of human dross would think up such a story and, not content to turn the living against the living, brother against sister and husband against wife, would also turn the living against their own ancestors? This is deliberate alienation and disenfranchisement on a grand scale.

On the death of a relative, wasn't life sad enough and, if the person were a breadwinner, precarious and uncertain enough in those days, without having some parasite propagating the kind of story that invested tragedy and grief with menace. As one mourned someone once so dearly loved in life, in death they were then to become an object of loathing and dread.

What we have here is a very disturbing collection of criminals who will say or do anything for power and what is even more disturbing is that these megalomaniacal, conniving dregs of humanity, either themselves or through sympathetic or sycophantic governmental elites, are still manipulating the minds of the people in ***Europe*** and ***America*** with variations of the same foul, evil nonsense they have always propagated. They may have taken a back seat, but they're still in power. Who will rid us of these pestilent priests?

In truth the king tribe never drank the blood of outsiders. There was no point in it, they were of a different race. Instead, in much the same way as they selected their rulers and druids, from an '*Atheling Pool*' of ***Brehon Families***, they also selected from this same group a class of females who became known as '***Grail Maidens***'. These sacred, royal princesses, virgins of ***High Birth and Pure Blood***, at an optimum age would be chosen to act as feeding females.

Giving willingly of their blood, fluids and energy, these girls were not mutilated, sacrificed or murdered during the process, but were worshipped and cherished as incarnations of the nurturing ***Dragon Goddess. Dea Vulna Gnosis.***

In fact they were perceived as, and treated like, goddesses themselves and their rank was second only to the ***High Queens*** who, on attaining the traditional age, they themselves became. Women today should be so lucky. When fully mature, the ***Grail Maidens*** became ***Dragon Princesses*** and were encouraged to pick the cream of the princes and war lords for their pleasure.

When contracted into lease marriages with their own kin they became the ***Dragon Queens*** and the matriarchs of their people, the mothers of the next generation of ***Elven Queens*** and ***Kings***. Such is a far cry from the treatment a ***Celtic*** woman might expect to receive, who having but one office open to her and far less physiological capabilities than a ***Dragon Queen***, was treated with less respect than a brood mare. Status Quo.

The ***Fairies***, though now thought of as obscure nature spirits, were at the forefront of Eurasian civilization and included the ***Pendragons*** and their cousins the ***Merovingians***. The decline and obscurity of the fairy race was caused, as we have seen, by the *Roman Catholic Church* who, unlike the now defunct ***Celtic Church***, were the sworn enemies of the ***Grail*** or ***Fairy blood***.

The ***Celtic*** or ***Druidic Church*** was a priestly variant of the middle eastern branch of the ***Grail race***, the ***Dragon Kings***. The word *Church* actually derives from '*circa*' and the old highland euphemism for going to the *Kirk* was "*going to the stones*", meaning *stone circle*.

The ***Messiahship***, the *rulership* of the *christian church* was invested in **Jesus** as the appointed son and rabbi and was intended, like ***Dragon Kingship***, to descend in his bloodline. This it did with the ***Merovingian kings*** and the ***Celtic Church***. In Britain **Jesus**' granddaughter married the **Archdruid Bran the Blessed**, cementing a blood alliance between the ***Dragon*** and the ***Grail*** branches of the one greater royal family, guided and protected by the druidic Priests of the Celtic Church and the indigenous Druids of Britain.

For reasons outlined in other works **Jesus**' other brother **James** attracted a following consisting of **Paul of Tarsus** and **Peter the Fisherman**. This faction broke with **James** and settled in Rome with Paul and established itself eventually as the ***Roman Church*** under **Constantine**, which boasted **Peter** as the *First Bishop of the Christian Church*. This was twaddle because, as ***Vatican*** records show, **Prince Linus of Britain** was already by blood descent from **Jesus** the First Bishop of the Christian Church following Christ himself.

Nevertheless, since then the Roman heresy, the ***Catholic***

Church of the Dogma and not the Blood, vied for ascendence and after its final victory in 664 AD at the ***Council of Whitby***, it did everything in its power to steal authority and leadership from the rightful bloodline descendants who held it. As part of this process in ***Europe*** deals were done with the *Mayors of the Palaces* aforementioned and the ***Merovingians*** were either murdered or incarcerated as the Church established these Mayors, ***the Carolingians***, under them as puppet kings.

After the *Dark Ages the Roman Church* became a ubiquitous and brutal power which attempted the utter destruction of the true kings and as a result of this relentless campaign, as the centuries have progressed we have been left to think of the fairies as the church would wish us to think of them, as being anything other than what they really were.

Hard pressed and in decline at this period, many in the outlying regions who could not adjust to the new regime or assimilate themselves into a camouflaged position simply took to the forests during the periods of the church's worst excesses.

In their place and in the places of those ***the Church murdered***, they appointed farmer chieftains and tinkers from the *Sudra class* of ***Celtic Society***, thus confusing the identities of the ***Scythians*** and the ***Celts*** allowing, in retrospect, a situation where it appears that the ***Celts*** trade off the earlier cultural accomplishments of the ***Fairy race*** as if they were their own, thereby paving the way for glorious ersatz 'Celtic Revivals' in the centuries to come!

So whilst some members of the ***fairy race of kings*** took refuge in deceit, many others took to the forests and lived in the obscurity and insularity of the *Greenwood*, thereby reinforcing the ancient association between fairies and the natural world in folk memory.

Such an association finds further reinforcement in the old druidic laws concerning the reverence due to trees and nature in general which, to the *fairy queens and kings* with their transcendent perception, contained life in all its manifestations, a life which they were the custodians of.

In the days of their ascendance the ***fairies*** operated a system of land management that consisted of nomadic pastoralism and hunting, interspersed by the settled agriculture of their ***Celtic*** clientele who tended the farmsteads in rotation, accompanying their fairy lords and ladies as they themselves travelled seasonally between a central Sacred seat and three out of four *satellite raths* and their burghs or brocks which were arranged in a *nomen* or *mark of Cain* circle-and-cross configuration.

The advantage of this system, which gave rise to the folk tale of the '*trooping fairies*', was that the regional game stock, the vegetation and the soil itself were allowed to recuperate and restore themselves in times allotted as being fallow.

For one year in four a whole region would lie fallow and a hangover from this tradition can be seen in the old '*Norfolk Strip*' style of crop rotation, though instead of resting strips of land in turn, the ***fairies*** rested whole districts, moving themselves and their clients from settlement to settlement in turn as the year progressed.

The traditional times to move were *May Eve, Midsummer, Samhain* and the return to the centre was at *Yule*, revealing a quarturnal rotation when the ***fairies*** could be seen and heard traversing the forests, hills and dales in joyous musical progressions filled with light and laughter.

Such tales, surviving the brutality and oppression of the medieval period, came down to us through folk tales until the last century when in ***Eire*** and ***Scotland***, they were still common currency amongst the rural communities who were wont to comment, as we have seen, that "*if the Elves die, the Land dies too*".

To the ***Dragon Queens*** and ***Kings*** - the ***fairies***, were attached numerous epithets some of which are included here, but are the subject of another essay, where these are dealt with in detail.

Chapter Two

Scythians and Druids

The **Tocharians** depicted in the cave shrines of **Takla Makan** are red haired and wear the same conical hat, sometimes called a Phrygian cap. A variant of this was worn by **Mithras**, the intermediary god adopted by the Persians and featured in the Indian pantheon of the **Asuras**.

In monarchical dualism he is depicted as balancing the forces of increase and decrease, represented by the gods **Ahura Mazda** and **Ahriman** and some classical authors identified him with **Jesus Christ**. His headgear is also depicted as the hat worn by gnomes and dwarves.

Accompanying the depictions of the **Tocharian Lords** in these cave temples are examples of the language attributed to them - Tocharian A script - which looks remarkably like one of the scripts that **Tolkien** attributes to his Elven peoples. That the **Tocharians** are **Scythian-Aryans** themselves means that the devotional language used by their High-Kings and Queens might justifiably be called an **Elven language**, <u>the tongue of Tolkien's Sundered Elves of the East</u>.

The second Gaelic word for '**vampire**' is **Sumaire**, which is pronounced **shimarie**, with the accent on the middle syllable - shim AR ri. **Sumaire** is translated as '**vortex**', meaning a whirlpool or spiral, a labyrinth: a sucker, a **reptile** (serpent or Dragon).

There is a clear link here with **Sumeria** and **Anu**'s mother **Tiamat**, the Dragoness of the deeps, and with **Anu**'s children **Samael** and **Lilith**, <u>the forebears of the fairies</u>. Various pictures of the latter two depict them as entwined around a tree, often the tree is **Lilith** herself, with **Samael** as the serpent or dragon resting in her branches as in Hebraic Iconography where **Lilith** <u>is the Tree of knowledge in the Garden of Eden</u>.

The **Sumerians** appeared first in Mesopotamia in 3500 BC. Prior to their emergence they were preceded by the **Ubaid** migrants from what is now southern **Romania**, from **Carpathia** and **Scythia**, who had fled south to escape the Black Sea flood of 4000 BC. Dated to about 5000 BC, archaeologists working in **Tartaria** in the **Ubaid** territory of **Transylvania**, discovered a 'tepes' or Rath under which they found a fire-pit.

Buried amongst the ashes were the human remains of a cannibalistic sacrificial victim and <u>two clay tablets</u>. On these were inscribed the name of **Enki** (**Samael**), the number of **Anu** - **60** - and the image of a goat, **Enki** again, and a **Tree - Lilith.** In Hinduism **Siva** is the <u>Goatherd of the Mountains</u>.

The pictographic nature of the inscriptions convinced the archaeologists that the language was the forerunner of **Sumerian** and so they called it proto-Sumerian. Making it fairly obvious that the **Sumerians** were originally Ubaid Overlords from Central Eurasia.

Sadly however, because a bunch of right-wing Hungarian nationalists then claimed Sumerian roots by virtue of a discovery made in a backyard they had only recently overrun, subsequent to the discovery in the 1960's and the attendant madcap claim, no academic would give the proto-Sumerian theory house room, not wishing to accommodate the views of a collection of neo-nazi cranks and quite rightly so.

What a group of Mongoloids thought they had in common with the **Aryan race** the author doesn't know. Having invaded the region as the **Magyar** at so late a period in history the author fails to see how any claim to Sumerian or proto-Sumerian origins, that an isolated group of Hungarian lunatics might make, could possibly hold up under even the most cursory scrutiny.

Nevertheless the author also finds the attitude of those academics who opposed the definition to be obstructive and misleading, especially as it is now conclusively proved that the culture responsible for the production of the Tartarian clay tablets and the Rath structure was **Ubaid** - the founders of civilized **Mesopotamia** and, as it turns out, the **Overlords** of the Indus valley civilization of **Mohenjo Daro** and **Harrapa** where **Ishtar** reigned as **Queen**.

Further east of **Transylvania** similar discoveries were made in the Ukraine or greater **Scythia** and the peoples who had settled the area were named after their dwellings, which in Russian were called **Kurgans**. They were mound houses exactly the same as the tepes of Tartaria and the Tells that the **Ubaid** built all the way down through **Anatolia** to **Al'Ubaid** and **Sumeria**.

To the **Kurgan peoples**, obviously the red-haired Aryan or proto-Aryan (if you must) horse lords, was attributed the invention of the chariot whose axle dimensions were copied on all horse drawn vehicles right up until the Victorian period, when they were incorporated into the axle width (4ft 8½ ins) of the standard gauge railways still in use today.

The influence that **vampires** have had on European culture should not be dismissed! They inspired modern wheeled transport, invented tourism in a big way and lent their images and their dress to the lids of every shortbread tin you've ever seen.

It seems fair to suggest, given the wealth of archaeological and anthropological evidence, that the **Sumerians** or **Ubaid** as we should call them, along with the pale-skinned and red-haired **Lilith** and her descendants, were the early **Elven, Aryan-Scythian Dragon Overlords** of what we know now as **Transylvania** and **Greater Scythia**.

This particularly in the light of the discoveries of bat winged, serpent-god statuary found in **Dacia** and **Tibet** (not too far from Takla Makan!) which is said to date back at least 5000 years, putting it into the period of the emergence of civilization in **Sumeria**.

Such figures we would readily identify as the **Dragon** or, in Gaelic - **The Sumaire** - whilst the Kurgans/Tells/Tepes that these early Transylvanian/Scythian **Sidheans** or **Ubaid** occupied were clearly duplicated in the Irish Raths of the Danaan, such as **Newgrange** with its spirally engraved stones, the **Ziggurats** of the **Sumerians** and the **Pyramids** of the **Egyptians**.

Whilst these ancient structures bore the marks of the **sumaire**, the **spiral labyrinth** or **vortex** design, thus emphasizing the creachaire - **sumaire** theme of **the Dragon** - **witch** - **Vampire** - **Overlord** theme, the Egyptians too adopted the labyrinth and used the spiral as a hieroglyph which they termed the '**Mer**', a symbol of irrigation associating it with water and, via weir spelt Vere and Mhaior, rendering Muir, returning once more to the Egyptian Mer - the fish trap or fish-woman trap, the enclosure of the mermaid, the maze or labyrinth and intimations of the wild hunt.
(**Muir** and **Mhaior** name variants courtesy of **Dr. Hugh Vere**).

So at long last, having trudged through the backwaters of obscure knowledge we can now say that we know exactly who and what **the Vampire was and is.** A very rare individual, a **God-King** amongst the race of human kings, the **Vampire** descends from the supernatural Dragon Royalty of Sumeria back to the **Ubaid Overlords** of what was to become known as **Transylvania** and **Greater Scythia**.

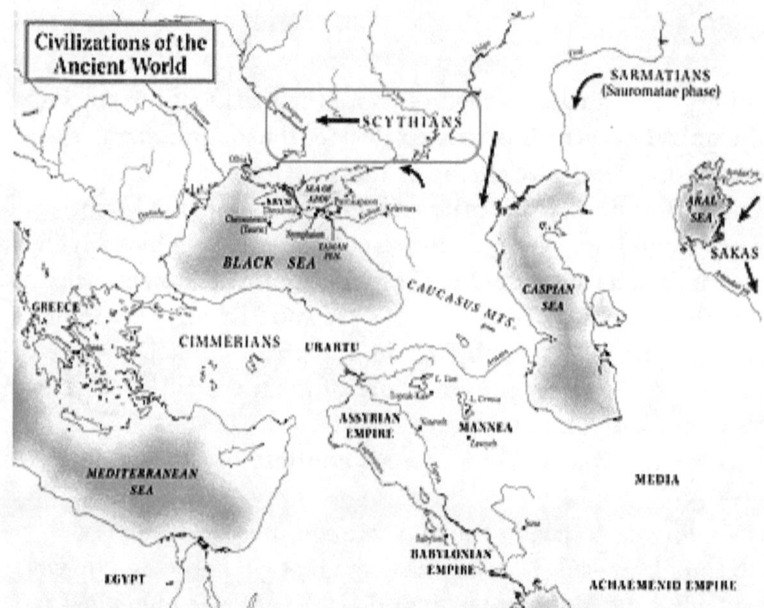

The Vampire: the <u>Dragon King or Queen</u> was an Archdruid, a Witch Queen or King, a Fairy Princess or Prince amongst the **race of Elphame**. Consequently the **Vampire**, the **Fairy**, the **Dragon** and the **Witch** <u>were all the same individual</u> and far from being the characters of fable they were in fact very powerful, very real beings whose vampiric natures and rituals sustained their <u>superconsciousness, transcendent vision</u> which in its turn maintained their positions as the overlords of mankind.

These **gods of flesh and blood** were the only gods that ever actually existed: Myth, however, transformed them into the ethereal deities whom we are conditioned to think of as Gods now, and who came to be worshipped worldwide. Nevertheless flesh and blood they were and their bloodlines descend to the present day.

<u>The Druids</u>

The word **Druid** is said to be Greek in origin and, as 'drys':

means 'tree'. Some authorities like to think it means 'oak tree' but no evidence exists to confirm this irrefutably. As we shall see later druid is also related to 'dru' meaning 'run' in **Sanskrit** and to Drys meaning a Wren - specifically the **Goldcrest** - one of the birds most sacred to the Druids. For the present however, we will concentrate on the Greek version of the word.

Though the **Druids** are associated with groves and, as some will insist, with oak trees, it is feasible to suggest that in the light of their Sumerian and Ubaid origins, the **druids** as **priest kings of the Dragon**, were connected specifically with the Tree of Life and the Tree of Knowledge, rather than with any mundane or temporal shrubbery.

Accepting this we may further suggest that, as priests of these pre-eminent Trees of Life and Knowledge, they may be further identified with those magicians and scholars whose **Transylvanian descendants**, the Scythian Aryans or Sumerian Anunnaki - the **Dragon God-Kings** - were instrumental in establishing the Chakric system of Hindu and Buddhist Tantra and Hebrew, Arabic and Greek Qabalah whose magical systems, as we all know, contain a glyph called the **Tree of Life**.

Generally speaking this Tree, a system of pathways both macrocosmic and microcosmic in nature, links the various subtle energy centers which are said to exist both in the universe, as levels of density and emanation relating to the manifestation of cosmic power and being, and in the human body - on the microcosmic level - as energy centers corresponding to the glands in the endocrinal system. In **Qabalah** the spheres which do not relate to the glands may be seen as points in the meridian system adopted by the **Chinese**. On another level, the Qabalistic Tree of Life is a **genealogical chart of the Gods**.

The magical **Tree** is a universal symbol. As in the early **Sumerian** depiction of the Tree of Life; the abode of **Lilith**, many of the subsequent Arabic, Indian and European Holy Trees share common attributes. All have residing in their topmost branches some form of bird.

In **Tantra** it is the swan, whose head rests within the **Ajna Chakra** which corresponds to the **pineal** and **pituitary glands** and the **corpus callosum**. In Welsh druidic lore the bird is represented as the eagle, a typically shamanic, totem bird which symbolizes the ascendent spirit. Here the eagle is the **god Lleu** (in Ireland he is the **Danaan king Lugh**), the father of the elven Llewelyn kings of Gwynnedd.

In **Arabic Sufism** the bird is a peacock whilst in **Viking lore** the Sacred Tree Yggdrasil has at its base a coiled serpent by a pool and in its highest boughs the bird of the released spirit accompanied by a white hart.

What a deer is doing up a tree is anyone's guess, but have a stab at it and I'll tell you later. **Yggdrasil** is called the Axis Mundi and is seen as the tree which contains within its branches and roots the nine worlds of the Viking philosophical system, including their version of the Hebrew Qlipphoth or underworld. Immediately the similarity between it and the **Qabalistic** and **Tantric Trees** becomes quite apparent and this is no fluke.

In actual fact the druid's most sacred tree wasn't the oak, it was the apple tree, linked to which is the blue boar, both of which came originally, it was said, from the Otherworld. For this reason the **Tree of Knowledge** in the Garden of Eden was always depicted as the apple, but could be interchanged with the pomegranate for reasons which eventually will become apparent to the hardiest and most persistent reader.

The Mistletoe Bard, whom we will encounter later, cut the golden bough from the Apple prior to descending into the underworld. Where it has been suggested that the berries of the mistletoe represent the sperm of the Great Oak God (**Jupiter/Thor/Jehovah/Enlil**) and thus his fertility and life-force, this isn't in fact the case.

The Mistletoe grew mainly on Apple trees which, as we shall see, are exclusively female. Therefore the berries of the Mistletoe represent the female and consequently the **Goddess' fluid**, not the seminal fluid of a male deity.

The boar is sacred to both **Mars** and to **Arduina** or **Diana**. This link between the apple and the boar, and the boar and Mars and Diana or the Moon is identical with the association between the Apple Tree of Eden as **Lilith** (of the Moon) and **Samael** the **Serpent** or **Dragon** who embraces her. Essentially the symbols of the **Boar** and the **Dragon** have become interchangeable.

The **Blue Boar** is a druidic symbol of office and the **Dragon** is a symbol of bloodline descent, a clan badge of the druidic race. In the **Scythian Dragon Tribe** the individual totem animal badges vary from region to region and reflect the local fauna and the status of the clan or sept. As an example a high or archdruidic family badge would be the boar, whilst a junior sept of that clannad would have as its totem the hedgehog, which is rather amusing.

The symbol of **Samael** the **Serpent** reclining in the Branches of **Lilith**'s **Apple Tree** in the Garden of Eden actually depicts the concept of the **Dragon** eating the fruit itself. This can also be found slightly more abstractly but conversely and paradoxically more graphically at the same time, in the **Tantric** equivalent of the **serpent** entwined around a female figure.

As the apple is also the favorite fruit of the boar in the wild, it is doubtless that the adoption of the **Boar** as a badge was because of this and further, that the identification of the **boar** with the **dragon** was through their mutual, actual and symbolic love of what the **Irish druids** called the apples of red-gold. The **boar** was also called **Le Solitaire** and for this reason has links with the **Merlin** which will be dealt with later.

The Apple Trees - either **Lilith** or her descendant scarlet priestesses - bore the fruit which symbolized the sephirah and the glands of the female body. These, the apples of **red-gold**, produce the enriched virginal womb blood that was consumed by both the male and female druids - the **Boars** in the Orchard and the **Serpents** or **Dragons** in the Trees. **Red-Gold** is also the **Tantric Kaula** term for womb blood: the **Rtu** or first flow of the womb.

In reinforcing the **Uber-Oupire** link - the identification between the **witch** (**druidhe**) and **vampire** - it is worth taking a look at the totem system of **Mithraism**, a close cousin of **druidism**. In the **Mithraic** initiatory grades there are 7 degrees.

The Highest is **the Dragon** and the penultimate is the wolf. Also included is the Raven and with variations across Europe these animals, along with Swans, Geese, Bears, Vipers, Hawks, eagles and so on, served as the **tuadh** or **kingdom emblems** for the various Scythian groups.

In **Romania** however, these grades with their animal totems or badges make up the degrees or conditions of vampirism. The most potent vampire is the **Dracoi** or **female Dracoica**, from whence the **House of Drakul** obtained its name, meaning 'Satan' or 'Dragon' whilst **Drakulea** or **Dracula** means 'son of

Satan' or 'son of the Dragon'. Lying at a close second place comes the **Stregoi** or **female Stregoica**, a being that manifests itself as either a wolf or a raven. We can see where this is leading, can't we?

The Stregoi or Stregoica represents both the **Morrighan** or **Morgana**, the **Valkyrie** and the Werewolf or Verewolf, which is simply <u>another manifestation of the vampire</u>. Typically and especially where wolves were in short supply, the werewolf was represented variously by the Bear and the Fox; and elsewhere by the crocodile (the **Sobekh** of Egypt - patron and protector of Royalty - whose fat was used as the **Messach** or <u>anointing oil of the pharoahs</u>, the **Messiahs** or **priest kings**).

In this neck of the woods it was also common to replace the werewolf with the **Panther** who was sacred to the lunar goddess Diana and also to Bacchus. **Panther** <u>was the clan name of **Jesus**</u>, and much earlier, the **Ubaid priests** wore the skins of **Panthers** as their totem animal. The Panther's feeding ritual involves it opening the jugular vein in its victims neck and drinking the blood prior to eating the carcass.

The association between werewolves and the moonlight which drove them loopy, according to fable, is repeated and reinforced by the traditional belief that **witches** (aka **vampires**) were sacred to **Diana** and worshipped her by the light of the full moon. The link between the full moon and the vampire of the Gothic Romance is also well represented in tradition.

The reason that **moonlight** drove **werewolves** round the twist and elicited devotion from **witches** was because the full moon was seen as <u>the menstrual moon</u> that signaled the impending flow and was worshipped particularly by the **witches** of **Italy** and the surrounding area.

These ladies were called **Strega**, that is the Italian name for a **witch** and rather than worshipping the full moon they were celebrating what the moon and **Diana** stood for - food for the soul - the blood of virgins! Give it a chance - it isn't as gory or unsavory as it sounds.

This was the secret foundation for the High Romance and Courtly Love that initiated the exoteric Medieval Romantic Movement itself, so don't get judgmental or picky. If you are health conscious and take supplements like HRT you might as well know that it comes in many cases either from the urine of Mares or French Nuns - yes the author did say: Nuns. It's official. So don't start turning your nose up at a bit of harmless but nevertheless profitable genital snogging. Its a lot more fun than taking the piss out of Catholics. Most of the time.

As **Melatonin** was the primary hormone extracted in the blood rites of Diana it's your choice: would you have preferred the blood of beautiful virgins, romantically celebrating and giving joyously of their feminine power and status by moonlight then, or the urine of papists - in a pill - now? One type of **melatonin** is live whilst the other is stone dead and useless - guess which is which. And **Melatonin** is only the beginning of the story.

In addition to the **Dragon Court**'s research into **DNA**, over two years ago the author who, many years ago, was the first to pinpoint the potential chemicals indictated in the precise hormonal makeup of the **Holy Grail** and **Grant**'s **Starfire phenomena** (which information he subsequently passed, in part, on to **Laurence Gardner**), also commissioned the assay of various organic fluids in order to discover and prove the presence of a range of these vital psychotropic and restorative chemicals discharged by the human female system.

These

included **oxytocin, prolactin, melatonin, seratonin, adenosy ne triphosphate, dopamine, telomerase** and **retinol**. The results of these assays should be known soon. **Richard Dufton** had also been working independently on identifying the same chemical presences for some years and when he and the author met in 1995 they began to work closely on the Melatonin basis for the **Holy Grail.** Out of this joint research the author discovered the wider implications of the discovery and restructured the Kabalistic and Tantric systems with precise chemical indices for each **sephiroth** or **chakra**.

The association between Scythian Totem beasts, Romanian animal vampire types and **Mithraic** grades of Initiation indicates clearly that **vampirism**, far from being random or opportunist, was in fact part of an ancient system of **elven rites** manifest in **Tantra, Mithraism** and **Druidism.**

Having said that the symbol of the panther and the werewolf were apposite, as the **Scythian warrior nobility** were a tad bloody-minded at times and Roman reports from the early part of the first millennium state how the **Pictish Danaan** had been witnessed eating the flesh and drinking the blood of their defeated foes following victories in battle.

Undoubtedly this was a corruption of earlier ritual practice as we shall see later. Certainly going out and 'eating Italian' had a unique and disturbing meaning for the Roman soldiery of the day, as the Ninth Legion in Albany discovered to their cost. Drinking the blood of friend or foe in battle was a common practice in **Eire** and **Scotland**, the former in remembrance of fallen comrades, the latter to obtain the strength of the enemy. Contrary to **Royal Vampirism**, the whole point of **Martial Vampirism** was to clog your arteries with someone else's adrenaline

Another ritual familiar to those who have read **Stoker**'s Dracula was the hauling of soil from the Scythian homelands in boxes. The **Scythians** initiated this practice with the idea that the earth was the source of sovereignty and power and that ones soul was linked to ones homeland.

This isn't entirely daft because we are what we eat, and what we eat affects the 'soul' (biochemically derived and mediated collection of responses and attachments called 'ME', the ego, personality or whatever, dependant for its existence on the continuity of the mind-brain interface) through the body, both body and soul being inextricably linked as they are. What we eat comes from the land where we are born and so the soil of ones country and its inherent sovereignty and identity literally flow in the blood that courses through one's veins.

Up until the last century, the displaced **Scots** who traveled to **America** would slip a little soil from their former Crofts into the soles of their boots in order that, wherever they went they would always be walking on the earth of their homeland.

The **Scythian Overlords** brought the **dragon culture** with them as they traversed the many regions of **Europe** and finally settled in the **British Isles**. All their kings, indeed all **Scythians** of the royal caste were dragons, particularly the **druids** and their high kings were called **Pendragons** or chief dragons and were picked by their druidic peers from druidic families.

Variant spellings for the name **Druid** include '**Draoi**' - thought to mean **Dragon** - which is close in spelling to the Romanian 'Dracoi' and 'Dracoica' which, if related to 'Drys', associated with wood nymphs or tree spirits, suggests that the 'Drys' or 'Dryads' were the female druids who were symbolized by the apple tree of **Lilith** whilst the 'Draoi' or 'Dracoi' - the highest degree of the male druids - were represented by **the serpent** entwined in the branches of those apple trees.

The **Priestess Queens** and **Priest Kings**, as we have seen, dwelt in the holy places, the **royal Raths** that served as both <u>temple and tomb</u>. These subterranean palaces mimicked the the Bergs or mound houses of the **Scythians'** 'proto'-Sumerian ancestors, who originated in **Transylvania** and **Carpathia**.

Similarly the <u>Mithraic underground temples</u> resembled places like **Newgrange**, in that they had an aperture above the doorway that allowed a shaft of sunlight into the building. This ray would hit the back wall of the temple where, in the case of **Mithraic rituals**, there were placed figurines, the sequential illumination of each in its turn, as the day progressed onwards, would tell an initiatory story, bathed in the dying light of the midwinter sun.

Beneath the doorways of various of these buildings have been discovered the remains of headless corpses whose skulls would have been secreted within these **Sidhe Mounds**. Their functions were to serve as Guardians of the Portals, spirit defenders of the power and sanctity of these shrines - the dwellings of the **Dragons** - the Goddess-Queens and God-Kings incarnate.

The <u>cult of the severed head</u>, as part of **Celtic religious practice** originated with the druids and therefore the **Scythians**. Examples of the head as the seat of the soul and the source of mystical wisdom, a bestower of gifts or cornucopia finds expression both in the legend of the head of Bran the Blessed or Bendigaid Fran, **Archdruid of Britian,** retold in the Mabinogion; and the Trial papers of the Templars, who owned a head which was said to speak words of transcendent wisdom. This head, along with that of Bran, have both been cited as being <u>aspects of the Grail</u> with whom both Bran and the Templars were connected.

The **Knights Templars** restructured by **Baldwin of Bourcq** in 1118 appended to their name "and of the Temple of Solomon" whilst the **original Order of Templars**, a **Vere foundation** which emerged in 1100 were called "**Guardian Princes of the Royal Secret**". However the original Temple Guard was founded 1500 years earlier in Jerusalem.

A close examination of the 'Song of Songs' attributed to **Solomon** will reveal to the reader certain esoteric references to **the Grail**. It has been further revealed that **Solomon**'s bloodline had Scythian Dragon origins and therefore connections with the Cult of the Head. That a head, said to be that of the **Magdalene**, successor to **Sheba**, to turn up in the inventory attached to the Templar trial papers should therefore come as no surprise.

The **Scythians** believed that the head contained the immortal soul. **Descartes**, writing in the 1600's, was of the same opinion and elaborated by asserting that the seat of the soul was the pineal gland. Others, writing later, have suggested that this organ is the mediator of inspiration and the translator of intuitive or cosmic information.

In Indian Tantric Yoga the **Pineal** is the physical seat or anchor of the **Ajna Chakra** which also corresponds to the **Pituitary** as well. In this philosophy the **Pineal** is symbolized as being the head of the swan, whose body comprises the various areas of the rest of the brain. As we have seen, the dove and the Raven also fulfill this symbolic function.

The **Pineal Gland** is specifically associated with **Grail Lore** and closely aspected to manifestations of **the Grail** in the forms of a **Cup**, a **Stone**, a **Cauldron**, a **Well**, **Mere** or **lake**; a **fountain**, (such as that found in certain kabalistic rituals) and an underground stream.

Within the theme of the severed head we also find the dressed head of **Llewelyn, King of Gwynedd**, which was severed from his body and garlanded with Ivy (sacred to Bacchus) before being dispatched to **Edward I** following the victory of his armies over the Welsh in the 1200's.

Some two hundred years later, on his death in 1477, **Prince Vlad Draculea**'s body was taken to an Abbey he had built on an Island in the middle of a lake in **Smyrna**. Such a sanctuary has distinct Arthurian overtones and associations with the Isle of Avallon, upon which there was also built an abbey of the quasi-druidic Celto-Scythian Church.

This replaced the early Rath temple, grove and sanctuary of the **Morganas**, the ladies of the lake who were the **Swan Maiden-Valkyries of the Scythian world,** **vampires** and **head hunters.** In such sanctuaries headless corpses, as we have seen, were placed as portal guardians and it is in just such a condition that we discover that, according to local tradition, Draculea's head was removed from his body and his corpse was buried beneath the stone flags beneath the doorway of the Abbey's chapel.

A similar incident is reported to have occurred with the establishment of the Celtic Christian Shrine on the **Island of Iona**. Here it is **St Columba** who is said to have severed the head of one of his disciples and buried the blood drained corpse beneath the doorway of the chapel.

The blood of the victim was then consumed as a eucharist in thanksgiving for the monks' safe arrival to the island. Here we can see that early Christianity was indeed tied up with the cult of the head, as was the collateral Johannite Cult of the Baptist, who himself was a sacrificial **king of Dragon descent**.

Draculea's name means son of the Dragon as we have seen, and his burial replicates the **Scythian** burials in the **Holy-Royal Sidhe** or power mounds found in **Eire** and **Scotland**.
In **Draculea**'s case there are a number of symbols associated with him that connect him directly with the Scythian druidic tradition.

Furthermore these symbols, some of which we can also find, surprisingly enough, in **Stoker**'s novel, lead to the conclusion that **Stoker** knew a great deal about his subject. Much of the information in 'Dracula' the novel, is of an esoteric and highly specialized psycho-biological nature, which does not detract from or conflict with, but rather elucidates upon, the character of the **Draculea** of history.

Bram Stoker was a close friend and associate of the Welsh magician and writer **Arthur Machen** who wrote numerous works, including a paper on the alchemical significance of the **dragon** and a novel on the Twllyth Teg - the fairies of Wales.

It is a common device to convey esoteric knowledge via the medium of supposed fiction and it appears that both **Stoker** and **Machen** involved themselves in such ventures. **Stoker** was also acquainted with **Aleister Crowley** and **MacGregor Mathers**, both of whom were leading lights in the Hermetic Order of the Golden Dawn. **Machen** and **Wilde** were members of this organization which, it is said, had its roots in the ancient Rosicruciana Anglicae.

Oscar Wilde was one of only four people associated with **The Golden Dawn** and the later breakaway group: the **Ordo Templi Orientis** headed by **Crowley**, who himself undertook to perform the rituals leading to the accomplishment of a variant of the ancient "Mass of the Vampire".

The amazing **Jack Parsons, OTO**., attempted it in the 1940's and joined **Wilde** in succumbing to the ruin and degradation that accompanies it. **Jack** died in an inexplicable explosion in the garage of his home in California.

Whilst **Crowley** accomplished the rite and walked away virtually unscathed, eventually dying of old age in Hastings, **Wilde**'s fate is known to all. Having said that 'Death in Hastings' has none of the romantic je ne sais quoi of say, 'Death in Venice', or even Paris. Perhaps **Wilde**, vilified as he was, had the better of it after all, at least in terms of style!

It has been suggested that **Stoker** was either a member of the **OTO** or the **Golden Dawn** and it would appear that the cohesion and integrity of the symbolism in his 'Dracula' must therefore point to **Stoker** having a source of esoteric information far more informed in historical and alchemical terms than any that he might have obtained, as it has been suggested, purely from the folklore of Romanian peasants or from contemporary literary sources.

Historical accounts of **Prince Draculea**'s life confirm that he was born in and became **Prince of Wallachia**, not Transylvania. In
linking **Draculea** with **Transylvania** however, **Stoker** suggests to the reader that the origin of the vampire tradition was indeed linked to the **Ubaid Homeland**.

Recent research has uncovered the fact that **Draculea** did indeed, like his **Scythian Warrior** ancestors, drink the blood of his impaled and decapitated victims. Decapitation is distinctly a **Scythian** practice and although it has been suggested that **Draculea** learnt the custom of impaling from his Turkish captors, this practice had been used as a punishment by the **Aryans of Persia** as early as 500 BC.

Although **Stoker** has Dracula impaled and decapitated at his castle when in fact **Draculea** was beheaded at the Abbey where he was buried, **Stoker** is rightly attempting to associate Dracula, via these rituals, with an entire vampiric cultural tradition of which his character was destined to become the definitive archetype.

This is no bad thing because the picture of Dracula and his accoutrements and behavior is not far from the actual truth of the matter. The finer details of the novel confirm that **Stoker** was probably being prompted by others in the writing of this work, which contains secret information that is still generally unknown outside certain circles.

It was generally thought that the only way to kill a vampire was to impale the body through the heart, in order to pin the wandering body to the earth, remove the head and cremate the remains. At that time cremation was forbidden in Christian Europe because it was believed that the bodily remains should be left intact to rise again on the Day of Judgment.

Obviously **the Church** thought that reconstituting the fetid and rotting remains of sinners on the Last Day would be a doddle for God, whereas he would be powerless to reconstruct the former human being from a handful of dust. Typically stunning christian logic in action here.

Cremation was practiced by **Hindus**, a race of people originally extracted from the **Aryan Horse Lords**. Considering this as a funerary practice in relation to decapitation and impaling, which was reserved as a royal punishment in **Persia**, perhaps the peasant memory, prompted by the church, recalled the link between royalty and these rituals and thence assumed that the only way to kill a **vampire** who was, after all exclusively a member of the Fairy or Royal Race, was to put the body through a series of ritual processes, some of which had been variously, components of **Scythian** royal sacrificial or funerary practice.

Royal decapitation we can see in the stories of Bran and Llewelyn, and although **Celts** buried their common dead, we might suggest, given the earliest evidence from **Tartaria** and other later sites, that **Royal Scythians,** like their **Viking** and **Hindu** cousins, cremated the sometimes decapitated remains of their sacred dead, depending on the requirements of specific ritual necessity. Perhaps to the peasantry, impaling was seen as poetic justice in dispatching one assumed to be of a race for whom impaling was a common punishment.

We have seen that impaling was thought to nail the body of the vampire to the earth and perhaps where the body wasn't burnt, impaling was considered sufficient to keep in its grave, the body of one belonging to a race that the crows in cassocks said was so terrifying and seemingly so indestructible.

It will be remembered though that many of the stories concerning **vampires** were contrived by the church to encourage the flock to remain in fear for its life and thus faithful to its only means of protection and salvation, the fat scheming pervert in the black frock.

It was immaterial to them that vampirism was rarely committed against outsiders except when they were opponents in war. Nevertheless the **vampire** scare went on longer than the **witch** craze and was just as effective in keeping the poor peasant in bondage to the evil doctrines of a lying church.

As a **Scythian** custom, impaling would have been as common in **Galatia,** later Turkey, where the **Cult of the Head** thrived in **Roman** times; as it was in **Persia** where it was reserved for one royal in particular - **Bress** - who betrayed his brother **Darius** following the successful invasion by **Alexander**.

Essentially **Stoker**'s Dracula is as much a part of the **Grail Cycle** as the Druidic stories of **King Arthur** and of **Eschenbach's 'Parzifal'.** In these stories as in most **Druidic** teaching fables, the Bards delighted in presenting material that could be read on several different but related levels which often have hermetic, macro and microcosmic components.

In particular where **Stoker** is concerned, an extract from **Solomon**'s 'Song of Songs' features in a couple of obscure lines in his Dracula and these directly refer to the central alchemical theme of the Grail Cycle and put the seal on the book as being an esoteric work, rather than just simply a Gothic novel.

Historically **Draculea** himself attended the 'Solomon School' in **Hermannstadt**, an alchemical, hermetic college that taught magic to the sons of Royalty. Two other schools like this existed in Europe, one was in **Toledo** in Spain and the other was said to be in **Transylvania**. At the 'Solomon' only one person per class ever graduated, or 'rode the Dragon' as it was termed.

Fanciful christian theory says that the rest of the students ended up with Satan in Hell! Reminiscent of a **Druidic 'Bangor'** or **university**, the 'Solomon School' finished **Vlad**'s education and fitted him to become a **Dacian** counterpart of the British **Pendragon**, with all the brutal wisdom of his fairy ancestors and predecessors who, as God-Kings of the specifically intermediary, guardian-class of **Anunnaki** deities, were inhumed in the same manner that Dracula himself was laid to rest.

Draculea the prince of Wallachia was little different in actuality from the Dracula character of **Stoker**'s novel. This Sacred Prince, a Hermetic scholar and initiate, a student of magic, Magus, Witch Lord and Dragon Prince, counterbalanced the bloodlust of his forebears with a refined knowledge and advanced practice of **Grail procedure** which, shining forth radiantly from the pages of **Stoker**'s little masterpiece, echoed the teachings that the historical **Draculea** would have received at the 'Solomon School': teachings and encountered in the **Dragon Court** of which he was a member, teachings which were held in common by Archdruids, Alchemists, Tantric Yogis, Hermeticists and Qabalists alike, each discipline originating from one ancient Fairy Tradition in **Sumeria** and **Transylvania** - the heartlands of the **Dragon Kings** and **Queens** of the **Sacred Danaan Peoples**.

In **Draculea**'s day christian kings sent their sons to christian universities but still, true kingship, the **Sobekh** or **Messiah kingship**, symbolized since antiquity by the **Dragon** or **Sacred Crocodile**, required that the true kings' sons learnt priest-kingship and in **Draculea**'s case, this education was still clearly of a Druidic nature, even as late as the 15th century.

In the Celtic British Isles after the Romans decamped, Princes were required to become **priests** or **druids** and as late as 660 AD we can find references concerning the education of the **Merovingian Prince Dagobert** at Slane University in **Ireland** where, up until the year 664 AD, **Celtic, Druidic Christianity** still held sway.

In those days and as late as 751 A.D. **Kings** still came exclusively from the **King Tribe** who supplied much of the Celtic world, as well as Eurasia, with **Draconian offspring** <u>to serve as Royal Priests</u>. This **King Tribe**, the **Arya** or **Sidhe** -

the **Scythians** - included the **Merovingian** dynasty who, although it was an amalgam of Jesus' Egyptian and Aryan blood, it was also closely related to the **Irish** and **Scots Royal Danaan** and the **Druidic castes** integral to these Houses still educated this dynastic progeny up until
the **Carolingian** usurpation and the ascendance of the **Church of Rome** in 664 AD.

Gradually at first the Roman church replaced the **true royal, elven blood** with its own bloodless puppets and made christian education the norm for the sons of the new christian kings and nobles whom the church had created. The Solomons of Hermannstadt, Toledo and Transylvania became the hidden leftovers of an ancient, originally druidic educational system which necessarily went underground and became the subject of myth and fairytale, along with the bloodlines it once educated openly.

The **Dragon Colleges** produced the '**Uber**',
the **Overlords** who, in **Britain** were called
the **Pendragons** and in **Transylvania** the '**Dracoi**' or '**Dracoica**' - the '**vampires**'. Only the highest graduates of the Druidic bangors would be thought of as true men or women of power, true **Sidhe** or **Fairy Royalty** and thus it was only the prince who 'rode the Dragon' who could be said to fit the same criteria for inclusion in the bloodline of the **vampire**,
the **witch** and the **fairy** families - **The Dragon Kings**.

Chapter Four

From Transylvania to Tunbridge Wells

'The Fair Folk'

Members of the ***Scythian Royal House*** were said to be of great beauty and wondrous to behold. We remember that they practiced selective breeding and that only the fairest and most pure could be selected as queens and kings.

Tall in stature and with the palest of complexions and the reddest of red gold hair, framing faces in which were set eyes of emerald green, these beings were magnificent to look upon admittedly, but beauty isn't just skin deep, only to the fool.

Beauty is a condition of the psyche and where those who have suffered a life of stress and tension, of bitterness and regret are concerned, we should not be surprised that they age quicker or look uglier, more mean of spirit that those whose lives have been led in truth and grace.

Added to their stunning symmetry, ***the Elves*** were naturally transcendent of spirit and their queens and kings were insulated from the common round of nuisances and petty concerns by minds which were bred for deeper matters.

Add then an inner state of being whose grace and equilibrium is reminiscent of the grace of the gliding swan, to a physical form of beauty attained by centuries of selective breeding, and you obtain a being whose elegance and poise is nothing less than otherworldly.

Indeed the swan in fairy culture, though representing an anatomical and physiological condition within the fairy brain, also represents that very serenity of being that that neuro-physiology effects within the ***fairy mind*** and is consequently seen manifestly in the visage and deportment of that race's queens and princesses and kings and princes, the swan maidens and swan knights of legend.

From Transylvania to Tunbridge Wells

In folklore such intimations of beauty come down to us in stories of elf maidens who, in reflecting such poise and charm as could only be manifest in enlightened beings, are portrayed as swans on the evening waters of moonbathed lakes who enthrall the onlooker and captivate his soul forever.

A perfect example of such eulogized beauty is the story of the ***Leanaan Sidhe***, an Irish female fairy who has developed in literature as being partly *muse* and partly *vampire.* She represents the state of grace and perfection of the ***Elven Princess.***

Memory however prompts those who tell of her to relate that her embrace is death. In ***Transylvania*** she is **Stregoica**, In ***Greece*** she is the **Lamia**; in ***Persia, Arabia*** and ***Israel*** she is **Lilith** and **An**, and just outside *Tunbridge Wells* she is **'La Belle Dame Sans Merci'**, immortalized in **Keats'** poem of the same name.

La Belle Dame Sans Merci

Oh what can ail thee, Knight at arms,
Alone and palely loitering?
The sedge has withered from the Lake
And no birds sing!

Oh what can ail thee, Knight at arms,
So haggard and so woe begone?
The Squirrel's granary is full
and the harvest's done.

I see a Lily on thy brow
With anguish moist and fever dew,
And on thy cheeks a fading Rose
Fast withereth too -

I met a Lady in the Meads,
Full beautiful, a faery's child
Her hair was long, her foot as light
And her eyes were wild -

I made a garland for her head,
And bracelets too, and fragrant Zone
She look'd at me as she did love
And made sweet moan -

I set her on my pacing steed
And nothing else sa all day long
For sidelong would she bend and sing
A faery's song -

She found me roots of relish sweet
And honey wild and manna dew
And sure in language strange she said
I love thee true -

She took me to her elfin grot

And there she wept and sigh'd full sore,
And there I shut her wild wild eyes
With kisses four.

And there she lulled me asleep
And there I dreamed, Ah Woe betide!
The latest dream I ever dreamt
On the cold hill side.

I saw pale Kings and Princes too
Pale warriors, death pale were they all;
They cried, La belle dame sans merci
Thee hath in thrall.

I saw their starv'd lips in the gloam
With horrid warning gaping wide,
And I awoke, and found me here
On the cold hill's side.

And this is why I sojourn here
Alone and palely loitering;
Though the sedge is withered from the Lake
And no birds sing -

John Keats

In England, during the 1300's this ***vampire maiden*** was to be found in the *Home Counties* and her name, the '*Maid of Kent*' pins her down as being, according to **John Ferguson**, the *Countess of Salisbury* who, at a summer ball in Calais was said to have let slip her Garter, which **King Edward III** retrieved with haste and, lifting the accoutrement into the air, pronounced "*Honi Soit Qui Mal Y Pense*".

As to her wandering around near ***Tunbridge Wells*** when the unfortunate knight-in-armour (from her point of view an early attempt at perfecting the art of tinning fresh meat) met her, she like him was returning from the Calais festivities when he must have caught up with her on the leafy track that has now become the famous A21. We will catch up with them in a minute.

Scholars once dismissed **Professor Margaret Murray** for several things, one being that the *Garter incident* elicited an over-reaction from **Edward** if the ***Garter*** was of no ritual significance. But however scholars may dismiss the incident, the question will not go away.

In a period not noted for its moral rectitude why would the King bother threatening anyone in connection with their possible attitude towards an item of women's underwear? **Murray** has already pointed out exactly how significant the ***Garter*** actually is and has given numerous instances to support a concept that goes beyond mere theory. There was no point in making a song and dance about the *Countess' Garter* unless the item had a dangerous connotation attached to it; which indeed it had.

The ***Garter*** or ***Gartier***, was a small, buckled belt worn by women around the top of the left thigh or just below the left knee on men. Apart from being a menstrual badge and a semantic symbol of the womb and the ***Grail***, it was also a representation of the serpent eating its own tail.
The ***Garter*** therefore was the *alchemical symbol of the* **Orobourus**, the serpent who, in consuming itself, has become a ***Dragon***, a ***vampire***. Here we will remember the opening prose at the beginning of this collection of essays.

The ***Garter*** was the '*witches belt*', the Devil's badge and a dynastic emblem of the fairy race that descended from **Lilith** and **Cain**, who were the *enemies of the Church and Mankind*, ***according to the church***, if not according to the fairies themselves.

The subsequent founding of the *Order of the Garter* by **Edward III**, to be followed in 1397 by the re-emergence of a ***Dragon Court*** in another related ***Angevin line*** under **King Sigismund of Luxembourg**, made both orders *Garter* and *Dragon* institutions using the *orobourus* as their emblems.

The ***Garter*** as the alchemical orobourus is still an emblematic component of the old *Angevin Imperial and Royal Dragon Court* today, under the Grand Mastership of its ***Vere head***, a senior heir of the senior ***Houses of Anjou and Lorraine*** who is himself a gartered knight of the ***Orcadian Clan Donnachaid***, which demonstrates the ubiquity of the *Garter symbol* amongst the ancient families. The ***Garter*** denoted rank in later ***witchcraft*** which, as we have seen, originated as ***Druidism***.

The ***Orobourus***, the reptilian symbol of completeness is the ***Sumaire***, the serpent that encircles and spirals to create an inhaling vortex, a black hole that draws all energy and life into it.

Sumaire is pronounced *shimmarie* as we have seen, and in being reminiscent of the word *shimmer* it suggests a relationship with that word which means to glow radiantly as with a light that had the power to fascinate perhaps.

It is a pertinent meditation when one remembers that from the dawn of time the ***Elven Gods*** were called the ***Shining Ones.*** Here there is also a relationship with the words ***Shaman*** and ***Shamanism***, a practice rooted in Northern Asia, the homeland of the speakers of '*Ar Sidhe Cantu*', being the ***Sundered Elven Tribe*** who went east.

Like the legend of the fascinating allure of ***Fairy Gold***, the ***Leanaan Sidhe*** and the Countess of Salisbury appeared so beautiful as to disarm their prey with an enthralling inward glamour of glowing radiance. Having disarmed their victims thus they drew either the blood or the life force or both from them, leaving them to wander forever, as **Keats** suggests, like living corpses in vain pursuit of a love and beauty so splendid, so transcendent and so complete.

Fairy fascination is a universal theme which in this respect suggests an innate ability to hypnotize people, though this isn't the whole story. In the tales concerning people's encounters with ***Elphame***, there is a quality of transcendence about their narratives which will be dealt with later.

Love on a Four Lane Blacktop

The element of translucence and light that is attributed to fairies can also be found in the stories relating to the *shamans* and *kings* of ***Eldorado*** in ***South America*** where these individuals are also referred to as the '***Shining Ones***' which is a common epithet, as we know, for the ***Elves of Eurasia***.

Jesus is said to have manifested this capability in the presence of the patriarchs and such an ability is closely connected with the *Qabalah* in its numerous manifestations and variations.

Both **Jesus**' mother **Mary** and his wife **Mary Magdalene** were called the '*crystal wombs from whence shined forth the light of god*', a description which suggests strongly the ***Tantric*** and ***Qabalistic*** concept of ***Starfire***.

We return to the eulogized dual carriageway on the outskirts of *Tunbridge Wells* - the A21 - and our tired but patiently waiting traveller, the '***Maid of Kent***', the ***Countess of Salisbury*** and the packed lunch she nestles so lovingly to her pale and perfect breasts. In her role as the vampire, we also find her, like the ***Leanaan Sidhe***, described as a fairy lover and, as the ***Garter Queen***, a witch into the bargain.

The ***Garter*** intimates that she is of the ***Dragon Clan*** and hence we have the ***Fairy***, the ***Witch***, the ***Vampire*** and the ***Dragon*** in one unitary identity manifest in a vision of fatal and deadly beauty who, in this instance is shagged out and nursing a serious hangover, after a week long knees up in Calais and a murderous crossing back to England on the overnight ferry.

We will leave this ***Shamanka*** to '*Steal The Edge*' and leg it, consigning her portion of *Corned Beef* to wander the Earth looking for her and the return of his mortal soul. "You should have read the instruction manual first sonny, contrary to the guff in the Gothic Novels and Moving Pictures, true love is how vampires are really made. Next time round - breathe in *The Breath of Ravens* and run for it, dummy". We will move on.

Such characters as the *English Countess of Salisbury* and the *Irish Leanaan Sidhe* in historical accounts are sometimes remorseful and cursing of the nature that condemns them to utter loneliness, sometimes they are unrepentant, predatory and without remorse.

It depends upon the motivation of the chronicler as to who does and feels what. It has been pointed out that the Knight in the poem, which **Keats** obtained from a far earlier source, might have transcended himself but looked the way he did purely to outsiders, whilst living in an entirely different dimension himself.

Having said that, the pain is all too real and the act of 'stealing the edge' by ***Dragon Princesses*** is actually what does awaken the ***Vampire*** in the ***Fairy***. It is doubtful in the very rare instances where this still can sometimes happen, that these females know what they are doing, but instead they act archetypically, like their ancestors, as an unconscious but necessary catalyst in a process of spiritual development which, for anybody's money, could lose nothing of its impact by being a bit more gentle. One might imagine that seven years of living hell and a hunger unquenched by Raw Steak, Pastrami or Carlsberg Special Brew is much too much to have to pay for enlightenment.

However, the author amongst others has always insisted upon a biochemical basis for magic and transcendant states and the psychobiological basis for such phenomena, including ***vampirism*** and the enlightenment that is its concomitant can be explained scientifically, without relying on such old favourites as *Iron Decifiency Porphyria* or on any of the other nonsenses that outsiders have suggested.

'The Shining Ones'

If you are a cheery ***Elf*** and you have managed to avoid the excesses of behavior and perception brought about by contact with your female counterparts in ***Elphame***, you might qualify for the epithet of '*Shining One*', you most fortunate of all jammy bastards. If you have realized to any extent that you are of *the Clan*, you will know that from the very beginning the ***fairies*** were called the '***Shining Ones***'.

This stems from the ***Sumerian*** era when '*The Controllers of the Fate of Men*' were known as both ***the Anunnaki*** and ***the Anunnagi***, the former meaning "*those who are manifest when Heaven meets Earth*" and the latter meaning simply '***Shining Ones***' or ***Star Children***. The two mean the same thing and refer to the nocturnal habits of our ancestors as much as anything else. These habits are directly related to the production and maintenance of certain ***hormones***, which then relate to the core meaning itself.

In particular the epithet '***Shining One***' was appended

to **Prince Shamash**, brother of **Erishkigal**, ***Queen of the otherworld.*** **Shamash** was the **Uncle of Lilith** and was also called the '***Prince of Justice***'. The ***fairies*** from very early on were hotly in favor of law and order, a trait which manifested itself in an attention to detail in social and legal matters that has earned them, as ***vampires***, a reputation in later centuries for being pathologically meticulous.

In ***Transylvania*** it is said that if you dropped grain in front of a vampire, it would stop to count the individual seeds, thus facilitating your speedy escape from danger. We may put this down to the pithy waggishness of peasant sarcasm, but we note the point all the same.

Shamash was therefore of the family of ***Sumerian Ubaid Gods*** who sired **Cain** and **Kali Azura**, and the ***race of Dragon Kings*** who were the keepers of the '*Tablets of Destiny*' or ***Fate***. In their turn **Cain** and **Lilith Luluwa** were the father and mother of the fairies, the ***Elven Grail Queens and Kings of the Dragon race*** so hated by the Church.

The ability to '*shine*', a phenomenon which can still be subjectively experienced, is the result of a transcendent, balanced state of mind related to certain processes connected with cellular rejuvenation. The ability is rare enough and is an innate genetic capacity manifested in the outworking of certain '*shamanic*' exercises related to '*climbing the Tree of Life*'.

Gentry is a word which specifically means '*of the blood*' and is derived from the Latin ***gens***. In this case, as in all cases *gentry* strictly used to mean '*of the fairy blood*' or of the ***Dragon family***. By misuse the word gentry has become related to a class or station, particularly in British society, and is erroneously associated, by attribution to the characters within that class, with a style of behavior and a code of conduct that bears no resemblance to historical actuality.

In its most basic sense the words *gentleman* or *gentlewoman*, in British society, refers to individuals who are associated with, gain status through and erroneous recognition from, their support of a hierarchical value system which was established illegally by *the Church* through the ***Tudor*** usurper **Henry VIII**, under the auspices of the earlier Roman doctrines of temporal supremacy expounded within the fraudulent ***Donation of Constantine***.

However, the British establishment, either through its *Courts of Protocol*, *College of Arms* or its academic or judicial establishments, has no legal or legitimate customary right whatsoever to recognize or refute anybody or anything and their qualification, via such institutions, to determine who is or is not royal or of the blood is non-existent as they are not 'of the blood' themselves. However, their blanket refusal to recognize any European title whatsoever has some redeeming element to it. The ***House of Vere*** doesn't recognize anyone else either! Including ***the Crown***, its ***Court of St. James*** and its ***College of Arms***. Why should we. Who are they anyway?

The *British* and *European Hierarchies* have their roots originating in the class of roving tinkers and tallymen who, during the early medieval period, established fixed warehouses in towns and eventually became settled merchant traders within these population centers.

Although to watch their antics in decades past it would seem as if they would wish to give the impression that they were nobility, their blood lineage and manners are not those of true nobility or royalty.

A <u>prime example of the concept of nobility</u> being affected by the merchants can be seen in *Renaissance Venice* which, for all its splendor and seeming nobility, was no more than a fancy but rather damp giant warehouse, run by self elevated tradesmen who called themselves '*Patricians*'.

Today ***Britain*** is run by these exact same sort of people. The descendants of warehousemen and *Norman* thugs sit in the *House of Lords*, another damp riverside warehouse, and call themselves *Peers of the Realm*.

In 1998 the transient public servant **Mr. Blair** wished to scrap hereditary privilege and replace the hereditary peers with new lords, doing exactly this in November 1999. Seventy-five percent of the old lords obtained their hereditary titles from ancestors who were the settled merchants who had bought their titles from impecuniary monarchs like **Henry VIII** or **James VI**, whilst the remaining twenty-five percent are descended mostly from the bully boys who accompanied the usurping bastard **William of Normandy**, who was only recognized by his own nobles under the duress exacted upon them by his father.

The remainder of the entourage present at ***the Hastings*** debacle comprised of ***Flemish*** and ***Breton Nobles*** some of whom had lived in ***England*** for many years. Assessing the risk of backing their friend **Harold Godwinson** they resigned themselves to the unpleasant but inevitable fact that he would lose and went along to ensure that the ignorant *Norman buffoon* didn't give away their English lands to his marauding henchmen.

Amongst these was **Eustance de Vere**, ***Jarl of Essex*** and brother-in-law of **Edward the Confessor**. On **Harold**'s death, **Vere** was pronounced ***King of England*** by the ***Witan***. This made **Eustace**'s right to the English Throne unquestionable under *Saxon Atheling Law*, especially when compared to that of an illegitimate invader who was so frightened of **Eustace** that he took hostages prior to the invasion, in order to ensure **Eustace**'s complicity.

The *de jure* Kingship of England has, therefore, descended through the ***Veres*** for over 800 years and in 1560 **Edward de Vere** gave the ***Tudors*** a timely and friendly, though somewhat esoteric reminder of this fact.

No one wanted **William de Normande** and all he did in seizing the throne of England was commit an act of theft and treason accompanied by torture, rape, murder and yet more theft and treason. And what will the '*new lords*' be if this **Blair** person gets his own way? More scrap dealers, bully boys and warehousemen, elevated in payment for their political sycophancy and installed as party Yes-Men. Why bother making the change, what's the difference?

The codes of conduct and styles of behavior developed down the centuries by these misfits and usurpers have come to be thought of as the manners of the 'gentry'. Such etiquette and standards of behavior are, however, rather of the nature of a complex set of rules and protocols which have evolved from the necessity for these individuals to reinforce to themselves and each other their sense of identity. This need is born of the insecurity of the usurper and the poseur, and the party games were initiated to ensure that those who refuted such mores or refused to adopt them were 'excluded'.

In recent history one of the ***Mitfords*** was said to have assisted in the development of a list of such styles of speech, patronage and behavior which one of her nephews published in a book entitled '*Noblesse Oblige*', which this author has perused.

Within its pages were lists of the 'U' and non 'U' words, affectations, preferred schools, clubs and so one which, by their patronage or utilization by others, would enable the fake aristocracy to determine whether any individuals they encountered were 'our sort of people', ie whether they were 'U' or non 'U', meaning '*Upper-class*' or '*Non upper-class*'. What a cheek! Particularly when one knows full well that the ***Mitfords*** were related to the ***Guinness*** family.

Situations similar to the foregoing represent yet another example of how the chattering classes, the sons and daughters of arriviste tradesmen masquerading as gentry, hide behind their sham rituals and their money, hoping that, as the years drift languorously by, people will forget that they were all descended from market traders whom the ***Scythians***, the ***real Nobility and Royalty***, hated for being liars and cheats.

When asked, **Mitford** said that the book was just a joke. Surprising then that these ridiculous social rules were rife amongst her 'class' before she wrote them down and that they were indeed used to determine whether one was fit company for their pseudo-aristocratic 'society' or not.

Today sociologists are doing exactly the same thing by using classification numbers to determine one's social status. One could be anything from say - an A1 category "social unit" - all the way down to a G3 and these numbers are appended to one according to one's job and income.

For instance, hilariously enough and for no good reason the author can think of, a film star is an ***A1*** "***social unit***", whilst a dustman is something like a ***G2***. In terms of social value and input one would have thought that the dustman would have been somewhere up in the high B's at least, by quasi-Marxist sociologists' standards.

If film stars went on strike for six months would you suffer more than if dustmen went on strike for six months? Of course not. If dustmen took the same amount of time out the country would be swimming in bacteria and disease. If film stars went on strike, you would just watch repeats on the telly or buy a talking parrot or a performing monkey. What difference is there in terms of skill or in terms of social contribution, after all?

Whether they are *Marxist* or *Weberan sociologists* or whatever, they are the worst manifestation of middle-class attitudes, because it is only the middle classes who would differentiate between themselves and other classes and this is how you know that they aren't ***Gentry***.

The ***ancient gentry*** knew the value of a person's contribution to society and respected the person for making it. The true ***gentry*** weren't above grabbing a shovel when the need arose and mucking in and mucking out with everyone else.

Only the elevated tinkery would expect someone else to do the work and only the tinkery would think that, because they had risen so far in their own estimation of themselves, the world owed them a living.

The ***Elven Queens*** and ***the Dragon Kings***, the real gentry of history, had no particularly complex hierarchy with which to stratify or differentiate rank amongst themselves, they simply knew that they were all of the ***fairy blood*** and were thus equal. This is apparent in both the social structures of the ***d'Anu of Eire*** and the ***Royal Danes of Scandinavia*** as late as 900 AD.

Under the present scheme of things where the medieval feudal system has been built upon over the ensuing centuries by the succession of various dynasties of tinker royalty in ***Britain*** and ***Europe***, we can see this insulating, snobbish mentality at work with its 'layers' of rank, determining 'layers' or 'degrees' of nobility or royalty. In the ***Merovingian*** and ***Pictish Danaan*** cultures, one was a king or princess and that was that. All shared the ***Sang Real*** and the ***San Graal***. Whether you reigned or not was immaterial.

Nowadays we have a system where the British throne is occupied by the descendant of a foreign family almost arbitrarily selected for a task in which, to all intents and purposes, they find themselves merely an impotent figurehead. Under this individual there is stratified a complex series of ranks, orders and accolades which, historically, were anyone's for the taking, as long as they had money; and which today you can still buy into at the lowest rung by paying the College of Arms Eighteen hundred English pounds.

If you can prove to them that you have "made a contribution to society" either and at the least, by getting a university degree or by having been trained to kill people, a nice coat of arms is yours for the asking. You will then be an official Esquire and henceforth (though not beforehand, one assumes) you will be considered to be "*A Gentleman*" because you have a pretty piece of paper saying as much. In ***Ireland*** the Chief Herald's Office formerly issued applications for armorial bearing upon which it was stipulated that the supplicant must be considered by the Chief Herald to have reached "*The Portal of Gentry*".

How can anyone '*reach the portal of gentry*' ? How can there be a '*doorway to blood*'? This is yet another instance where language is eloquently engineered to become completely ineloquent nonsense.

Every year the arguably unqualified monarch dishes out knighthoods and orders, to worthies who are chosen at the fawning whim of some transient, jumped-up public servant, mainly to self seeking individuals who have been thought to have made a 'contribution' to society.

Many of these knighthoods go to prancing luvveys, football managers and industrialists - although both the former have already been paid a more than adequate amount of cash for their dubious and ineffectual contribution - whilst the latter who likewise have also been paid adequately for their self seeking contribution have also assisted, by their greed, in turning the planet into an orbiting swill bin.

Why are these people being rewarded for serving themselves and how can they possibly be thought of as behaving like 'gentry', when the most that they do is produce useless consumer junk, infotainment and pollution? They have got rich by creating jealousy, envy and enmity, and through the media their dissemination of double standards has created a level of moral confusion which has inevitably led to further social and economic division and environmental damage. And for this they get a knighthood already?

Two of the most atrocious investitures recently went to a grocer's daughter and the head of a country whose government refused, for forty years, to recognize their nation's responsibility for the treatment of civilians - whom they used in chemical warfare tests - and prisoners of war whom they forced to work to their deaths in military building operations.

Firstly, how can a grocer's daughter be thought of as suitable material for inclusion in an order that was so strictly intended for those of the royal blood and secondly how can the most hated enemy of the British people in recent history qualify either?

The *Most Noble Order of the Garter*, already trashed down the centuries by its association with a motley assortment of pseudo-royal dynasts who had no right to belong to it, let alone confer it on anyone else, had reached it lowest ebb when those two individuals were granted membership.

The *Order of the Garter* was and still is an ***Angevin*** and hence an ***Elven bloodline institution*** and on the death of **Richard**

III therefore, all rights to continue to own the ***Order of the Garter*** died out in his line and by the laws of Sovereign inheritance the Order then belonged to the senior heirs of the ***House of Anjou***.

No subsequent *House* has the right to give the order to anyone, let alone to a jumped-up bourgeois tradeswomen or a war criminal. The ***French*** used to say that the ***British*** were a nation of shopkeepers. It would appear that the British are a nation of shopkeepers reigned over by a shopkeeper.

The *Most Noble Order of the Garter is Britain*'s premier ***Order of Knighthood***, in fact heraldically speaking it's actually the second in rank after the ancient ***Caledonian Dragon Court*** that spawned it but who's quibbling. The very word '*knight*' stemming from the Saxon *cnecht* means '*to serve*' or a '*servant*'.

When, in the name of God, **Karaoke** accepted, did **Hirohito** do anything to serve the interests of the British people and when did he, or the *Grantham woman* deserve to be invested with Britain's most senior rank of knighthood?

To direct ***Her Majesty*** to give out such degrees, either to pay off a favor to a fellow member of the bourgeoisie, or suck up for diplomatic reasons to a nation simply because it now has a bit of cash tucked away, seems to me to be the worst manifestation of the bourgeois mentality yet to be witnessed, especially when the present dynasty, it could be argued, appear to have no historical right to give ***the Order*** out in the first place.

Her Majesty's son **Prince Charles** - who has a brain - has publicly lamented the decline in standards in the English Language for years and the author tends to share his concern. How can anyone '*become*' a gentleman, a member of the ***gens*** -

the ***Sangraal?*** How can a piece of paper instantly make one into a member of a separate race.

There is no indication in the small print that - in reality - one would have to undergo a class-transplant at genetic level, so how can they have the nerve to assume that they have the power to create or change a species, simply by issuing a bit of calligraphised toilet paper and without having the toadying supplicant to the altar of snobbery undergo a series of radical medical procedures that don't even exist anyway?

Have the British establishment perfected the art of *Transubstantiation* I wonder? Are they too alchemists who can turn human lead into *Fairy Gold*? This is yet another example of middle-class arrogance: the idea - typical of Americans in particular who though, it must be said, inherited it from the British - that if you have the money and the mouth you can buy the 'goods'.

However, race is not a saleable commodity, whatever any *College of Arms* of questionable authority might say or imply, and whether one is of the gentry or not, it never was and is still not a matter of social standing or social badges, any more than real kingship is about 'rule' or wearing tin hats and dead weasels. *Vermin in Ermine*?

The real '***gentry***' or to give them another familiar epithet - the ***Lords*** and ***Ladies*** - were just that. They were by blood alone, the members of a *genetic strain*, the ***Dragon and Grail families*** - the ***Fairy Blood***.

One could not and cannot 'become' a member of the gentry any more than one can 'become', by initiation or otherwise, a 'witch', a 'vampire', a 'magus', a 'dragon', a 'fairy' or an 'elf'.

All these are names which described the '***gentry***' and the latter

- ***elf*** - is a word which originates from *albi* meaning a *white* or '***shining one***'. From *albi* derives the French ***Cathar*** name ***Albigensian*** (Albi + Gens) meaning - '***of the elven blood***' - *et quid erat demonstrandum.*

The Pharisees

This curious and delightful name for the ***Elven race*** is a common English rural folkword probably created by the addition of an extra syllable to the word fairies, thereby making a double plural suffix. ***Pharisees*** is simply *Fairies-es*, a bit like **Tolkien**'s double plural '*pocketses*' attributed to his character '*Gollum*' in *Lord of the Rings.*

A more obscure possible origin for the ***Pharisee epithet*** however, may be found in the nature of the ***Elves*** themselves. Some of their families were from mixed ***Pictish*** and ***Merovingian*** bloodlines, and where the latter is concerned, it descended from **Jesus** and had a *Pharisaic origin.* The word *Pharisee* itself stems from the Hebrew ***parush*** meaning '***separated***' which by blood the Elves indeed were.

In this particular context we should also remember the ***Celtic Church*** which was *Nestorian* and *Pharisaic* in its doctrine and structure. The ***Celtic Church*** supported the Fairy bloodline of Jesus whilst also having strong Druidic associations, to the point in fact where **Jesus** himself was considered to have been a ***Druid*** and a ***Magus*** by his British kinsmen - the **Elven Pendragons**.

The Plantagenets

According to their own account of themselves and the accounts of subsequent chroniclers and historians, including **Professor Vivian Green**, the ***Plantagenets*** were descended from the ***fairy race***. Certainly they shared a common ***Scythian*** trait when riled, and that was a vile temper!

The ***Plantagenets***, whose name was thought to derive from *'planta-genista'* - the *'plant of generation'* or *'Tree of Life'* - used a *sprig of the Broom*, the *'plantagenista'*, as one of their earlier family badges. The seeds of the ***Broom plant*** are hallucinogenic and were a well known part of the ***witches'*** pharmacopoeia throughout the Dark Ages and the Medieval Period.

It was said that the ***Plantagenets*** had two ancestral grandmothers named ***Melusine***, one the daughter of **King Elinus of Albany** and the other the daughter of **Baldwin du Bourg**, *King of Jerusalem.*

In the first instance the ***Plantagenets*** derived their name from a princess named **Plantina** (possibly derived from *Plantanu* or *Planta-Anu*) who was actually the younger sister of **Maelasanu des Scythes** or **Melusine McLean** and this obviously means that the ***Plantagenets*** were not actually directly descended in the male line from **Melusine** herself, who in a matriarchal ***Pictish*** system of inheritance, was the senior daughter of **King Gille Sidhean of Albany**, and the heir of her mother **Queen Pressina** or more formally **The Queen Bruidhe-Anu des Scythes**.

Melusine certainly was the matriarch of the ***Angevin*** or ***Anjou dynasty***, but her senior heir and the first Count of Anjou was **Maelo de Vere**, not Tortolf de Rennes, making the ***Plantagenet dynasty*** descending from the younger sister **Plantanu**, a junior branch of the ***Imperial and Royal House of Vere***.

The ***Veres*** left ***Anjou*** in 800 AD and the ***Comite of Anjou*** was divided and at length settled upon the heirs of **Tortolf**, thereby giving the erroneous impression that they were the first and therefore senior branch of the **Angevin** family which, according to the records, is simply not the case.

The second **Melusine** was in fact called **Melisend**, so the ***Plantagenets*** had no direct male connection with any **Melusine** at all, despite the attempts of subsequent royal genealogists and amateur historians to make it so. Nevertheless the ***Plantagenets***, our younger ***Vere cousins***, were still of the Blood Royal and they were still of ***Elven Stock,*** and the discrepancies in their story seem to add to, rather than detract from, their claims or the claims made for them.

The popular, chronicled descent claimed for the ***Plantagenets*** from **Melusine** was in fact via a cadet female ***Vere*** line - that of **Ida de Vere** - a member of another junior branch of the *Vere family*, specifically the *Imperial and Royal House of Vere of Constantinople and Jerusalem.* **Ida de Vere** was the aunt of the inaugurator of the ***Knights Templars***, the **Swan Knight Godfroi de Vere de Bouillon** and the ancestral granddaughter of **Prince Maelo de Vere d'Anjou** and his mother - the much coveted **Princess Maelasanu McLean de Vere des Scythes** - via **Adolph de Vere de Guisnes**.

The ***Plantagenets*** could however claim a line of unbroken male descent from the late 800's until the sad death in 1485 of **Richard III** - argued by some to be the last true King of England. This junior branch of the family managed to survive for about 600 years, which isn't a bad innings. Since then the British have suffered a succession of nondescript church puppets who, out of generosity, one might call eighth-breeds at best.

With the death of **Richard III** the *Garter* died out in the junior ***Plantagenet*** line and became, as a dynastic family *Order of the House of Anjou*, the legitimate property of the already *Gartered Imperial and Royal House of Vere of Oxford*, (the legitimate kings of England by the will of the English people themselves) later to descend to the ***Scottish*** and ***Irish Branches***, the latter whose seniority, on the death of the *Vere Clan Chief*, **Lord Adrian Hope-Vere** - *Laird of Blackwood* - became confirmed in 1973.

Melusine's father **Elinus** or **Gille Sidhean** was a descendant of the *Ulster Royal House of the Uilidian*, the ***Fir Bolg druids***. Her mother was a ***bruidhe*** or judge-poetess of ***Pictish*** royal descent from the *Bruidhainn* or (by Roman error) *Cruthainn* remnant of the **Tuadha d'Anu** or **Tuatha de Danaan**, as they are sometimes mistakenly called.

These were the ***Aes Dan*** or ***Aesir Danaan***, the *Elven Gods of Eire* and the *Lords of the Calle Daouine of Caledonia* or *Northern Pictavia*. **Melusine** was a ***Dragon Princess***, a ***Lamia***, and we will tell her story later.

The ***Plantagenets*** or ***Angevins*** became, after their demise, a much sought after bloodline to be descended from, as if it were implicitly understood that ***real Dragon blood*** made real queens and kings. **Queen Elizabeth the First**, the great granddaughter of a Welsh farmer and **Margaret**, *Countess of Anjou*, had broom pod motifs sewn onto one of her gowns in celebration and assertion of her Anjou ancestry.

She is known to have had two coronations, the first and most important of which was a pagan, '***fairy***' coronation held in public on the Mayday prior to her Church investiture as queen of England. Following this event **Edward de Vere**, 17th earl of Oxford, staged the *Windsor Stag Ride* incident and killed the beast before the Queen as a gentle reminder of who the real Kings of England and the Greenwood were.

Even today the biographers of the present constitutional *Heads of State of Britain* proudly boast of that family's ***Anjou***

descent and the author supposes that we, the senior heirs of the senior branch of that dynasty, should be flattered, despite the fact that such a descent is tortuous in the extreme and traces a line therefore, that looks as crooked as a donkey's hind leg.

Boasting something like 2000 connections to **Edward III**, who was only a member of a junior Anjou line, this originally German farming family is outranked in terms of blood even by the ***Spensers*** whose daughter, the late **Princess Diana**, could claim 4000 connections to the same character. Furthermore, one geneticist recently working with the blood samples of German royal and noble families couldn't find one whose male line reverted any farther than the early 16th century.

Chapter Five

Dragon's Deep

Edmund Spenser is said to have flattered **Queen Elizabeth I** by referring to her as the '***fairy queen***' though it is equally possible that his was a veiled reference to the fairy wife of the alchemist, the *Earl of Desmond* at whose seat - *Castle Matres* - **Spenser** and **Sir Walter Raleigh** resided during an expedition to retrieve the Wizard's library from a war zone on behalf of **Dr. John Dee**.

Castle Matres or ***Matrix*** as it is now known was said to have been named after the ***Matres*** or triple goddess. The castle rests on the banks of the river Deal in County Limerick and the library which was housed there is said to have contained singular works on Magic and Alchemy, works that **Dee** didn't want, under any circumstances, falling into the Queen's hands because, as **Laurence Gardner** has pointed out, **Dr. John Dee, Edward de Vere, Francis Bacon, Edmund Spenser** and **William Shakespeare** *et al* were well aware that **Elizabeth**'s house were badly bred usurpers and despite the descent from **Margaret of Anjou**, the blood wasn't pure. I wonder what the boys would have made of the successive packs of kein-kultur, dynastic rabble that followed the Tudor Turnip Farmers.

Though ***Plantagenet*** descent and the ***fairy blood*** that ran in the veins of **Edward III** in particular, appears to have been greatly desired to legitimize the subsequent claims of the dynasties that superseded them, the ***Plantagenets*** themselves and **Edward I** in particular, looked to ***Scotland*** to legitimize their own claims to kingship. Scottish and Irish ***Dragon Kings*** were invested on the *Stone of Scone.*

This ***Stone*** - the ***Lia Fail*** - the *Stone of Destiny* (or ***Fate***) of the ***Tuadha d'Anu*** once rested at the summit of the ***Hill of Tara***, the ancient seat of the ***Elven High Kings*** in *County Meath*. When the **Milesian Dalriada** left ***Eire*** for ***Scotland*** it is believed that they took the ***Lia Fail*** with them.

Despite **Edward I**'s best efforts to conquer the Scots and wrest from them the ***Lia Fail*** - the ultimate symbol of royal legitimacy - thereby confirming, one suspects, his right to ***fairy*** kingship which, retrospectively he had anyway and was thus wasting his time, the ***Stone*** of the ***Elves*** never once rested under the gilded commode in ***Westminster Abbey***.

Because the *Raven-Stone of the Phoenicians* wasn't the *Stone of Scone* that **Edward I** stole, this fake lump of rock that the English thought was the ***Lia Fail*** was nonchalantly and unceremoniously driven up to *Edinburgh Castle* in the back of a Land Rover a couple of years ago. Even select members of the ***Order of the Golden Dawn*** knew this over a hundred years ago and descriptions of the ***Lia Fail*** can still be found in the literature of their successors.

Part of the later ***Plantagenet*** ancestry included the descendants of the *Danish Jarl*, **Rollo Duke of Normandy**. The senior *Angevin dynasty* - the ***Vere*** - also have the **Viking Rollo** as an ancestor in the female line.

The word '***Viking***' has been explained in various ways. Originally spelt '***Wicking***' it was thought to derive from the word '*wic*' meaning the *inlet* or *mouth of a Fjord*, whilst the earlier meaning of the word from the *Old Friesian* and *Old English* had '*wic*' as an *encampment*. In ***Russia*** however the '*Vikhr*' was a ***whirlwind***, a manifestation of the ***Zmei*** or ***Dragon king*** which is dealt with later.

The ***Vikhr*** is a character which is common to both the Russians and the Irish and it will be remembered that Russia was actually founded by the ***Viking Ruotsi Clan***, intimating that the actual definition of the word '*Viking*' is the same as the ***Irish*** word '***Sumaire***', a ***Dragon*** and a ***Vortex***.

Anciently the Danes and the ***Danaan*** were closely related and an examination of the Royal Clan in both cultures will reveal the same egalitarian system of self regulation that distinguished the ***Danaan*** from the rest of Celtic society.

The similarity doesn't end here. Like their ***Fairy*** cousins defenders in Ireland and ***Scotland***, the ***Danes*** warriors were utterly indifferent to death and fought without mercy. Their overall belief system engendered behavior that appears to have been almost nihilistic and devoid of any moral conflict.

This system, based on the '*Nine Worlds*' or emanations of being, was duplicated in earlier or contemporary variants of the ***Qabalah*** and ***Kaula Tantra***. As with the former where the spheres or ***Sephirah*** were incorporated into the Hebrew 'Tree of Life', the ***Viking*** spheres or worlds were thought to rest within the branches of a tree which, in the ***Norse***, was called ***Yggdrasil***, the *World Ash Tree*. ***Yggdrasil***'s roots were embedded in *Hel* or the *Underworld*, whilst its branches brushed against the stars of Heaven.

Yggdrasil is a shamanic glyph which represents the macrocosm - the universe both subtle and material - and the microcosm - the human body. The tree glyph itself in all cultures represents the path the shaman takes, from the roots, embedded in matter, up the trunk and into the branches and the stars, to the rarified spiritual spheres and beyond, to unite with godhead itself.

Such a journey inevitably must transcend mundane care, fear, greed, opinion or morality, and he or she who embarks upon and completes such a journey successfully becomes united with the **One Unmanifest**, the **True Will** and the **Total Self**. As we shall see later, the *Tree* is actually a woman, a ***goddess incarnate*** or ***Avatar***.

The individual who completes the journey is beyond mortal conditioning or the short-sighted relativity upon which is based human moral law. This system and its results duplicate themselves in many other mystical systems and in early witchcraft in particular.

Perhaps therefore, when considering the behavior or attitudes of the individuals in cultures like those of the ***Danes*** and the ***Danaan***, it might be more apposite if scholars took more into account the effects that philosophical systems like these actually had on people like the ***Norse***, and then rethought the etymology of the word '***Viking***' or '***Wiccing***', before settling on an answer that smacks of over-specialization.

In tandem with their ***Aryan Hindu*** cousins, the ***Vikings*** used the symbol of the swastika. An example of its utilization by the ***norse*** can be found in ***Iceland***, whose early inhabitants emblazoned the blue swastika sacred to ***Kali Azura*** or '*blue Kali*', the sister of the **Sumerian Cain** or **Qayin**.

Variants of this figure, the hammer of ***Thor***, fig 1, earlier a copper, single-headed labrys or tomahawk common to the ***Ubaid***,, which is the shape of the fig 2 spinning and creating the vortex, the spiral storm or tornado, can also be found at numerous archaeological sites including ***Newgrange*** in its early spiralised form fig 3. This is the spiral design of the ***Sumaire*** of ***Sumeria***. In its variant form fig 4 the ***swastika*** represents the curved Scythian sword reaping the whirlwind.

The ***swastika*** is also found reversed fig 5 and both forms respectively are thought to be moon and sun symbols respectively. As the author will continue to reiterate, when reading on such subjects, particularly in relation to the philosophy of the Druids and other Indo-European, ***Aryan philosophies***, it is wise to bear in mind that the teachings and symbols operate on both the macro and microcosmic levels at the least. Often the symbolism is in fact multi-faceted.

In the case of the ***swastika*** the moon and the sun symbolism applies inasmuch as the sun radiates or pushes energy out whilst the moon draws energy to it in the form of the sun's rays. Its gravitational field also pulls the tides. The fig 6 of ***Kali*** is the *Sumaire*, the *whirlpool* which is the sucker-in of blood and energy, like the moon draws the suns rays and sucks up the tides, whilst the fig 7, the ***solar swastika*** symbolizes the donor or benefactor who gives willingly of their essence.

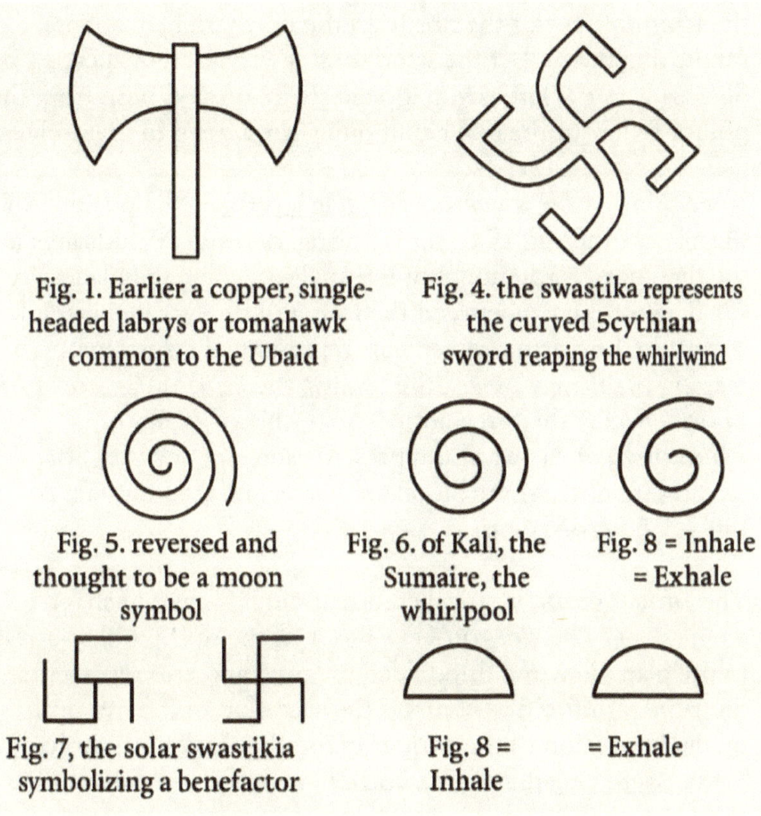

Fig. 1. Earlier a copper, single-headed labrys or tomahawk common to the Ubaid

Fig. 4. the swastika represents the curved 5cythian sword reaping the whirlwind

Fig. 5. reversed and thought to be a moon symbol

Fig. 6. of Kali, the Sumaire, the whirlpool

Fig. 8 = Inhale = Exhale

Fig. 7, the solar swastikia symbolizing a benefactor

Fig. 8 = Inhale

= Exhale

Some figs not available. Please use as research references.

If we look closely we will also notice that the ***circular swastika*** is the mark of **Lilith** given to **Cain** and also the mark of **Kali**. In their original form fig 10 they represent the ***scythe*** of the reaper, the ***Golden Sickle*** of the ***Druids*** spinning on its hilt. Therefore the fig 11 is also the fig12. The swastika has another three-armed formed which appears again at ***Newgrange*** and also as the badge of the **fairy king Manannan Mac Lir,** *Lord of the isle of Man* fig 13 and Lord of the Waters of the Sea. As fig 14 it compares to the ***dragon***'s eye of the south ,fig 15 and also fig 16 the ***dragon***'s eye of the north. In the northern hemisphere, mimicking the pull of the whirlpool, the rotation of these devices is to the left as you look at them, or clockwise from the point of view of the one summoning the *sumaire* in themselves.

If we think of the ***swastika*** as being a turbine, the position of the arms, either fig 17 or fig 18: or fig 19 or fig 20, indicates not the direction of rotation, but the angle at which the blades are set. The difference between the four and three armed swastika is that the four armed essentially represents the sowing or reaping of "*the four winds*", the *pneuma*, the ***spiritual*** or ***morphic energy***, whilst the three armed cross, the ***swastika of Manannan*** of the waters, represents sowing (donating) or reaping (removing) the blood and waters of the Fountain of Life - ***The Holy Grail***.

The ***pineal gland*** is so-called because it is similar in shape to a pine cone. The ***dragon***'s eye fig 21 of the north looks similar to the plan view of a three sided pyramid and also represents the ***pineal gland*** that controls the secretion of the mystical fluids. In relation to the ***pineal gland*** the Grail is symbolized by the sacred head, the ***Baphomet*** or source of wisdom.

Related to the Solar disc and the ***Ajna chakra*** in Tantra, in ***Mithraism*** this stage of the Grail process is represented by the ***Dragon*** of the sun and so here the three armed ***swastika*** is the ***Dragon***'s eye of the north fig 22 representing the pine cone shape of the pineal gland and also the 15th letter of the Hebrew alphabet *Ayin* fig 23 the 15th path of the Tarot - the *Devil* - and the number of **Ishtar** or **Venus** in the roll of the seniority of the Gods. The ***Ayin*** is the '***All Seeing Eye of God***' (**Enki** or **Samael**) peering both in and out of the void.

At the end of their journey from the brain, through its third ventrical, down the spinal column to the womb, *graffenberg gland* and ***urethra***, here the fluids rest until naturally or manually discharged. The womb becomes the grail Cup containing the waters of life, the Cubic stone of the Philosophers.
The ***Dragon***'s eye of the south fig 24 = fig 25 - the Cup.

Thus ***the Grail***, amongst other things, is both the ***Head*** and the ***Cup***, and both 'eyes' of the dragon - north and south - are the eyes that contain "The light that illumines the human spirit". It is also the pineal i - D, the Delta or Hebrew Daleth or Tau - The Doorway to the eternal.

In any form the ***swastika*** is an emblem of life, of breathing (the breath of ravens) and of self-sacrifice. As such therefore, the swastika is one of the primeval symbols of ***Priest-Kingship*** and ***Dragon Maidenhood***. Greatly to be abhorred then is the fact that the ***Nazi Party*** of Germany hijacked the swastika of Kali and, along with numerous other fairy symbols, made it the most hated and feared glyph on the Planet.

The *Death's Head* of the ***SS*** is the head of wisdom of the ***Templars*** - the ***Baphomet*** - whilst the ***Sig rune*** itself is the path of the serpent of wisdom descending the Tree of life. The red banner with the white circle and black swastika represents the bloody funeral ground of the ***Aryan*** saints, who gave the last drop of their life's blood to **Kali**, represented by the white disc of the moon amidst the crimson field of the banner and whose swastika is the *sumaire* drawing life into it as the ***Moon*** draws the seas to her.

The red flag is thus intended to represent the *self sacrificing Tantric priests* of the ***Kaula Vama Marg*** shedding the last vestige of their egos and their lives, to be left drained. As empty vessels they were then ready to be filled with the wisdom of the ***Cosmos*** and with the power of the ***Siddhis***.

In practice however the ***swastika*** represents the suffering of four million people sacrificed to the stupidity of a nation duped into thinking that a dysfunctional *House Painter* and a disaffected *Chicken Farmer*, leading a doomed race of potato peasants, could really be the vestige of the *Aryan Peoples* -Their so-called *Master Race*.

And feeling the pinch after the ***Weimar Republic*** had its debts called in who, fuelled by the politics of envy, wanted to keep the good times rolling by backing **Mr. Adolf Menachim Schickelgruber**, the Aryan God-Hero of the Teutons who would get rid of all those nasty *Hebes* and redistribute their wealth in the German people's favor? Correct - the German bourgeoisie - the smug, Jew-hating, complacent bloody middle classes. It's nice to have a readership that keeps itself informed in matters of contemporary history.

This Jewish Holocaust exactly replicates what happened to the ***Elven families*** for over a thousand years and for exactly the same reasons. Money and Power.

The ***Aryans***, The ***Noble or Elven Race***, were a king tribe and were ***Ubaid Sumerian-Scythian*** in origin. These ***Dragon Kings*** and ***Fairy Queens*** weren't extensive in number, didn't breed outside their caste and weren't nationalists or racists. How the Germans ever thought they were all descended from them is beyond understanding.

The ***Fairy progeny***, in small pockets, spanned the Earth from as far distant as ***Japan**** to ***Scotland*** and they rarely mixed with the indigenous populations who invited their rule and their wisdom. Germans, like any other tribe would have had their

Aryan caste to guide them but that doesn't entitle a whole nation to consider itself Aryan.

* The ***Ainu*** of Hokkaido or North Island are a tall, fair-skinned Caucasoid people, thought to have been the original inhabitants of the Japanese Islands who were driven north by waves of immigrants from China, Korea and South Asia.
The ***Ainu*** (pronounced: Eye-Noo) are animistic and shamanic and share many beliefs with the ***Amerindians*** and the ***Scythian druids*** concerning the nature of life. Their principal divine totem is the Swan.

During the 12th century the ***Ainu*** were almost extinct following continued hostilities with invaders. Their mythology tells them that their race was saved by a swan who descended from heaven and mated with the last living **Ainu Lord**. This coupling produced the ***Ainu*** who still occupy Hokkaido today.

The ***Swan Maidens*** are the ***Dragon Princesses*** of the Grail, the ***Scythian Druid Queens*** and the ***Nordic Andvarinauts***. In ***Irish lore*** they can transform from swans into maidens and so, anthropologically speaking, it would appear, and the assertion is supported by academics, that ***the Ainu***, born of the womb of a ***Swan Maiden***: are of the ***Royal, Elven Dragon Blood - the Blood of Anu!*** The ***Ainu*** have dark hair and almond eyes and are distinctly Asian despite their complexions. Nevertheless, the remnant of the ***Ainu*** who retain pure blood, no more than 17,000 of them are left, are of Aryan extraction. So much for the 20th century blue eyed, blonde haired German fantasy. The pure, insular ***Ainu*** have more right to the epithet Aryan than any German chicken farmer ever had.

Well dressing

Yggdrasil, the Tree of Life of the *Viking Kabala* or *Nine Worlds system*, is coiled about at its base by the serpent-dragon ***Jormangr*** *the encircler*. At ***Yggdrasil***'s roots there is a pool. In ***Ireland*, *Scotland*** and ***Wales*** this symbol is repeated as the *Hazel Tree* by the well, in which lives the *Salmon of Knowledge*. Atop the branches of the Hazel tree there sits an eagle who drops a blood red nut of wisdom into the well 13 times a year. There it is consumed by the *Salmon of Knowledge*.

Because of this story, real wells and trees eventually became the focus of devoted rituals that we now now as well-dressing, a misunderstanding of the idea that the tree and the well were figurative and that their curative properties were obtained not from well water, but from something entirely different.

Because these waters were considered therapeutic and rejuvenating the wells were blessed and venerated and, one supposes in order to make the forgotten approximation closer to the reality of the symbol, the trees adjacent to these wells were decked in coloured patches of cloth. These symbolized the ***Chakras*** or Sephirah of the tree of life of the female body which the druids were really symbolizing in their use of the tree and the well glyph.

In the case of the Gaelic form of ***Yggdrasil***, the nut of the Hazel represents the pineal discharge. Dropped by the eagle, representing the spirit or the ***Sun God Llew*** (the ***Ajna Chakra*** or ***Kether Sephiroth***), it descends through the tree of life (like the lightning bolt of inspiration) and falls into the well or womb. Here it is consumed by the salmon of Knowledge. In the Irish story it is *Nechtan* (meaning 'pure one') the God of 'waters' who catches and eats the salmon, a euphemism for cunnilingus. Repeating the entreaty of the grail story however, it is only the pure one who may see or benefit from the 'Grail', which is here, as anywhere else, the female genitalia and the mysterious essences they bestow.

This story and its variants can be found across Europe in one suppressed or hidden form or another. Whilst the eagle represents the spirit we are clear on the nature and identity of the secretions represented by the nut. The spirit was said to be located in the pineal gland by **Descartes**, who was repeating an *ancient gaelic belief.* The *salmon* however represents the *vulva*, resting at the '*bottom*' of (eg. beneath or below) the womb.

Both in contemporary and in classical and historical colloquialism the fish represents the female vulva. This usage is universal. If eating fish is said to be good for the brain, then eating ***Nechtan***'s ***salmon*** takes on a whole new meaning for us. The fish crops up as a Christian symbol, that of ***Ichthys*** (meaning '*fish*' in Greek) which latter day Christians believe means ***Iesus Christos Theos***, or '*Jesus Christ God*'. And on the subject of fish and fish women or ***Mermaids***, we enter the labyrinth.

The Labyrinth

The word *labyrinth* has an etymology of which there are two interlinked variations

i) derived from *labrys*, a pre-Hellenic word said to mean '*double headed axe*'

ii) derived from the Latin labia meaning '*lips*' or '*folds*'

The double-headed axe was sacred to ***Zeus***; the Grecian ***Thor***, whose hammer was a variant of the *labrys*. The spinning hammer was thought to form the shape of the ***swastika*** as it flew through the air, whipping up the whirlwind.

This ***whirlwind*** and the ***spiral swastika*** that symbolized it were the figurative progenitors of the stylized maze or labyrinth. Nevertheless the hammer, shaped like two opposed crescent moons was, like the *labrys*, a female emblem. At the highest level the labyrinth symbol works on several different but interconnected strata as:

- The Folds of Time

- The Spiral Cosmos
- The Folds of Human Self Deceit
- The Journey of Life
- The Brain and Spinal Column
- The Womb and Vagina
- The Tomb or Creachaire
- The Vortex or Sumaire

We will be concentrating upon the ***vampiric symbolism*** in relation to ***samadhi*** or ***transcendence***.

As the Romans, formerly and anciently the ***Scythian Trojans***, continued to follow Hellenic customs, the word *labrys* would have been known to them. Consequently the construction of their Latin word *labia* would have had incorporated into it any of the original suggestions intimated by the pre-Hellenic word *labrys*.

This assertion is borne out by an inspection of the glyph representing the double headed axe. It is constructed in an hour glass configuration by placing two equilateral triangles of equal dimension together point to point, with the points meeting on the vertical plane, equidistant from the two horizontal planes.

From the central meeting point of the two triangles, a horizontal line extends out, twice the length into the plaster of the walls of the labyrinth at ***Knossos*** and it is this figure, the ***labrys***, which authorities present as giving the ***Knossos*** labyrinth its name.

With the handle removed and placed upright before the double triangle we have the figure 18 which, when the numbers are merged into a monogram, form the *caduceus of Hermes*, the "phallus" of ***Baphomet***, the fennel stalked *thyrsus* of *Bacchus-Dionysus*, the fennel stalk in which ***Prometheus*** gave the gift of "fire" to man and the flying reed-stalk of the ***witches*** (the original witches broom).

It is also the ribbon entwined maypole, the serpents **Lilith** and **Samael** entwined around the tree of life and the rise of *kundalini* up the helix encased spinal cord to the *ajna chakra* of the brain, all of which the foregoing also represent.

The ***witches*** flying reed stalk suggests soaring consciousness in the same way that the caduceus does, which has wings attached to what is thought to be the solar disc, which is rather the *sephiroth* corresponding to the brain. The fire given to man by ***Prometheus*** might be thought by some to have been the ***fire serpent kundalini***, who features as a maiden in the service of the evil **Klingsor**, in the stories relating to **Amfortas** and the *knights of the Holy Grail.*

Klingsor represents the *perversion of the vampire rite* into an act of base sexual lust. He is the aspect of male human nature who, like the ***Minotaur***, represents the danger of capitulation to sexual drives when the knight, like ***Theseus***, is presented with the true quasi-erotic nature of *the Grail* in the form of the virgin vulva.

However ***Kundalini*** promotes the production of ***noradrenaline*** and the sexual hormones which work in direct opposition to the Grail and if the pilgrim allows his baser nature to prevail, the "Grail" will destroy him by producing in him the opposite hormonal response to that which engenders ***wisdom*** and ***spirituality***.

In the story of **Amfortas, *Kundalini*** realizes her true function and dies (to a former physiological capacity in which she was ever active in the service of "*Klingsor*") meaning that she becomes passive and receptive to her other, deeper spiritual role, and capitulates to the service of the ***Grail***, symbolized by her expiry at the Fisher King's feet

This simply means that she, the spinal column, accepts her role as the *conveyor of Grail chemicals* from the ***pineal*** to the ***womb***, instead of only sexual ones, from the ***genitals*** to the ***brain***. With the expansion of knowledge in the science of *Endocrinology*, it is possible now for the informed outsider to restore these stories to their original meaning.

So the fire of ***Prometheus*** is not the fire of ***Kundalini*** *going up the spine to the brain*, but the ***fire of wisdom*** going down the spinal column to the womb to become ***Starfire***, which is shed from thence and drunk in the '***Rite of the Vampire***'.

The double triangle *labrys* design, identical with the one found in the labyrinth of ***Knossos*** but without the handle, was used up until medieval times to denote the womb and vagina. One of the medieval sexual talismans incorporated into the '*Clavicula Salomanis*' includes this axe-head glyph as a representation of the female principle, encircled by the Latin phrase "*Exeat et Replete Terrum*", taken from *Genesis*. The talisman cited was used to attract female lovers, one might speculate for what purpose precisely. Certainly no purpose that would serve a ***vampire***.

The genital symbolism is therefore quite clear and whether the word *Labyrinth* is derived from either *labrys* or *labus*, it strongly indicates that the ***maze*** or ***labyrinth*** was originally a graphic representation of the womb and vaginal channel, at least on one level of relationship to any attendant symbolism.

The following figures demonstrate the relatedness between the *labrys*, the *caduceus* and other historical symbols and objects.

Fig, 26. The labrys ox double-headed axee

Fig. 27. The talisman of Solomon (medieval text)

Fig, 28. The symbol of Isis-Osiris with numerical and gematric values

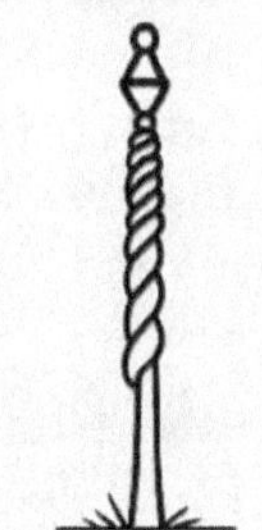

Fig. 29. The maypole, the Thyrsus, the Caduceus of Hermes, the Phallus of Bafomet and the witches Reed stalk

Dragon's Deep

The labyrinth of ***Knossos*** is thought to be a later version of the temple labyrinth of **Amenemhet III** (ca. 1818 - 1772 bce) built at ***Faiyum***. This was a mortuary temple complex consisting of some three thousand rooms and halls resting beneath the shadows of the ***Pyramid of Hawara***, a name which itself is reminiscent of the ancient **Sumerian Dragon Queen Hawah of Elda** who was an ancestor of the builder.

The *Hawara labyrinth* was adorned with carvings of the ***dragon god Sobekh***, to which the labyrinth was principally dedicated, which is not surprising when one learns that ***Hawara***, formerly ***Arsinoe Ptolomais***, was also named ***Crocodilopolis***, the cultic centre of the veneration of this *Egyptian dragon god* of sovereignty and the protector of the royal caste, which was also the *Sumaire* of ***Sumeria*** and the ***Scythians***. The 22 kings of Egypt of the XIIth dynasty met there and it is within the precincts of this palatial labyrinth that **Amenehemet**'s daughter, ***Sobekhnefru***, held the ***Royal Dragon Court.***

Although vast in size, it was not unique, as many pyramids themselves had *labyrinths* built into their structure. We are reminded of the nature of pyramids as sacred mountains, echoing Egypt's cultural origin in an earlier mountainous region of Eurasia, and we will also remember the *sacred hill of the Ogdoad* and the links between the pyramids, raths, sidhes, tells, tepes, kurgans and ziggurats.

The ***labyrinth***, like the pyramid and its collaterals, is thought to be a development of the idea of the mountain cave itself and examples in support of such a theory are to be found in the intricate passages and designs of *Palaeolithic sanctuaries.* As we know, each of the pyramids and their related structures had funerary and living quarters and were representations of the "cave in the mountain".

From the kings or queens habit of living in these funerary buildings, we obtain the myth of the ***vampire*** as one of the undead. ***Labyrinths*** have been discovered as far afield as ***Siberia*** (north-east Russia) and ***Wales*** suggesting strongly, because of the locations, that the concept was of a ***Fairy origin***. In support of this theory we find in Iceland various turf mazes and labyrinthine stone structures called ***Volsunghausen*** or '*Wayland's Homes*'.

Wayland or ***Alberich*** (Aubrey/Oberon) was also called ***Laurin*** and this name, meaning a *Bay tree*, has a double entendre when it is translated as 'passage' in relation to the maze cult. A spiral path can be trod to the top of *Glastonbury Tor*, which is said to be the home of Oberon.

Frequently these structures are associated with barrows and atop one of these outside **St. Anne**'s *Well* (a sacred site dedicated to ***Black Annis***) in ***Nottinghamshire*** is a turf maze named "*Robin Hood's Race*" which is virtually identical with another which was sunk in a depression at the top of "*The Fairies' Hill*", a barrow outside *Asenby, Yorks.*

It was the custom up until 1908 to tread the ***Asenby*** maze of an evening and sit in the centre to hear the ***Fairies*** sing. The design of these mazes, which are of considerable antiquity, some say Bronze Age, are lately called "*Shepherds Races*", (many with a distinct spiral pattern towards the centre of the structure), and were copied by the church during the medieval period.

The ***labyrinths*** at ***Chartres*** and numerous other churches in France, Germany, Spain and Great Britain, are of an identical design with these far more ancient mazes which invariably were placed adjacent to or in the midst of originally prehistoric sacred sites, often forming the centre of the Groves. The labyrinth of ***Chartes Cathedral***, built by the ***Knights Templars*** in the 13th century, like many ritual mazes, has no blind alleys or fake routes.

At its centre there is a six petalled "***Plantagenet***" or wild rose, carved into which there seems to be an ***M*** figure reminiscent of the symbol of Virgo -c- which is the ***M*** for "Our Lady", the **Virgin Mary Magdalene**, to which the ***Ichthys*** or *Salmon of Wisdom* has been appended, denoting the genital nature of the whole glyph itself. As the maze is situated in a cathedral dedicated to ***Notre Dame***, it seems appropriate to think of it in these terms, as the womb of the Virgin.

The ***Rose Garden*** symbolism of the core of the labyrinth of ***Chartres*** is an echo of the ***Garden of Solomon*** and the ***Rose of Sharon***, meaning '***Blood of the Virgin Princess***', and also of the later forest labyrinth of ***Melusine***, with its fountain, mentioned in medieval French literature.

The ***Labyrinth of Solomon*** is in fact a medieval alchemical symbol doubtlessly denoting the "*scented fountain garden*" of ***Sheba***. In the French stories **Melusine** lies in hiding at the centre of her maze garden, waiting to prey on victims returning from the Hundred Years War. She would draw them in and drink their blood. Conversely she also lay at the centre of the maze, as the prize of the quester for ***the Grail***.

The centre of the maze incorporated a ***black cubic stone*** n from which spurted the waters of life, *La fonteine de soif*, and the blood of the virgin womb. At ***Chartres*** the *Rose* in the centre of the maze can be seen bathed in the sanguine light of the sun beaming through a strategically placed pane of red stained glass, making the *combined Grail symbolism apparent.*

Gematria, a system whereby attributive numbers are added together to give the lowest figure and thus reveal the essence or spirit innate in any particular beings, words, higher numbers or objects, to which there have been traditionally attached a numerological component, was an integral part of *Hermetics* and *Kabala*, which was used extensively, as part of ***sacred geometry***, in many Templar buildings.

The ***Chartres Maze***, was also called the Jerusalem mile and was used as a symbolic substitute devotion in place of an actual pilgrimage to the Levant. The mile, though here only suggestive, is 1760 Roman yards which, when added together *gematrically* gives 1+7+6+0 = **14**. The multiple component of the mile is **X 3**, as the mile is measured in yards or 3 feet spans. In order to calculate the number of feet in a mile one times 1760 by 3 which gives 5280 feet. In reality the maze path is far shorter, but the inference is implicit.

It actually measures 150 yards which was a *Gaulish measurement* of 1500 paces, called a *leuca*, *leuga* or *leuva*, which is a term remarkably close to *Lucca*, whom **Professor Margaret Murray** states was the god whose name the reputed royal sacrifice, **William Rufus**, invoked in oaths. ***Lucca*** is related to ***Loki*** and ***Lucifer***, the bringer of light, also known as ***Mazda*** or ***Ormuzd.***

The cult of the ***Mistletoe Bard*** and his journey to the *Elysian labyrinth of Persephone* is clearly documented in the author's notes on *Cai ap Emrys* and the Vere dying kings.

If one multiplies the ***gematric*** sum of a mile (14) by the number of feet in a yard (3) one obtains 3 X 14 = 42, the diameter of the maze. In the medieval period three types of calendar were used: Solar, Lunar and terrestrial.

The calculations of both Solar and Lunar calendars are well known. ***Gematrically*** the symbolic ***Chartres*** "***mile***", if it actually were a mile in feet, added together would give 5+2+8+0 = 15, which is the number of the path of the devil or ***Baphomet***, the head of wisdom, the skull and crossbones, the androgynous god of the Templars (Mercury-Venus or Hermes-Aphrodite) whose combined male and female gender celebrates ***Enthea: Hierogamy or divine union***.

However, it is 150 yards which added *gematrically* amounts to the same thing: 15. 150 yards is 450 feet which adds to 9: ***N'H'Sh,*** the tripartite triple goddesses of "*The Love that is Death*" and the *Vampire Sumaire:* the Spiral Serpent of the Vortex.

When the Catholic faithful walked the symbolic 5280 feet of the

Jerusalem mile, as the maze is called, *kabalistically* and *gematrically* they were following the path of the Devil (15) and walking down the road to *Damnation.* Which was nice.

The actual measurements used vary from modern scales but the component measurements remain the same. The scale used was medieval and the diameter was 42 old feet, each comprising of 11.5 inches per foot, which still relates to ***Venus*** and the cubic stone, **Melusine** and so forth, without actually changing the meaning of the design. This measurement also seems to be a regularly occurring standard for early turf mazes in Britain. These usually display the 10 or 11 concentric circles which correspond to the *sephiroth* of the *Qabalistic Tree of Life.*

The ***Chartres Maze*** was probably based itself on earlier patterns associated with **Melusine** and **Sheba**, which themselves were based on the ***swastika***, the pre-eminent glyph of the *Vortex* or *Sumaire*, the "sucker-in" and source of life and life's blood.

Associated with this is the concept of the *maze* as a dance pattern which, similar to the original sacrificial sword dance of the ***Danes*** and the ***Scots***, was an echo of the spiraling ***witches'*** dance around the vortex and a celebratory rite of the *Wild Hunt.*

For some, entry into the maze would result in their life being drained away by the virgin occupant, whose repast she would pass on to her kind, as she acted as the fountain of thirst and fed them in turn from her holy blood. In a sense then, where the ***Minotaur*** at ***Knossos*** is concerned, (who is frequently interchangeable with the ***Scythian*** Centaur in classical art), he is also representative of the vampire king.

Thus at the highest level, as a whirlpool attracting and

distributing life and life's blood, the ***Labyrinth*** was both tomb and womb, life taker and life giver. In that order. On at least two occasions in *England labyrinths* have been euphemistically referred to as "*fish traps*" or ***Veres*** (*Norse:* '***Ver***').

Chapter Six

The Jewel in the Crown

That it was a druidic device can be ascertained by its 6th century associations with the bard Lwarch Hen. One will recall that **Melusine** was a "**mermaid**", half fish (or rather Water Serpent) and half woman, and that **Mer** is the Egyptian Hieroglyph which, shaped like a square spiral maze, denotes water and irrigation.

As an **Elf Maiden** she would have been the ritual quarry of the Wild Hunt and thus "a fish for the fish trap", a blood offering for the **Vere King**. It appears therefore that the maze is the Bower of the Virgin and indeed some mazes have been named just that: **Maidenbowers**. The symbol of **Virgo**, the **M** with a fish appended, denoting the virgin vulva and womb, is pertinent here.

As the cubic stone is the **Lia Fail**, the emerald tablet, the **vulva of Venus** and the **jewel in the crown of Lucifer**, then it relates also to the Sumerian **Inanna**, the Akkadian **Ishtar** who, like **Melusine**, was said to consume her lovers, and **Hathor** who, like **Persephone** was the vendor of "deadly" otherworldly "food" (which, like its counterpart, **fairy food**, compelled one to remain in **Elphame**), and whose sacred emblem was **the Ankh** from whence was derived the name of the druidic death cult, the **Ankhou** or **Anjou**, of which **Morgana**, and **Melusine** (the Fountain of Thirst) of the **Labyrinth**, were high priestesses.

The Ankh was also used by the **Albigensian Cathars**, thought by scholars to be either the descendants of, or to have been influenced by, the **Persian Manicheans**, the **Arians** and the **Bogomils**, which suggests a further reinforcement of the link between pre-Nicaean and thus gnostic-dualist, or original Christianity and Druidism.

The **Maze** is associated with the root word from whence we derive the adjective "to amaze". This itself probably has associations with the name Mazda, the principle of light, suggesting that whatever was at the centre of a Maze rendered enlightenment and that ecstatic amazement, or wonder, accompanied it.

As **Ormuzd**, it might even be associated with the Spiral Serpent of the vortex: **The Sumaire**. Some dictionaries have suggested in the past that maze was derived from the Saxon word for a whirlpool, mase, and although scholars later insisted that no such word existed, like it or not, the early maze was indeed a figurative vortex; a tornado or whirlpool.

At the centre of the **Knossos Maze** there dwelt the **Minotaur**, the bull-man who destroyed all who entered his environs. From previous notes we will recall that the bull, **Jehovah**, represented the unregenerate man and his world view.
Once **Mithras** or **Mazda** slew the bull, from its veins poured

forth all fertility.

The Bull's head also represented the female organs, one will recollect. Again a source of fertility on both levels.
The **Theseus** story therefore is a typical rendering of the central mystery of the dualistic cult of **Mithras** which is repeated in Sleeping Beauty, Beauty and the Beast and the tale of Holger Dansk. **Theseus** learns that 14 victims every nine years were sent to **Knossos** to appease the **Minotaur**. This has echoes in the popular medieval story of **Melusine's Maze**.

The number 14 is, as we have seen, a strong component of the dimensions of the **Chartres Maze**, which is 42 feet in diameter, being 3 X 14. The radius of the maze is 21 feet which is 3 X 7, representing the <u>three fallow weeks of the menstrual cycle</u>. The week of menstruus would be represented by the point at the centre of the maze, which is, on certain days, illuminated red, as has been recorded in other works.

The fourteen children, 7 virgins and 7 youths, sacrificed at **Knossos** represent two 1 week periods each. Of these there are, symbolically at least, 21 of each in the terrestrial year, which, as 7+7+7 and 2+1 (3) connects the **Labryinth** story once more to the <u>triple goddess and Persephone</u>. The total days of the earth year of 42 weeks add up to 294 which, added together, <u>gives the number 15 again</u>, the **path of the devil** which, added again, gives six and thus the **hexagram of the Labrus**, the womb and vagina of the virgin priestess.

The **Seal of the Temple** is **777** and the number of **Venus** as Netzach on the Kabalistic Tree of Life is also 7. The three component of the Seal represents the three aspects of **Venus, Freja, Persephone** or the **Tantric Kali**, which in themselves encode the three stages of the **vampire ritual**, a component of an entire hidden culture that, resting upon the universal archetypes of common humanity, forms, as **Jung** would argue, the distinct tribal or racial memory (my note; of a unique and separate sub-species), for whom alone this culture, its icons and rituals is emotionally understandable and psychologically relevant and accessible, as is the case for any given race.

Diana and the **Moon** symbolize **Virgin Blood**, **Venus-Aphrodite** represents divine union with the Maiden priestess (symbolized by Iduina-Arduina-Diana) and the taking of her blood, whilst **Hel-Hecate-Kore-Kali** as the last aspect of the Earth and death represent both the death of the mundane soul and the fertility of the super consciousness that displaces it.

Less familiar are the numerical values attributed to the earth or terrestrial calendar however, which operates using a 42 week system with extra days dispersed throughout the weeks of the year. In this context, the maze therefore has a link with the horology of the earth and in particular to the myth of Persephone.

Some authorities claim that **Persephone** spent half the year in the **Underworld**, whilst others state that her sojourn in **Hell** was for only a third of the year. In ancient times there were only three seasons in any event and it is likely that her Underworld semester was therefore for one third of an earth year.

The earliest known calendar used to calculate the earth year was dug up at **Cluny** in **France** and dates back to the Celtic bronze age. It is therefore Druidic in origin. **Persephone** is dealt with elsewhere in these notes, however it is worth noting that she is said to emerge at the end of winter, thus representing the return of Spring and youthful fertility to the earth. She is therefore the fertile maiden. (fertility of the blood in the rite of Enthea, not the fertility of bestial or vegetal congress and sexual increase).

Her association with the **labyrinth** as a **swastika** is confirmed by Knossian coins which bear her head on one side and the fylfot maze with an eight pointed star in the centre on the obverse. An example may be viewed, with similar maze design variations in the British Museum's coin collection. Like the **Norse Freja** and the **Aryan Kali**, **Persephone** is a tripartite Goddess whose three aspects themselves have three aspects, pointing to a distinctly **Scythian origin** and to the Celtic belief in the sanctity of the number Nine, gematrically associated in the Hebrew with **'N'H'Sh;** the **Serpent** or **Dragon**.

Forbidden Fruits

Persephone herself has three main aspects: Diana the Maiden, Persephone-Venus and Kore as Hecate. The Norse equivalent, **Freja**, also has three corresponding aspects, Iduina-Freja of the Apples of eternal youth (Gaelic: Arduina-Diana of the Nine Fires and of the Blue Boar), Gamlod-Freja and Freja.

In turn, **Freja** herself is one third of the team who made up the Witches of Macbeth, these being **Freja, Frigg** and **Hel**. At death, the Norse believe, the chosen hero is welcomed at **Valhalla** by a Valkyrie bearing the Drinking Horn (see below; Horn Gate) that contains the beautifully and suggestively named "Mead of Inspiration", which in Gaelic is the **Dergflaith of Sovereignty** and in Greek, the **wine of Persephone**.

It is probably worth taking a quick side-step and looking at the iconography here. **Mead** is the fermented juice of Apples, (the Graffenberg discharge of the Royal Princess), flavored by honey, which symbolizes the polysaccharines and glucosides which are now thought to be produced during the **enzyme reaction**, (at a specific point in the menstrual cycle), that creates **serotonin** from **melatonin**. The "honeyed sweetness" of the fluid would indicate a high melatonin presence during the hours of the evening and nightime, which are ruled by **Ishtar** or **Venus-Persephone**, as the Goddess of "Love".

At 10,000 years old, so it is claimed and probably therefore the earliest manufactured beverage known to man, **Mead**, is another of the archetypal representations of the **essence of the Goddess- Priestess**, representing the flow of the priestess, sweetened by the nectar (ambrosia or "food of the Gods") collected by bees who are the sacred animals of **Binah**, the mother of Understanding.

Nevertheless, if you cut an apple in half across the core the seed chambers form the pentagram that appears on the brow of the **Baphomet**, symbolizing the cubic stone.

The seeds themselves contain **cynanide** in a such a quantity as to make 25 grams sufficient an amount to kill a man. The apple was chosen to represent the goddess but, as we can see and as tradition testifies, the goddess and her Grail maidens have a symbolic down side. Again we encounter the love that is death and the **concept of death** to one form of perception and the reawakening to another.

As **Kali, Ishtar, Diana, Hecate** and **Hel,** these Goddesses represent the deadly potential of the **sacred elven female**. The essence of **the Grail maidens** and their chemically generated **morphic energy** can heal much, but there is a price to pay.

One draught stimulates dormant centers in the **fairy brain** that, in becoming sensitized to, and instinctively acknowledging these chemicals, it develops a dependence on them and the subtle sweet energy they produce, which as a pathological dynamic is much like alcoholism, such is the intensity of the experience. Because of this, though the **maidens are indeed the Grail**, they are also called the fountain of thirst and, like La Belle Dame Sans Merci; the **Grail Maiden, the Leanaan Sidhe** can leave her victim like **Keats'** palely wandering knight who no longer sees the world in which he once belonged but sees, and consequently inhabits, another world altogether.

His has become a world of infinite wonders but, at her inevitable departure, it has also become a world of unbearable longing, of intense hunger and thirst. Like 'La Belle Dame' these beautiful living goddesses come as softly and as unawares as spirits, to open the door to the rose garden and initiate their chosen prince.

Having united with him in enthea and "removed" his soul, they inevitably depart from these "chance" encounters as softly and as swiftly as at first they arrived. Like bees they are put on the earth to pollinate the flower of fairy consciousness but invariably like bees, they also suck dry the nectar of the fairy's soul.

Bees however, are the badge of the **Merovingian** descendants of **King Solomon** whose Song, or at least the one attributed to him, is packed to the gunwales with **vampiric references** to the gathering of the nectar of maidens in an apiarine fashion later eulogized by **Shakespeare** (**Edward de Vere**?), who was a descendant of **Solomon** and a veritable son of the tradition.

Bees live as equal entities in **Hives** under the rule of one **Sovereign** who is chosen and created from their number by the administration of "Royal Jelly" (**Dergflaith**) by and from the body of the previous Queen.

In this respect the clans of the **Danaan**, the **Elven King Tribes** of the Western Aryans, once replicated in their social structure the organization of the **Hive**. Furthermore the hexagonal construction of the bees' incubation chamber, their place of origin or birth, is repeated in the hexagonal shape of the Kabalistic tree of Life (the Planta Genista, the [family] tree of Origin) which was intended to be identical in its shape and layout with the hexagonal web of relationships on the diagrammatical family tree of the **Sumerian/Scythian Dragon Goddess-Queens** and **God-Kings**, from whom the **Fairy Danaan** and the **Merovingians** are descended.

Bees suck the nectar from the flowers in the garden and in like fashion the vampiric Fey kings and queens drank the nectar of the lily and the rose from their virgin goddesses, in the maze sanctuary of the sacred groves.

The **Bee** symbolizes Understanding, and in history so do **the Fey**, whose legendary power and eternal wisdom, like that of their cousin **Solomon**, was phenomenal, such was the efficacy of the "**Mead of Wisdom**" distilled by the **elf maidens**, the **Valkyries** or **Ladies of the Forest**. With the canny dance of the Bee forming the figure eight, which in human terms represents infinity and is the glyph of **Isis**, we return once more to the subject of the triple goddess.

In the triad of **Diana-Persephone-Kore** the individuals are represented by the **Moon**, the planet **Venus** and Earth respectively and reflect the qualities associated with each. In **Dragon** terms these aspects represent **Potential** (the Blood of the Moon), **Union** (the enthea of Baphomet as Persephone-Venus) and **Release** (the winning of spiritual sovereignty and fertility) after reaching the centre or **Nix**, the love that is death, symbolized by **Persephone-Kore** the fruitful Earth, which is both womb and tomb.

Kore itself means virgin, and the image of **Kore** as Hel or **Hecate** as crones, is only valid on an exoteric, popular mystical level which concerns itself with nature worship. However, the symbolism still hidden in non revivalist witchcraft as it has come down to us today continually points to a high magical purpose with strong connections to the death and blood mystery cults of classical and pre-classical times. The symbolism is often interpreted as being concerned with venal fertility because of the rustic allegorical images which were employed to hide the esoteric information being conveyed.

It has been forgotten that doctrines were split into three layers, each corresponding to the needs, interests and capacity for understanding of the intended audience or participants. In the mystery of **Diana** (**Iduna** or **Arduina**) - Persephone-Kore related to **Chartres** we have seen that we have an example of the maze or labyrinth as both womb and tomb. In the myth of Persephone and the pomegranate, the Dianic Mistletoe bard of Arduina must enter Hel or the Underworld to draw the wine of the fruit of life from her, which in the Gaelic is called **dergflaith**, the red beer of the queen of sovereignty.

Also reminiscent of this journey to the underworld is the **fate of the potential lover** of the mermaid who is destined to be drawn into her realm and certain death, but only death of the ego, it must be remembered. According to trial transcripts the **Templar**'s kept a preserved head in a silver reliquary carved with the figure of **Virgoc**, the **Virgin-and-Icthys** or **Vulva-fish**. This head it is said, they called the **Baphomet** or head (source) of wisdom or **Father Mitras**.

The **Baphomet** or **Bafomet of the Templars** according to **Fr. Eliphas Levi** was an androgyne figure which, with a bit of consonant wander no doubt, incorporated the Mithraic element suggested in **Vatr Mitr**, which has a distinctly Aryan ring to it. **Virgo** relates to **Iduna** and **Arduina**, **Diana** or Artemis the virgin huntress, as well as **Mary** and **Persephone**.

Related to Persephone in the cult of the Elysian Plain which, like the rose at the centre of the Chartres maze, lies at the centre of the otherworld, is Orpheus or Bacchus-Orpheus. **Bacchus** was also called **Liber**, which in Latin means:

a) liberty or release

b) Tree

c) Wine

d) a book,

secret wisdom or knowledge, The Hidden Torah

Orpheus in the Underworld

Bacchus-Orpheus, it will be remembered, was crucified, hung on a tree like **Odin** and **Christ**; and, with **Dionysus**, was a god of the blood and death cults of the mediterranean region which correlate with the Elysian mysteries, introduced to the inhabitants of **Greece** and **Crete** by the **Scythian Danaan of Troy** who had settled in **Carthage** and **Egypt** following the fall of their city. The **Elysian Plain** corresponds to the Irish Tir Na n'Og. The Land, or Tree, of Youth which itself has associations with the Ankh.

In recounting the Elysian story of Aeneas and the Trojan rout, **Virgil** explains that **Aeneas** travelled to **Italy** to seek out the **Sibyl** or **shamanka of Cumae**, to gain knowledge of how to enter the underworld and obtain an audience with his deceased father.

In order to enter the door of Dis and descend to Averna (cf. Avallon), the shamaness explains, he must first bury a friend and then pluck the Golden Bough, but warned him that although many may enter, few except the children of the gods (my note; **The elven race**) may leave again (this denotes a **ritual involving fairy food**). On leaving the **shamanka**'s cave, the **Trojan-Scythian** lord buries a fallen comrade and plucks the **Mistletoe**.

As in the tale of **Gilgamesh**, the **shamanka** accompanies him on the journey and both descend into **Hades** where they meet **Orpheus** on the Elysian Plain and accomplish the task they set out to do, after which **Aeneas**, (being the son of **Assaracus** by **Aphrodite** and the descendant of **Electra** the daughter of Atlas the Titan, son of Iapetus or Japhet the Lord and father of the elven race), was permitted to leave.

Next to the doorway to **Hades Virgil** locates a representation of the **labyrinth**, as a map of the underworld with, as we discover as the story unfolds, **Elysium: Avallon**, at its heart. As a teaching the story of the underworld quest incorporating the mistletoe can be found in the epic of **Gilgamesh**, giving a **Babylonian** and, no doubt, an early **Sumerian**, middle eastern origin for the labyrinth concept which, as the spiral vortex, is related to the decorative motifs employed by the **Ubaid** culture of **Scythia** and **Carpathia**, from whence the royal Sumerian culture itself originated.

In support of such a view it is pertinent that in **Scandinavia** labyrinths were sometimes referred to as "Babylons" and in the **Roman Empire**, the figure of the labyrinth formed into jewellery was worn exclusively by the emperors, because it was considered to be solely a royal insignia. At such a time the explicit inference would have been to directly connect the labyrinth concept to that of Kingship and thus, in classical memory, to the ancient Dragon cult of Sumerian priest kings.

In the story of **Theseus** and the **Minotaur**, by the time **Theseus** is said to have turned up, the tribute to the Minotaur in youths' and virgins' blood had been paid twice in 18 years. **Gematrically** this gives a total of 28 victims or one lunar cycle of 28 days. The youths' blood represented the fallow part of the cycle.

The 18 year period represented Isis and Osiris, Keshalyi and Locolico or Nergal and Nin-Kursag. Osiris was the Blue Faced God of the dead who was the counterpart of the Aryan, blue faced Shiva-Vishnu, the blue boar. **Osiris**' brother **Set** first tried incarcerating him and throwing him in the Nile, but **Isis** and her sister **Nephthys** found him and revived him sufficiently to father **Horus** from **Isis**. The symbol of **St. George** slaying the dragon is derived from the Roman depiction of the slaying of the crocodile **Set-Typhon** by the mounted **Horus**.

Secondly, (Set was not a quitter), Osiris was ripped to bits by his fratricidal brother and his members were scattered. Again, Isis, and Set's wife Nephthys, went around picking up the bits but couldn't find his penis, symbol of his creative force or sovereignty and another symbol for the spinal column, as emphasized by the serpent entwined "phallus" of the **Baphomet**, which is topped off by an orb, representing the brain. In consequence of this **Osiris** is a candidate for identification as the **first Fisher King**, crippled "in the thigh", as the proprietous euphemism puts it. Osiris's "organ" is represented by the figure one or I.

Isis' figure is infinity or the number 8, which was often drawn as the double axe-head figure found in Knossos or Cnossos, a name derived itself from the Greek root word gno or gno, which also renders **gnome, gnomen** (judgment) and gnosis or wisdom from whence derives (self) knowledge.

The **phallus** representation in exoteric **Tantra** suggests a symbolic link between the rush of ejaculation and the release of energy when the **kundalini** is aroused. This **kundalini serpent** is said to course up the spine from the base chakra, like semen rushing up the urethra, inundating the brain in a phenomenon described as a psychic orgasm. An apt analogy.

The phallus symbol here refers to the **spinal column** that carries the neuronal pathways of the brain and consequently its vital essences, via the third ventricle and the **nerve helix**, to the **Graffenberg gland**, the womb, the urethra and the bowel where certain corresponding essences are manufactured and find their way back up to the brain, much in the same manner as the **kundalini**.

The **kundalini** differs however in that it is the process whereby a rush of aggressive, sexual, electro-chemical signals are forced up the brain stem to the base of the corticospinal tract. It is suggested that the kundalini effect is similar to that of stimulatory drugs like MDMA and amphetamine, and that the signals incite the brain stem to release substances including **dopamine**, **noradrenaline** and **acetylcholine** in a violent cascade reaction which arouses the sophisticated sensory centers of the higher brain.

These are not the chemicals associated with transcendence but with processes that reinforce the desire for and attachment to material gratification, the very obstacles that stand between the **individual** and **'spiritual' release**.

Despite constant references in the ancient teachings to the conflict between the different forms of body chemistry, it is often thought by some that playing the beast with two backs is the primrose path to the Kingdom of Heaven.

It can lead so far, inasmuch as it introduces the beginner to altered states of perception - that is undeniable, but biologically, one endocrinal process inevitably dominates the other and it is the subtler process that causes **transcendence**, not the one driven by the desire to achieve more intense, longer orgasms. Its fun, but its not the real thing.

Consequently ancient Aryan, **Draconian "sex magic"**, unlike the type envisioned by a few modern authors and the western gurus of right hand path **Tantra** and the eastern mysteries, has little to do with penetrative sexual intercourse.

Therefore **Osiris' One** or **I** represented, not simply the phallus, but both the tongue and the spinal column, and the eight thus represented **Isis'** womb and vagina. Under the principle that a king isn't a king without a queen, **Isis** and **Osiris** are shown together as the figure **18**, or **666**, the mark of the beast, or the **Knossos Axe Head**: **8** - where the **I** is horizontal.

Theseus, like Orpheus, must travel through a subterranean realm to find his love and, like the mistletoe bard, at the centre of Hades he will win the Chalice of Persephone's pomegranate wine. **Theseus** decides to tackle the **Minotaur** and armed with a sword given him by **Ariadne** he enters the labyrinth with a golden thread tied about his waist.

This sword is firstly the straight edged weapon of focus and purity of intent. The symbol is working on two different levels at the same time here. The Golden thread relates to the Golden Fleece and also the Grail, it is the rivulet of womb blood on the biochemical level, whilst on the psychological level it represents the path of logic and truth.

The golden thread is given to **Theseus** by **Ariadne**, so it is emphatically a female symbol. Whether the **Theseus** version of the story was at variance with others, or with the primeval Grail theme itself, by suggesting that the golden thread was not already laid out on the path, is a question that springs immediately to mind. In Rapunzel the golden thread is her hair and the maze is substituted by an equally daunting but related structure, a Tower.

Nine Pieces of Gold

Symbolically, **Ariadne** is at the centre of the maze, just as **Rapunzel** is at the top of the Tower and, as **Rapunzel** lets down her golden hair to assist the knight in getting to her, **Ariadne** in another sense, assists **Theseus**.

A tablet at **Knossos** describes **Ariadne** as the 'lady of the labyrinthe' to whom money offerings were made. In developing this theme, **Grant** (Myths of the Greeks and Romans) says that **Ariadne** was a goddess of the underworld; which relates her to both Persephone and Melusine and, strangely enough, to **St. Nicholas of Dumnonia** or **Cornwall** who, as a mistletoe bard and traveller to the underworld, a **horned Merlin** and an **Odinic priest**, is said to have offered three gold coins each to three poor virgin sisters to prevent them from becoming prostitutes.

The three girls in relation to Santa as Theseus, it would seem, also appear themselves to symbolize the tripartite Diana-Persephone-Kore or her priestesses. The nine Byzantine, imperial gold coins that the **druid Nicholas** or **Nicassius** gave to the holy virgins became the nine heraldic 'bezants on a field sable' which variably were the arms of his, the **Emrys family**, and which eventually became the arms of the duchy of Cornwall.

The apocryphal story of **St. Nicholas/Nicassius** offering money to the impecunious virgins probably relates to **St. Nicholas**' family as the Druidic, Priestly administrators and Keepers of the Sacred Grove, its holy temple and its virgin priestesses who, like **Magdalene**, came to be thought of, utterly erroneously, as prostitutes. **Cassius** was the name of one of the Roman rebels but has links also with, and was possibly a re-expanded diminutive or affectionate form of the name Caspar, which is of Persian origin and is said to mean treasurer.

This meaning was probably derivative and

like **Nicholas**, **Caspar**, probably a temple official, was the **Syrian Magus** or **Druid** who was said to have presented gold to the child Jesus. The link between **St. Nicholas of Dumnonia** and the bezants would suggest therefore that this is the more likely secondary meaning of his name which is itself ultimately related to Nisse or the Nix.

In a way it can be said that the golden thread in Theseus is a rivulet or rtu of **Ariadne**'s **essence**, a sutra that leads **Theseus** to the centre of the mystery and the Grail. One might suggest that symbolically the golden thread was spun by **Ariadne** from the wool of the **Golden Fleece**.

This artifact is a classic variation of the grail symbol which, guarded by a **Dragon** in the heart of **Greater Scythia** near to where **Prometheus** was chained, had the same healing properties attributed to the **Holy Grail** and the blood of the **elven goddesses.**

In relation to the theme of **the Grail** as a panacea and physick, is the White Cross of **St. John** or the gnostic Iao (**Jao**), related to the sephiroth of Tiphareth and closely linked with Isis and Persephone.

The question must be asked, "How on earth is a thread tied about **Theseus**'s **waist** going to help him find the **Minotaur**?" Quite simply it isn't, and yet the story doesn't say he spent six weeks wandering around in circles getting tangled up in wool before he found the monster.

If the **Labyrinth** were a **Maze**, the thread would be fine for helping him find his way out, but equally difficult without a **golden thread** to guide him, would be the task of finding his way to the centre in the first place. However, the structure at **Knossos** is described as a Labyrinth and labyrinths - unlike Mazes - are single paths which inevitably lead to their goals with no blind alleys or fake turns. This would render **Theseus**' need for an actual golden thread redundant whilst on the psychological level the labyrinth would cease to exist once the **Minotaur** had been slain, thereby rendering the thread pointless anyway.

G.R. Levy explains that **the thread** (Sanskrit: sutra as in Kama Sutra), or rope, or 'clue', and the winding path appear as components of European tales of entry into an actual or subjective spiral maze, many of which were found in medieval churchyards or grave/grove-yards, signifying that the ancient groves were places to meet with the dead. Furthermore the word dru (as in druid) in Sanskrit means 'run', as in run the race or "dance the maze".

The **Llans** were special geographical locations where the **groves** were built and these were on the intersection between **Dragon Lines** (not ley lines) where,

a) the power was thought to be strongest and

b) the site occupied a kind of in-between place which, like crossroads were neither one direction or another and thus were said to be in-between the worlds

As such they were doors to Elphame and later, crossroads (invariably with their gallows poles) and graveyards became the meeting places for **witches. Gallows** were often placed at crossroads, doorways to the otherworld, in order to facilitate the criminal's speedy journey to **Hell** or **Elphame** - life after death - in order that his or her ghost may be encouraged to leave the mortal realm immediately, thus discouraging him or her in death, from further troubling the living, as they had done in life.

Grant continues by saying that the maze relates to the life after death and gives initiation. The author emphasizes that life after death is more properly life before death or transcendence, being the **life** of **superconsciousness** following the death-in-life of mundane perception.

Such a teaching accords with the message of **Jesus** and most other mystics. **Grant** relates the thread to the spindle of Sleeping Beauty, making her a **Fate** or **Mori**, a goddess figure like the golden-haired **Scythian princess Ariadne**. In Sleeping Beauty's story the thread is in the Castle which, surrounded by a thicket representing the labyrinth, is the centre of the maze itself and thus the rose garden and the Elysium.

Sleeping Beauty occupies a tower in the castle in the undergrowth, or a **Caer Glas** (Verrieres) in the **Forez**, if you like, in similar fashion to **Rapunzel** elsewhere mentioned herein, who lets down her golden hair to admit the knight to

her tower chamber. In the course of time stories change and become corrupted by various admissions and omissions, this is the process whereby history becomes myth and legend.

It is not so arrogant to suggest therefore
that **Theseus' story** likewise appears to have undergone changes and suffered the ravages of time. To facilitate a meaningful interpretation of these stories therefore, it is necessary for the student to compare them together by genre and settle for a

common sequence of events and a common objective.

For them to make any sense at all, they must relate to human physiology and psychology and to be grounded in empiricism. If the stories are subjected to over mystification by those who are unaware of their inner workings or of the available esoteric knowledge or the intention of the stories' creators, then confusion sets in.

On **the Grail** or biochemical level, **Theseus** must follow the rivulet to attain and drink from its source, having battled with his own common lust in such a situation. If he does he wins **Ariadne** as the **Virgin Grail**, intact and appropriately related to him. If he does not and the **Minotaur** (Arthur's Klingsor) within him prevails at the source, then **Theseus** will defile that source for base gratification and the **Minotaur**, his own sexual lust for Ariadne, will consume him.

Theseus is a wily lad however and unlike **Arthur**'s druidic saw, which is an adaptation of the story of **Theseus** and **Ariadne**, his is a story of success. **Theseus** attains the source of the golden-red fluid, the heart of the labyrinth and with Galahad-like purity of heart (focus and insight) he sees the Grail, instead of just Ariadne's sex organs. This act itself is enough to **slay his Minotaur** and he exits the labyrinth to unite with **Ariadne**, the virgin source of sovereignty.

However, now he must enter once more and face another **Minotaur** on a different level of being. In the story, **both Minotaurs** are one and the same and are slain at the same time, but I am analyzing the story level by level and it is in this sense that **Theseus** repeats the two-fold exercise.

Having attained and consumed **Ariadne's blood**, she has

become his **Sheba**, his **Rhiannon**, his **Guinevere** and his **Viviane**, and armed with the sword of her sovereignty (creative energy, [non-sexual] libido), he now enters once more to trace his path through the avenues and back alleys of human self deceit and confront the very power source, the very foundation of his own delusion.

This he does and in **slaying his Minotaur** <u>once more</u>, he wins **Ariadne**, the **Sleeping Beauty**, his **Anima**, and her sword of sovereignty is the straight edged blade of his purity of mind, his focus, clarity of vision and singularity of purpose.

Having attained **Hierogamy** or **Enthea** and individuation or personal sovereignty, **Theseus** left **Ariadne** to **Dionysus**, the bull headed child of **Zeus**, the Great World-Bull of delusion. In the French versions of **Arthur**'s tale, **Guinevere** decamped from **Camelot** with **Lancelot**. In all these tales, the "marriages" were not sexual in the sense that we would understand and they weren't built to last.

Because narrators don't know the real reason for these alliances, a social tendency towards post-Victorian morality interprets the separation of the couples as betrayal and marital breakdown. In reality the contract had come to an end with the <u>change in blood chemistry</u> and the females were then ready to leave and pursue other interests.

<u>Axe Lords</u>

The **Minotaur** has been said to be a version of the **Phoenician**, <u>bull-headed God Baal Moloch</u>, the son of **Enlil**, which might be partially right in a ritual context where, it is thought, sacrifices were made to the **Phoenician King** enacting the ritual role of the god by wearing a bull's head as a mask.

It is suggested that the **Minotaur** was **Minos** himself or some other Cretan king in masquerade, fulfilling some ritual role. Said to represent the virile principle, the bull symbol appears on other Aryan artifacts as far away as **Harappa** in the **Indus** in 3000 BC.

If the virile principle is seen in context as the workings of various hormones in the human physiology, it will be understood that those **hormones**, which initially suppress the production of **melatonin** and **serotonin** which themselves play a profound part in the attaining of transcendent states of consciousness, are therefore also the chemicals responsible for many human delusions and anxieties, bringing us back to the symbol of the human mind as the World Bull of Deceit, and to **Mithras** as **Theseus** and so on.

Theseus was the Son of Neptune, king of the waters, an otherworld symbol, whilst **Ariadne** was the daughter of **Minos**, king of the dead, another otherworld character. As a king of the dead or "Dead King" **Minos** was ritually associated with the **Repha'im**, and the axe-head carving in his labyrinth suggests that his people had some association with the **Scythian Axe Lords** of **Idumea** and **Mittani**, from whence came the cult of the Kings of the Dead (**Osiris** or **Orion**), the **Rephaim** or **Angels**.

The chronology is shot to bits in the original tales and the characters are most likely to have been the lineal descendants of the major deific personages, but removed by relationship to a further degree than the stories allow.

Consequently, **Minos** was the son of **Zeus** (**Enlil**), or of **Zeus**' royal-priestly officiate or descendant and **Europa**, who was the daughter of **Phoenix**, whom we assume was the historical **Phineas Farsaidh**, the **Scythian King of Phoenicia**. Minos' brother was called **Rhadamanthus** the red-haired, according to **Michael Grant**, so we can safely say that this genetic strain was present also in **Minos** and **Ariadne**, both of whom therefore were **Scythian** and thus we have a strong **Scythian** component in the **Labyrinth** concept, both in **Egypt** and **Crete**. **Ariadne** was a form therefore of **Lilith**, who was the daughter of **Nergal**, whose name suggests **Naga'el** and **the Naga** or **serpent gods** of the deeps who, as the **Avatars** or **Shining Ones** - the **Anunnagi** - form part of the Aryan Hindu pantheon.

The **Axe Lord** epithet has more to do with **the Grail** than with the axe as the 'tree' or 'man hewer', (in Hebrew - **Nefilim**) as **the Grail** is often drawn in the form of a **Labrus** or upended, double-headed axe. There are similarities between **Theseus** and **Ariadne** and **Samael** and **Lilith**. Where **Theseus** is the son of the king of the sea, Samael is the Lord of the Waters.

Ariadne is the daughter of the King of the Dead and so is **Lilith**. Lilith eventually became the consort of **Enlil-Jehovah** and the substitute matronit or **Lady Sabbath**. She was likened to **Sophia**, the **Shekinah** and the Holy Spirit or Wisdom. Likewise **Ariadne** left **Theseus** for **Dionysus**, the son of **Zeus**. **Ariadne** was therefore also a source of divine wisdom.

In a sense **Dionysus**' attainment of **Ariadne** from **Theseus** and **Enlil-Jehovah**'s Attainment of **Lilith** from **Samael** is symbolic of the way in which divine wisdom (**Lilith**) was purloined by the usurper. This has repeated itself in the claim that **Rome** has made over **Mary** and the **Chartres Maze**.

The **Chartres Maze** is circular and has a central path leading from the outer circumference to the rose in the middle. On either side of this channel are the turns of the inner paths arranged to look like the ridges of the walls of the vagina, as depicted on the Mycenaean Grail chalice. Again **Rome** has sequestered this anciently inspired symbol and profaned it by what they consider sublimation.

Today the faithful flock to **Chartres** from all over the world to walk a Maze inspired by vampirism and laid down in stone by "Satanists". By doing this they think they will get closer to God by an "Act of Faith", repeating the endless theme that the maze itself wished to warn man against, that the **Labyrinth** can represent the dominion of empty form over substance and that man's mind is a vast cavern of paths that fold back on themselves endlessly, in mankind's attempt to hide from man himself the central mystery of his own unjustified misery and terror, that at the centre of his being, cloaked in delusion and fear, lies nothing.

The folding paths of the maze are the paths of **deceit** and **dogma**, of ritual and habit that must, like the **Gordian Knot**, be rent asunder if man is ever to glimpse the real. The habit of walking the Chartres maze merely reinforces the very stupidity that prevents man from ever actually reaching the maze's true, hidden centre.

That man can reach peace and "salvation" by mindlessly walking round in a circle, just because a priest says he can, is yet another fold of self deceit in the maze itself. Symbolically the **Chartres**

maze is so configured as to invite you to ignore all the folds of the pathways and walk straight up the vaginal channel and into the centre of the symbol. Nevertheless it is characteristic of homo religiosus that none ever does.

The **Chartres maze** was not created for Roman christian ritual but for a meditation alien to its tenets and foreign to its culture. Like much that is of value, much that has meaning and the potential to transform consciousness, the church has wiped away the dynamic and replaced it with safe, empty party games that ensure that none break free from the grip of tyranny maintained through mindless conformity and mimicry. Such a sad parody is endemic in all religion and religious thought, not just in christianity.

A tradition which repeats the theme of the **Sacred Virgin** at the centre of the labyrinth is discovered in rural British custom where the vampire symbolism of the original iconography became reduced to rituals for fertility and games of sexual license.

On village common land throughout much of Merrie England it was the custom to lay out a maze and on Sunday afternoons and at other leisure times, the maidens of the parish would gather at the maze and one would elect to stand at its centre. The local village lads would then race each other round the maze to see who could win the virgin first. The winner was awarded a barrel of beer, and the virgin, of course.

This custom also appeared in **Finland** and **Iceland** and, as elsewhere, echoes the original pursuit of the Wild hunt. The beer was a folksy, rustic reminder of the wine of **Persephone** in a ritual involving peasants trying to imitate the mysteries of their ancient superiors, the meanings of which they have absolutely no idea, just like those who adhere to christianity or modern witchcraft and occultism today and all of which are the low versions of the quest for the Grail and Enthea, where such mindless dogma or ritual and bestial

copulation have no place.

In many mazes, thought to be the 'Core' of a **'Llan'** (cf Avallon or Ava-Llan) or **sacred site**, there were once erected pillars upon which were situated the effigies of **Doves**. These sites were the **Apple Groves** where the Mistletoe Bards gathered with the sacred virgins to conduct the secret blood rites of Arduina and sing into being both the Gods and the noble characters of the Kings. **Llan** also appears as lawn, originally meaning a clearing in a wood. **Lunn** means a sacrifice and taken as a whole concept, the **Llan** was a sacred sacrificial grove.

Chapter Seven

The Cors

The ***sacred virgins*** were ***the cors*** (cf ***Kore*** or ***Persephone*** of the Pomegranate, see previous notes) who sang in choirs and who, like ***Ariadne*** at Knossos, performed the sacred spiral dance of the "*choros*" which, in ancient times, were also the chorus of narrators of religious ritual, ballad and tragedy.

This ***chorus***, in later Rome comprising of only the cream of noble youth and maidenhood, danced the maze around a central *core* or '*Cor*', in effect the eye of the storm or whirlwind, symbolized by a column or pillar, upon which roosted the dove of the spirit, the ***Magdal***, which represented the ***corpus callosum*** and the *wings* of the *grey matter* of the cerebral hemispheres of the human brain.

As late as 1660 a turf maze in *Hilton, Huntingdonshire* sported just such an obelisk capped with a sphere, placed there by its builder, a **William Sparrow**.

Similar to ***Chartres***, but in a more direct fashion still, the path to the centre of the maze is straighforward. At ***Saffron Walden***, prior to the turn of the last century, the centre of its turf maze was occupied by an *Ash tree* or *Aes tree* (*Na'Nuine*), symbolic of the Goddess of sovereignty and reminiscent of the ***Fairy Aes Dan***, the Danish Aesir or first gods, the ***Asher*** of the *Egyptians* (Isis and Osiris) and the ***Asuras*** or ***Shining Ones*** of the ***Scythian Aryans***. **Merlin Emrys** was married to **Ninian** or **Na'Nuine**, replicating the union between ***Odin*** and ***Yggdrasil***.

The Cors

Also pertinent to *the maze*, as the *genitalia of the Cor* or *virgin* (***OED***), and variously therefore the ***triangle of Daleth*** in which is set the *All Seeing Eye of God*, is the ***Cor***, as the pupil of the eye. The graveyards in which are located the barrows or bergs of the high *Kings of the Dan at Uppsala* are triangular.

Further linguistic relationships include ***Cor:*** A *Horn*, as in *Hearne* or *Cernunnos*. This is related to ***Keras***; the horn of the ***Horn Gate*** of true visions which is one of the portals of the Underworld. ***Keras*** is related to the verb *Krainousi*, meaning "*to attain fulfillment*". Possibly fanciful, though tantalizing, is the idea that the "*Horn Gate of true visions*" was originally the arch of the open legs of the ***Meremaid***, attired in her ***Scythian***, horn plated ritual armour.

However, **Michael Grant** suggests, in his commentary on ***the Aeneid***, that this relates to *cornu*, the eye with its horny tissue, the *cornea*, whilst the other gate, the *Ivory Gate of falsehood*, corresponds to the teeth and the mouth. He elaborates that what is seen first hand is truer than that which is related in speech, a pertinent observation well fitting the magical idea that *Gnosis* is greater than belief and initiation is more powerful than faith. Nevertheless, in relation to the ***Horn gate***, it is still poetically and charmingly supportive of ***Cor***, as the Eye in The

Triangle.

In elaborating on the concept of ***Cor*** as *cornu* and in further pursuing the *Horn* and *Ivory* symbolism, we should look at the twin pillars of the temple: ***Boaz*** and ***Joachim***. One is black and the other is white, corresponding to the *Horn and Ivory Gates of Hades* in **Virgil**'s ***Aenead***. Bull's horn is often black in colour whilst Ivory is obviously white.

In the major *arcana* of the *Waite Tarot* which, with its wealth of *organo-alchemical, Solomonic symbolism* could well be termed the ***Tarot of the Vampire*** or the "a la carte menu" of the *Epicurean*, the second card, the High Priestess portraying the virgin ***Isis***, is seated before a veil decorated with ***Persephone***'s ***pomegranates***, which is suspended between the two pillars.

Partly concealed beneath her blue robe she holds a scroll on her lap bearing the legend *Torah*, or *Law*. One recollects the Welsh story of the virgin's lap and its association with the female organs in the story of ***King Math***.

Here it is indicated that the law resides within her womb and that she and it are situated between the pillars and thus represent and occupy the point of *Zen balance* or stillness derived from divine union, which is symbolized in British witch tradition by the seesaw and the candle.

Kabalistically speaking she sits at the ***Core of the Llan***, the *Inner sanctuary* of the temple in the ***labyrinth***, before the invisible middle pillar of the tree of life and it is in this position, in ceremonial magic, that initiates position themselves psychically in anticipation of a final communion with their Holy Guardian Angel which for them anyway, is the ***Ende-Werk*** of the Hermetic process, as envisioned by modern occultists.

On her head the High Priestess wears a crown comprising of the disc of the ***Ajna chakra*** or *sephiroth of Kether* positioned between the ***draconian horns*** of divinity, on her breast she wears the *Johannite* white cross of *Iao* or *Thymus* the Healer (see notes on endocrinology), and at her feet rests the crescent of the new moon.

The classical symbolic link between the ***feet*** and the ***genitalia*** derives from the empirically obvious, explained by modern neurological anatomy linked to recent studies of the compensatory adjustments made by amputees who develop *ghost limbs.* Neuro-surgeons locate the nerve terminals for the feet immediately adjacent to the nerve terminals for the genitals. This delightful discovery also goes some way in explaining how the *body's meridian lines* work.

Again in this particular instance the High Priestess Icon demonstrates that the middle pillar, the ***Perrone*** of the *Tree of Life* represents the spinal cord of the Swan Princess and that she and her *sephira*, the *Apples of Iduina*, are the Daleth or doorway to the underworld.

Cor as ***Kore*** or ***corn***, as in **John Barleycorn** and the *Barley Mow*, is associated with the circular field, a variant or adjunct of the ***sacred Llan grove***, in which the sacred grain was grown for the cakes and ale served at pre-christian ceremonial journeys to the *Other/Underworld.* Human sacrifices were strongly associated with the ***Barley Mow*** and the blood was sprinkled as a libation across the field.

Further to this the word *Hospital* or *Ysbyty* in Welsh is associated primarily and anciently with *hospitality* and the *Ysbytys* were *druidic houses*, rather like *Templar Preceptories* or *small monasteries* or *Bangors* where local people or travellers could go and refresh and heal themselves. The sign outside such an establishment was usually a ***druidic Blue***

Boar and it was a part of *Brehon Law* that any given region should have a certain number of these establishments to which were attached the ***Barley Mow*** adjacent to the Sacred Grove nearby.

The ritual function of the ***Barley Mow*** and the public rites in the *Grove* can be viewed as an intentionally pagan (***pagani*** - a Roman social numerical unit corresponding to a Sept) or popular derivation of the higher rites of *Enthea* and were probably devised as a devotional ceremonies for the Celtic peasantry of the rural *septs*, or *pagani*, by
the ***Scythian druids*** whose Bards, one recollects, also sang into being gods for them to worship.

From this we discover the origins of the rustic games which parodied the quest for the grail in the common mazes of *Merrie England*. Lastly ***Cor*** as ***Corvus Corvidae*** (see *OED*),
the ***Raven*** or **Morgana** whose position in the story of Holger Dansk, was under a tree at the centre of a circular garden protected by a ***serpent*** or ***dragon***. (On one level the serpent also represents the ***Nidhe Hogga***, the spiral serpent of the Cosmos).

As such **Morgana** is, like *Ariadne*, *Melusine* and *Sleeping Beauty*; the ***Virgin*** at the centre of the ***labyrinth***.
The ***Corvus*** of ***Morgana*** was interchangeable with
the ***dove*** in *Hebrew Kabala*, as a bird of divination (Cor: the eye: "to see") and the underworld or *Qlipphoth*. The ***Raven*** was originally sacred to **Lilith**. Etymology derived from *OED*. (The serpent-necked ***Serpilion*** dove is interchangeable with
the ***swan*** and is related to the Solar Caduceus).

In parody of the sacred ritual dance, in later ages, maidens and youths danced the *Maypole* and *Morris Men* danced the ring around the Maze at whose centre the Maypole was often erected. The idea that the Maypole was a phallic symbol is only true on one level.

At its highest level the maypole was the ***Tree of Life*** and thus the ***Spinal Column***, at the head of which rests the Dove of the Brain. The true significance of the *Maypole dance* can be observed by watching what happens as the girls and boys (see sacrifice to the Minotaur above) weave the web of coloured ribbons around the pole. With each step the maidens and youths get closer to the pole itself as if drawn into the Maze.

The interlaced pattern of the woven ribbons represents the web of ***Elphane*** or ***Arachne***, the web of
the ***Fates*** or ***Fairies*** (*Mori-gans*), in one sense drawing them closer to the maze's centre and their doom. (In Sanskrit '***Tantra***' means to weave the web of energy.) As they dance closer, the woven ribbons around the pole itself tighten up and begin to symbolize the helix pattern of the *nerve channels that encase the* spinal chord, on their way down to the base of the spine and ultimately the ***womb, the central point of the labyrinth.***

The Tree of Life

This *spinal column* or ***Core Pole***, the ***Ankh*** shaped ***Bethel Stone***, is not simply or solely the penis of some god of mundane fertility, but the main trunk of the *Tree of Life* that is ***Diana***, it is the backbone of the Virgin Goddess, huntress and protector, and any virgin royal priestess, or ***Cor***, who represents her.

On a smaller scale the *Maypole* is the *Thyrsus of Dionysus*, topped with its pine cone. In Scandinavia the maypole relates to the *Axis Mundi*, the lynch pin which was said to hold the sun in place and whose foundation lay buried beneath the world.

The *Axis Mundi* is *The World Ash* or *Aes* and the *Trunk of the Ash*, the *Maypole*, represents the spine of the Goddess or priestess. Thus the sun represents the ***Ajna Chakra***, the halo of christianity, whilst the Earth represents the virgin womb and this symbolism is repeated in the ***Ankh cross***, dealt with in a further essay.

The maze or spiral dance around the *Maypole* is a development from the earlier chorus around the stones and the later witches spiral and ring dance, whose origins are to be found in the dance around the ***Core*** or ***Perron*** stone at the centre of the Labyrinth within the ancient Grove. Sometimes these ***Perron*** stones had pine cones carved at the top, as a variant of the dove but which are identical in their symbolism.

It must be remembered that the virgin at the centre of the maze, the ***Melusine***, was also a ***Morrighan*** who fed on virgin blood, a practice echoed in the story of the blood letting of ***Parcival***'s sister and the symbol of the healing blood of Christ (properly the blood of his mother or wife).

The web of fairy magic drew maidens and youths in as sacrifices, but if the rite was reversed and they were drawn in to feed themselves, then they were to feed on fairy "*food*", of which priest-ridden, terrified humans said that at the first taste, one remains in ***Elphame***, damned forever.

The "*food*" stills the chattering monkey in the head, changes consciousness and deepens perception and one can no longer see the mundane world of petty mortal care, where the trivial is of such import. One sees instead a realm of wider, deeper meaning that in other cultures is called the ***Kingdom of Heaven***. One is healed and "saved" by the Blood. Amen!

In other traditions the condemned were forced to tread the labyrinth on the Common before being hanged from "*The Gallows Tree*". In some distant memory, the executors of the condemned man's fate believed that in walking the maze first, the convict's spirit would be loosened from his body and more readily set free upon execution, in a similar fashion to those who, it was believed, were hanged at crossroads.

In this is dimly recollected the more profound idea of ***the maze*** concealing at its centre the truth of enlightenment and the freeing quality that transcendence has upon consciousness. In this idea, as in religious observance, the central mystery and its mechanics have been lost, to be replaced by superstitious mimicry.

Nevertheless, as evidence, it reveals historical ideas about the nature and function of the ***labyrinth***. At the end of the maze lay death on a tree. At the end of ***Theseus'*** journey through the labyrinth he slayed the ***Minotaur***, himself. Having ***died to one state of consciousness***, ***Theseus*** united with ***Ariadne*** and was born into another state of perception altogether. We have dealt with the concept of death on a tree where the tree represents the female for and upon whom the hero sacrifices his life and through whom he obtains wisdom.

In another sense the ***labyrinth*** represents the ever moving, spiralling vortex of the galaxy and the cosmos at whose centre there is utter stillness as in the centre of the maze, the journey's end; death of the lesser self, stillness and release. Thus the centre of the maze is the *nix*, the *nil point*, the *womb* and the tomb, where the worm of fear dies and is reborn as the embryo of new consciousness.

Footnote

The ***maze*** as ***Time***, related to the spinning of the web of fate, is a very interesting concept and by its design implies that time folds back on itself in layers. Depending on what time width one imagines, instead of time being solely lineal, it might be suggested by the maze design that periods are folded on top of one another, like the skins of an onion or the web of a spider, so that the Greek classical period might lie just beneath the medieval period, which itself might be covered by the Victorian age.

This might go some way in explaining why some ages seem to *wish to revive* the former glories of other particular ages past. If they are adjacent to each other in the time fold, then it seems likely that they may influence each other, just as they do in lineal time. The corollary of this is the shamanic concept of chronological filaments or spirals packed against each other

Part Two

Chapter Eight

The Cult of Ankou

Introduction

In ***Scythian Warfare*** the mounted warriors had one or several amongst their number who rode backwards and naked, painted black from head to foot. He or they would carry a pigs bladder on a pole. These men would ride headlong, so to speak, into the opposing ranks and select individuals whom they would beat across the head with the bladder.

As they rode back to their own ranks they grimaced at the enemy and poked out their tongues. The enemy often viewed this behavior with a degree of considerable alarm, borne in response to a belief system which was commonly held by both sides, even when one side was Roman. This practice has been named "*counting the Kou*" (possibly also related to the Persian kuh: Mountain, perhaps as a sacred hill, place of the gods and hence ka; the spirit, double etc.) and was a method employed to select the most useful spirits for captivation after death, which must have been a terrifying prospect.

Not only was it likely that one would die horribly anyway, that being the nature of classical warfare, especially against the ***Lords of Death***, the ***vampiric***, cannibalistic ***Scythians***, but if one were selected (*Valkyrie* comes from the word '*to select*') ones soul, post mortem, was destined to become either the food of savage gods or the slave of foreign chieftains.

The *poking of the tongue*, also seen in medieval pictures of demons (probably inspired by these ***Dragon Warriors***) who select capture and condemn the souls of the damned, is related directly to the symbol of the tongue as the *lingham*, the *utterer* of the Word of Law, Fate and the Pneuma or Spirit, the ***Ka***.

These black warriors were probably the counterparts of the black ***Morrighans*** or ***Bruidhinas***, the female judge-bards whose word was law, whose "*spells*' were '*Fatal*' in the proper sense. To be struck by one of these meant certain damnation after life with no chance of avoiding the inevitable.

In a sense these warriors were male ***Valkyries***, the dark ***Repha'im*** who, like the ***Morganas***, did a bit of moonlighting (literally!) and doubled up as ***Swan Knights*** on their days off. The tongue pointed at one intimated that the act of ones selection was inevitable and irreversible, and meant also that your enemy, by doing this and thus "revealing his spirit" his ***Kou*** or ***Ka***, after taking your own, considered you to be no threat at all. Is it any wonder that the church drew upon such images to populate their demonologies?

It seems entirely appropriate to model the fiends of the *pit* (*OFr. Kou*) *of Hell* upon such terrifying characters who claimed to be able to take the fallen warrior's very soul, having first tortured the body briefly but nevertheless unspeakably in life, on a field of battle that must have seemed to the observer to be the opening up of Hades itself.

It was in such battle conditions that the entire Roman Ninth Legion, after crossing the ***Antonine Wall*** were utterly defeated, eaten and one suspects, spiritually enslaved by the ***Pictish Scythians of Caledonia***. Not one Roman escaped the carnage.

Related to the word ***Ankh*** are; *Anjou, Angouleme, Anschau, Ankou*. The cult of the ***Ankou*** or ***Ankh***: Consonant migration - This can take place with the change in phonetic accentuation, regional pronunciation, changes in fashion, the vocalization of the words by non-native speakers and the copying of manuscripts by foreign scholars or the scribes of subsequent generation.

In this case it appears that the original word ***Ankh*** has developed into ***Anjou*** via a linguistic path influenced by Goidelic. Spelt '*Ankh*' the ***H*** in Gaelic would have become aspirant which would have been pronounced *Ank-Huh* or *Ankuh*. Verbally the ***K*** became mistaken for a hard ***G***, giving *Anguh*. In due course the ***G*** became *non-Goidelic* and soft, as in '*germ*' and, with the emergence of the letter ***J*** as a softer variant of the soft ***G***, the Word ***Ankh***,
via *Ankhu*, *Ankou* and *Angou* (as in *Angouleme*) became ***Anjou***.

The cult of the Ankou in *Brittany* and *Anjou*, the cult of the ***Spirit of the An***, derivatively therefore the cult of the ***Dragon's Breath***, prior to its introduction to the continent, is asserted to have been of immediate British origin, although it was strongly represented in the Island now known as ***Ireland*** in pre-christian times, where it was probably originally introduced first by the **Egyptian Princess Scota**, the wife of the governor (or king) of the *Red Sea nome*, **Niall of Scythia** (see charts).

It is said that it was introduced into Brittany during one of the migrations from Albany in the first millennium AD. Described as a cult of the dead, the rites and symbols associated with the characters who were claimed or appear to be its royal priests and priestesses reveal that it was also a cult of blood and death, as well as ancestor veneration. In ***lowland Scotland*** the spoken tongue was Northern Cymric and in this language '*angev*', it is said, is one of the words used to describe ***death***, possibly suggesting '*going to the Dragon*', the Church's 'Devil'.

It is significant linguistically because the later house of ***Plantagenet*** were called the ***Angevin Kings***, emphasizing, along with the name ***Angouleme***, the consonant migration described above and adding some veracity to the *Angevin* claim that they were descended from the Devil.

> "We who came from the devil must needs go back to the Devil. Do not deprive us of our heritage, we cannot help acting like devils"
> - **Richard Coeur de Lyon**.

Or, as the Monkish sponsor of the *Knight Templars*, **St. Bernard of Clairvaux** put it when describing the ***Angevins*** - "De Diabolo Venit Et Ad Diabolum Ibit".

The syllable *Ang* in *Angev* is also to be found in ***Angel*** and derives from the Greek *aggelos - aggelos* which is reminiscent of *Agg* or *Ygg*, the ***Odin*** priest as an angel, a ***Repha'im*** or priest of ***Nergal. Freja,*** as a goddess of the Earth and the underworld, was the proud owner of a Heron or Crane-skin bag and a *Merlin* feathered cloak which ***Odin*** was oft wont to cadge from her from time to time, making him a *Merlin* figure and linking her to the sacred and sinister bird of the druids. One of the explanations for the name of the ***Fir Bolg*** was "*Bag Men*". Related to the Crane-Skin Bag, the ***Fir Bolg*** are ***Merlins*** or ***Druids*** and thus Fir 'Bog', "***Men of God***"

The ***Merlin*** itself was described as a "bird without a nest", a solitary wanderer in exactly the same sense as was the magical ***boar***, "*Le Solitaire*". The ***boar*** as the '*The Hermit*', the solitary *archdruid*, the lonely wanderer, is the Merlin who likewise ranges alone, thus indicating that ***Merlins***, ***Odins*** and ***Archdruids*** were synonymous.

On the ***island of Delos*** the dance of the *labyrinth* was called *Geranos*, the "*dance of the Crane*" and is suggestive of the druidic ritual of 'Crane pointing' as a form of related magical observance. The Crane dance, known in Britain as the "*Dance of Troy*", was also performed by the *Ostiak peoples of Siberia* up until the 18th century and was so-called because they wore *Crane skin* clothing for the occasion.

Principally the ***Ankh*** or ***Ankou*** in ***Brittany*** was described as being a collateral cult of the ***Morrighan*** which was particularly prominent in the Breton coastal regions. As such this would suggest that the *Ankou* had some influence upon the *Armorican* cult of the *Ferryman of the Dead*, particularly as ***Morgana*** herself is associated with the Swan Barge of Avallon, which transported the dead ***Mordred*** to his final resting place in the sacred grove.

In ***Eire*** the Cult of Ankou was associated with *Sidhe mounds*, *Raths*, *hills* and *Barrows*, and hence ***labyrinths***. Known as Mari in the Basque region and associated with the ***Morias*** or *fates*, *Ankou* was the original model for the ***Black Madonnas*** there. The goddess *Ankou*, ***Black Annis***, was derived from the Greek '*Anku-Kis*' who was a form of the earlier Egyptian Goddess of the underworld - *Anu Ket*. In the Semitic-Ugaritic texts found in *Ras Shamra* in 1928, Ankou is called *Anat*, a witch goddess and regeneratrix who shape-shifted into the form of the ***Morrighan*** or ***Morgana***, a black predatory bird.

We are here in the presence of '***An***' the ancient ***Dragon Mother*** who is both a sustainer and a reaper, a phoenix figure whose Raven like attributes link her to the Kershalyi and Locolico of the first dragon homeland of ***Transylvania***. In Breton churches her priestess ***Morgana*** is portrayed as a *wouivre* or double-tailed mermaid or dragoness and in this respect she is identical with another Priestess, ***Ygraine***.

The ***Cult of the Ankh*** or ***Ankou*** was the ***Court of the Dragon*** of *Ankh-fn-Khonsu* and his successor ***Sobekhnefru***, whose most sacred inner symbol, historically, was the winged Orobouros with a pendant Greek cross; the Ankh of Nin-Kursag or Hathor, and her daughter **Innana** or Venus. In tracing the history of one, via Egypt to its ***ancient Sumerian*** roots, we inevitably therefore recount the story of the other. They are, therefore, the same thing and represent The realm of the Dead (or more pertinently, precisely and poetically "*The Undead*"):

- Tir N'an Og
- Elysium
- Drakenberg
- Lothlorien
- The Court of the Kingdom of Elphame

• The Grove of the Swan Maidens

• Hall of the Dragon Lords of the Rings,

• Repha'im or Rapha Elohim, named after Raphael who, in the Koran is the reaper and summoner of the dead and corresponds to Waite's Tarot card 'Judgement'

Later on, following ***Ygraine***, the ***fairy Melusine of Anjou*** who descended from her, was also portrayed in this manner as a *wouivre*, especially and also in medieval religious architecture. Related to this theme, in the cathedral of Le Mans on the *Anjou-Maine* border near ***Rennes***, there is a carving of two serpent tailed doves, called *Serpilions* and derived from the Persian '***Smenda***'. Another representation of the ***Dragon*** is the ***serpent necked Swan***.

The dove is sacred to ***Venus*** and is particularly associated with the **Virgin Mary Magdalene**, whose name **'Magdala'** means the *place of doves*, e.g. the temple of the cult of ***Hathor*** or ***Venus*** - ***Ishtar***. In Albany the 'place of doves' was *Camlann* or ***Camelot*** and the association with ***Morgana*** and ***Melusine*** and the Ladies of Avallon, and thus the priestesses of the cult of the Ankh (of Hathor or Venus), is apparent.

The Ankh of Hathor, according to **Gettings**, is generally believed to be the source for the astrological symbol of her daughter **Inanna** or ***Venus***, whose magical colour is that of ***Elphame***. Further to which, **Emma Jung** reminds us that when the Grail appears as a 'stone', it is presented on a green silk cloth, which reasserts the link between the stone and the emerald of Venus.

The colour green in alchemy is the ***Benedicta Viriditas***, the colour of the *Holy Spirit* or ***Sophia***, the wisdom gained by the hero who, on completing the "*quest for the Holy Grail*", is awarded the *Green Cloak* or *Greenmantle.* Green Stags (The Robin Hoods) are one of the Grail badges or totems of the lords of the forest which entered heraldry in the armorial achivements of some families. The ***Green Stag*** amongst other things represents the transcendent king, the fairy lord of the forest, blessed of a fairy queen. ***Stags*** drinking from *Grail Chalices* are quite common subjects for bas relief sculpture.

The links to ***Green*** as the ***Elven Colour*** are obvious and indicate

a) that the Holy Spirit is immanent within Nature or the Cosmos, i.e that the universe and god are One Being and

b) that the Fairies already possess the Holy Spirit of God by virtue of blood and birth, not through the consent of some priest.

Therefore they are naturally eternal beings and in no need of forgiveness of sin, because they, the ***sons of the Repha'im*** as the true Children of God, don't and can't commit any sin.

The Key of Life

It can be asserted that the ***fairy*** or ***dragon*** cult of the ***Goddess Ankou***, although not originating there was, in any event, maintained in Albany, where ***Morgana*** was born and was ritually active. Having established this it is likely that the later kingdom of Anjou, formerly known as ***Pictavia***, derived its name from a priest or priestess or court of the Ankh which settled there from the Breton coast.

If this was ***Melusine***, the founder of the Pictavian House of Anjou, then *Melusine* would have been known as '***Melusine d'Ankou***' or '*Melusine of the cult of the Ankh*' prior to moving to there. That in itself is almost certain, as it would be for the other Avallonian princesses, but the idea that she actually founded the kingdom itself is not, as the realm of the Anjou, as stated, was passed down by inheritance it seems, from the reigning *Vere Tigherna 'Vortigern'* to the grandson of **Merlin Emrys III**; **Guy de Marys**, who was already a prominent figure in Breton legend.

Guy de Marys, reputedly a ***Vere ancestor***, was also know as ***Kai***, ***Cai*** or ***Kay***, the latter spelling meaning both ***Quay*** and ***Key***, in relation to which the ***Ankh*** was called both the Key of the Nile and the Key of Life. **Guy** was a merlin and a druid or magus, specifically a bard of the golden bough who descended to Hades, by classical Greek description and definition, and as stated, he would have been a revealer (anschau) and binder of mysteries. As a "spell" master, a binder and loosener of lives, a male Fata or Mori, one of the ***Fairy Race***.

The presence of the cult in Brittany, suggests that the ***Anjou*** or ***Ankou***, as the otherworld kingdom of the dead, was moved as a rite, from northern *Pictavia* to southern *Pictavia* in Gaul where it gave its name to a region which then became its cultic kingdom, years before either ***Morgana*** or ***Melusine*** were born.

It is more likely therefore that **Emrys II - Ambrosius Aurelius** - introduced the cult to the region when he decamped to Brittany sometime after the defeat of *Rhydderch*, which would then help to explain *Melusine*'s later presence there.

She is said to have fled to Gaul from *Northumbria* with her ***Dragon Court***, after the ritual killing of her father in the same manner that ***Morgana*** killed ***Merlin***. (*Elinus*' spirit was later deified, it would seem, and given symbolic gift offerings of milk, after a manner associated with the live "*dragons*" who were given the *semen* or "*milk*", and the blood of maidens; and were thought to inhabit caves, or labyrinths, throughout Europe).

However it was unthinkable that a *royal pictish princess* would flee and wander through someone else's kingdom unannounced, as this could be construed as an act of invasion and war. Such a story seems to be a later justification of her presence there.

But as a *priestess of the Ankou* in ***Scottish Pictavia*** she would have been welcome in the other land known as ***Pictavia***, where her cousin **Rainfroi**, the third great grandson of **Ambrosius**, reigned as the *Archdruid of the Golden Bough*, the hereditary, ritual king of the dead. As it is they, both patricides, were destined to marry, which would strengthen the dynasty, and thus the migration was a planned event. In any case the cult, with its ancient Irish associations predates *Vortigern*, and we should be looking farther back still for its origins.

Essentially the *British-Gallic Cult of the Ankou*, is related to a symbol sacred to ***Horus'*** supposed wife: ***Hathor-Venus***, and to ***Isis*** and ***Nephthys*** - the ***Ankh***. These deities appear to be related to each other in the same triple goddess configuration found in the rest of Europe and the Levant. The ***draconian Ankou cult*** is a regional variant therefore, perhaps the origin, of the Greek cult of Persephone as described in the foregoing essay on the ***labyrinth***. (Isis and Nephthys are also both, amongst other things, goddesses of the dead).

In the Funerary Cult of Egypt, the nobility employed Ka-Priests to tend the dead. This is linked to a strong thread of ancestor veneration which is also found in ***Scythian*** culture. Though the ***Faiyum Labyrinth*** has long since been reclaimed by the sands, the massive labyrinth complex of funerary palaces in the 25-26th dynasty necropolis standing next to the temple of Hatshepsut in Deir el-Bahari is still in existence. At the centre of the complex is situated the sacred sanctuary which has an adjoining cell which is commonly recognized as the utmost Holy of Holies, the singular feature of which is the carved ***Ankh Cross*** which dominates its facing wall.

In the '***Papyrus of Ani***' dated 1300bc, ***Isis*** and ***Nephthys*** are depicted as standing either side of the Ankh and holding aloft, above its loop, the solar disc which relates to the *Sephiroth of Kether*, also called the *Ajna Chakra*, symbolized by the '*thousand petalled lotus*'. This lotus in Egypt was associated with the **psychotropic Nile Lily**; and the generic symbol of the lily in all its national variations, was associated with ***the Grail*** and ***Dragon Families***. The subject of the lily will be studied in some detail later on.

In pre-christian Gaul it appears on the carved heads of chieftains whose effigies were incorporated into architectural columns and at a very early period Prior to its adoption by the committee of Paris, the lily or '***Fleur de Lys***' (Fleur de Luce or Flower of Light; Flavia Anderson) was the badge of the ***early Kingdom of Anjou***. The shape of the *fleur de lys* seems to have been influenced, in its present form, by a very important Gallic magical rune which was within a group of symbols derived from, or related to, the prototype of the Ankh.

The lines of the ***fleur de lys***' basic structure pass through two planes and two angles to form a *St Andrews Cross* overlaid upon a *Greek Cross* in the manner employed to create ***the Norse*** binding runes. From the evolution of this figure it is thought that the *Chirho* was developed as a later form of the *Ankh*.

This eight armed cross appears in the Canary islands cut into the bottom of the bowl recesses which were carved into the top of stones outside sacred caves, duplicating the concept of the cup and ring stones one can find throughout Britain.

As was the case in the offerings made to ***Melusine***'s father outside the cave in ***Northumbria***, in the Canary Islands milk was also poured into these depressions and left to trickle away down the side of the monolith. The eight armed figure was believed by the islanders to be sacred to Isis, the virginal High Priestess of Waite's alchemical Tarot, and it was said to be her "milk", the dew of the ***fleur de lys*** or ***rosicrucis***, that flowed from the eight armed cross to form the milky way, the spiral vortex or labyrinth of the "cosmic" dragon, the ***Orouborus*** which features in the cross of the ***Dragon Court.***

The ***fleur de lys*** itself is so configured as to contain within it both the ***Ankh*** and the ***Chi Rho***. The figure of the fleur de lys, as a Gallic rune, comprises in the Norse of Nyd as +, an equal armed cross meaning both need and death, Gifu as ***X*** meaning union and Wyn as a loopless ***P*** meaning victory.

Translated, this forms the ritual process encapsulated in the rite of the labyrinth. The ***P*** lost its loop during symbol migration, a phenomenon documented by the **Count d'Alviella** in his book '*The Migration of Symbols*', some components of which I will draw upon later and reproduce the figures for.

In essence there are several related crosses that, although thought to have developed from each other serially, belong to a very ancient group of symbols employed within the royal ***Dragon*** culture within which the rites associated with central mortuary theme of the cult of the ***Ankou*** form an integral and timeless component which is well known.

The Sacred An

The ***Chi Rho***, is the symbol for the symbol for the ***Swan Knights***, is developed from the ***Ankh*** itself which in turn forms the basis for the ***fleur de lys***. In Melusine's time the field of lilies, the arms of Anjou, represented the Pictish virgin princesses coveted by other dynasties, which are the lilies featured in the earlier *Song of Solomon.*

These ***lilies*** or ***Anjous/Ankhous/Ankh*** maidens, sacred to the various Goddesses mentioned herein, are the ***Bruidhinas***, the ***Morrigan/Valkyries*** and ***Swan princesses*** of the ***Dragon Dynasty*** which the ***Swan Knights*** were sworn to protect. Their symbol IS the ***Chi Rho Ankh*** which, instead of just representing the ***XP***, the first letters of the name of *Christ the Man*, latterly conceals the true nature and gender of the **Christos** itself, which is of the ***rtu*** of the ***Ankh***, the Goddess.

Consequently the ***Chi Rho*** itself is a ***female Dragon symbol*** related to both ***Morgana*** and ***Melusine***, as well as all the other *Ladies of the Lake*, mermaids, naiads, nixes, virgin priestesses and so forth. The earlier history of the ***Chi Rho***, the ***Ankh*** and the ***Haegl rune*** which forms the ***fleur de lys*** can be found in the development of Mesopotamian cuneiform from earlier Sumerian pictograms.

In Sumerian the symbol represents '***An***' : ***The Star.*** The star pictogram later became cuneiform with the wedges forming the ends of the top branch or ray, and the subsequent three rays going down the left hand flank of the glyph. At this stage the symbol came to represent the '*Heavens*' and its final cuneiform representation was as an equal armed cross with a wedge at the end of the top ray and two wedges on the left arm which represented the gods. This figure is close to variant representations of the Ankh in medieval black magic where the top arm is an enlarged triangle whilst the other arms have smaller wedge ends.

The common translation of the word ***Christ*** is "***anointed one***". ***Libatio***, from the root *libare*, meaning '*to taste*', 'to pour' (as **Mary of Bethany** is said to have anointed **Christ**) is however, closely related to this concept. *Libare* is related to the Greek *leibein*, to pour, drop by drop, translated as 'to pour out (wine etc.) in honour of a god' OED.

Wine is not uniquely specified, but any liquid; meaning that *Libare* and *Libatio* are not solely confined to the act of the libation of wine to a god. It has been suggested that some Greeks would argue that '*Christos*' meant *gold* and that would then intimate that the idea of anointing, in relation to the Grail, was derivative and attributive.

In the Greek Orthodox Bible *Christ* is described as the '***Golden One***' from *crusos - Crusos - Gold*; rather than *cristos Cristos - To anoint*. Here we are back to **Christ** as the '***red-gold flow***, an *anointing* or *libation* of virgin blood of the Labrus or *Labia*. *Libare* is also related to *Liber* or *Bacchus* the god of "wine" and here we are reminded of the later christian doctrine of transubstantiation and their substitute of wine for blood.

In ***Mithraism*** the blood of the bull was poured from above onto the supplicants as an anointing chrism and a liberatory eucharist drink, and so the idea of libation solely being TO a god is incorrect, as often the gods, or indeed the goddesses' blood, was shed as both an anointing and libation for their flock. Further on we will encounter 'anointing' not as Christos, but as murizein - murizein which has its own surprises.

Jesus' ***surname is ben Panther***, meaning the ***Leopard***, which is the totem steed of both ***Bacchus*** and ***Diana*** and is repeated in the arms of the ***House of Plantagenet*** as three (originally one) heraldic leopards '***Or***' on a field '***Gules***' or three golden leopards on a field of blood. The archaic spelling for *Leopard* is ***Libard*** and this night stalking animal is renowned for drinking the blood of its victims prior to eviscerating and consuming the carcass. Here again is a variant of the word *Libare* and quite a pertinent one at that, as again blood becomes a *Libation* associated with **Christ** the son of the Libard, as the *anointed anointer*, the ***libater***, the ***initiator***.

Christianity is substantively a prime example of the reversal of libation and in this it attempts to mimic earlier Bacchanalian ritual. *Royal anointing* in post Carolingian christian ritual, where the oil of the chrism (representing the Holy Spirit) and the vatican's right to use it to create kings from peasants and merchants, also by transubstantiation one assumes, is treated as though it were delivered in obedience to the will of God by proxy through his chosen priesthood, who intended it to take the place of royal blood in the veins.

It is suspected that the etymology of the name Christ was tampered with in order to accommodate this ***anointing ritual*** and to derive the usurped social power that attends upon it. Along with the service of communion this is another catholic version of reverse libation with blessings being showered upon the grateful by a beneficent priesthood.

Libare is related, via 'to taste', to labia - lips and *libant* means 'tasting' or 'touching lightly', obviously with the lips. Related to ***Libare*** we will remember ***Bacchus*** and ***Liber***, as the tree to which he was crucified and which gave blood red wine that liberated the spirit and taught it dark knowledge and ancient law. *Lake* or *Del Acqs*, sometimes written as *Lac* represents the lily and the rose: The Roman dye "Lac": The crimson flow, and ***Lac*** or ***Lactose***: The white "milk" of the maidens. Within the *cellular and genetic fabric* of these substances was retained the ***Ankh'***a or ***Ka*** of the ***An***, the Holy Spirit and ***power of the Dragon Gods*** - the ***ka*** of the ***An***: The soul of the Heavens.

The crimson flow and the 'milk and honey' (***Nectar*** or ***Ambrosia***; cf. the name of three generations of ***Merlins*** above) of the priestesses can be adequately and correctly described as their sacrificial libation, the "***blood of the Christos***" shed for the remission of *sins* (Hebrew: *'Sin'* - "*falling short of the mark*"; perceptual blindness, the living death).

The spurting of "milk" relates to ***La Fontaine de Soif***, so called because it "sprays out", like a fountain, from the cubic stone. This symbolism is derived from the ejaculatory propensity of the ***Graffenberg gland*** which ejects its seminal fluid, the sacred *'milk and honey'* or nectar, like a jet.

Poured onto the *Ankh* figure in the cup stone by the sacred cave or ***labyrinth***, the substitute ***milk of Isis*** is not symbolic breast milk but an allegory for her seminal fluid, inundating the symbolic *vulva*, the *Ankh*, from whence it originates. It should also be noted, however, that breast milk itself contains ***Telomerase***, a sort of bicycle puncture repair kit for ***infant DNA***. One is supposed to see a connection here, I think.

The ***Ankou cult*** and the ancient form of the ***Ankh*** is therefore associated with caves and thus ***labyrinths*** and with the holy female essence. Both ***Morgana*** and ***Melusine of Anjou*** or ***Ankhou*** are closely associated with such elements, as High Priestesses and ritual representatives, in a line of succession which goes back through the *Pictish Fairy Princesses* or *swan Maidens*, beyond ***Sobekhnefru*** and the *Egyptian Ankh Goddesses* to the ***Sumerians*** and ***Babylonians***, whose goddesses ***Ast*** (*Isis*) ***Nebt-Hat*** (*Nephthys*), ***Nin-Kursag*** (*Hat-Hor*) and ***Lilith***, from whom ***Melusine***, ***Morgana*** and the *Ladies of the Lake* are descended, all bear the ***W symbol*** which forms the loop of the Ankh, which was first entrusted to the god ***Thoth***, who was the Sumerian ***Nin.Gish.Zi.Da:*** *The Lord of the Artifact of Life*, son of **Enki** and **Eresh Kigal** (Persephone-Demeter).

Likewise **Magdalene**, the daughter of the *Jireh Priest of the*

Temple of Jerusalem was a Priestess of this lineage and the matriarch of the Ankh Priestesses in Albany. Known as a ***Scarlet woman***, she was so-called because of the colour of the Lac-dyed ceremonial robes she wore as a senior officiate, the blood tincture indicating her ritual obligation.

The term ***Scarlet Woman*** became associated with prostitutes because **Magdalene**, as a temple priestess, in her relationship to **Jesus** as a ***Pharaonic, Dragon Messiah*** or ***God-King***, fulfilled the role of the goddess ***Hathor*** or the Judaic ***Astaroth***, the ***Sabbath*** or ***Matronit*** in the esoteric, Kabalistic aspects of Jewish spiritual philosophy.

This role involved her in forms of ritual "congress" or *Enthea*, of the type specified in the ***Song of Solomon***, which are also found in the *Tantric Kaula Vama Marg* and repeated later by the *Avallonese Virgins of the Holy Blood.*

Astaroth was the *Goddess of the Shekinah*, the divine presence of The Eternal within the Solomonic Temple of Jerusalem. To the early *Gnostics* she was recorded as representing the ***Sophia*** or ***Holy Spirit***, the (feminine) principle of Divine Wisdom. Later ***Astaroth*** (a denizen of the Devil in the *medieval demonologies*) continued to be recognized by the ***Cathar christians*** as a symbol of the *Holy Spirit* and during **Jesus**' life, ***Astaroth*** was therefore manifest in the person of **Magdalene** as **Christ**'s consort in accordance with *Apocryphal doctrines*, in much the same way that ***Ishtar***, ***Matronit*** and ***Lilith***, as early priestesses of the ***Shekinah*** began as the consorts of **Enki**, **Enlil**, the ***Dragon God-Kings*** and later **Jehovah**.

In this **Mary** too, fulfilled the role of ***the Anunnaki*** blood mothers who fed the ***Dragon God-Kings***. As the physical embodiment of ***Astaroth***, the ***Sophia*** or ***Shekinah***, within the *Egyptian Therapeutate* she was ***Hathor-Venus***, whose cross derived from the Ankh, and as ***Ishtar***, the morning and evening star, she personified "*war*" in the mornings (***Seratonin***) and "*love*" in the evenings (***Melatonin***).

After ***Ishtar***'s example the progeny of ***the Anunnaki*** dynasty, the ***Rephaim*** or ***Angels***, who became the ***Elven***, ***Dragon Maidens*** and ***Knights of Albany***, Eire and Gaul, fulfilled two roles, that of destroyers and reapers, and that of divine lovers and healers.

Under the patronage of ***Ishtar*** or her mother - ***Hathor*** (***Nin-Kursag***) of the Ankh or Ankhou, (and later, under two of the principal Astaroth matriarchs, Magdalene of the Green Dress and Anna, her grand daughter, who migrated to Albany and married into the collateral ***Pendragon dynasty***), the ***Rephaim of Pictavia*** and ***Eire***, were both the Swan Princesses; vessels of the *benedicta viriditas*, and the Morganas and Valkyries, the Priestesses of the Ankou and the Guardians of the ***cult of Blood and Death***.

In this way the ***Cult of the Ankhou*** gained a collateral line which descended through the posterity of the ***Druidic*** families to the ***Mistletoe Bards and Priestesses***. From the '*Letter to Ceretius*' we know that **Jesus** performed a sacred role as the central figure within the circle dances that, in conjunction with his secret teachings and his rituals of initiation (**Morton Smith**), he conducted at night.

In the '*Letter*' **Jesus** is recorded as saying at one nighttime gathering "*The Eight Are With Us*". These are the ***Egyptian Ogdoad*** or eight Great Spirits of Gnosticism which are also found in ***Taoism***. The ***Eight Spirits*** are the second wave of creators (after the *Cosmic Twins*) that appeared tilling on the sacred mountain of the "rising land" that emerged after the flood.

They appear in an illustration in the '*Book of the Dead*' of **Khensumose**: Third Intermediate Period, 21st dynasty circa 1075 - 945 bce. Evidence for the existence of this belief prior to the pre-Ptolomeic period is derived from its worship site at ***Hermopolis*** whose '*Eight Town*' quarter existed at the time of the Fifth Dynasty: 2498 - 2345 bce.

'***The Eight***' when reflected upon in relation to ***Ubaid*** or ***Sumerian tradition*** represent ***the Anunnaki***, the original gods of Egypt salvaging the remains of their civilization after the Black Sea inundation. The story has been transposed to Egypt, like so many stories travel with their tribes, and becomes the creation myth of the pharaohs.

The ***Ogdoad***, also found in ***China*** as we have noted, are some of the sons and daughters of **Enki-Samael** (***Ptah***) and **Ninkhursag** (***Hat-Hor***). **Enki** sired **Ningal** from **Ninkhursag**, and **Eresh Kigal** from **Ningal**, it would appear. **Eresh Kigal**, mother of **Lilith**, gave birth to eight deities - Abu, Nintulla, Ninsutu, Ninkashi, Nazi, Azimua, Nintu and Enshag; (**Sitchin**). That **Jesus**, as an initiate, invokes them, suggests that he had a firm Egyptian, gnostic ritual background which has its origins in ***Dragon kingship***, manifesting itself later in *medieval witchcraft.*

This reinforces and supports an argument for the role of **Jesus'** ***wife*** as his ***Priestess of Hathor-Astaroth*** and points to her lineage becoming a contributive bloodline to the pre-existent cult of the Ankou in Albany and Pictavia.

It is significant that the ***Ogdoad*** are also known in ***Scandinavia***, where they are called the ***Aia***. The ***Norse*** have a diagram of the sacred mound as a square which also shows the compass points and the migration of the eight tribes of the Gods from the Holy Mountain. **Professor Douglas Adams** of

Idaho University has demonstrated that the ***i*** or ***y*** may be substituted by an ***s*** as in *Arsi-Cantu* becoming *Aryi-Cantu*, which would give us *Aia* as *Asa* and thus *Aesir* and ***Aes Dan*** or *Aes d'An* (***Arya of Anu***).

This is of some interest because people are used to having ***the Anunnaki*** presented as a small council of deities, when in fact they were a race of people who were still known as ***the Anukim*** in ***Canaan*** in 1200 bce, 760 years after **Enlil**'s *Anunnaki court* had apparently fled Babylon in 1960 bce. Corroborating the Migration myths of the ***Danaan*** in the Irish *Liebhar Gabhala*, the *Aia migration* glyph suggests that eventually at least one of the tribes of ***the Anunnaki*** settled in the north, whilst another, ***the Danaan***, headed west following "a flood".

The location of the sacred mound would then seem not necessarily to have been Egypt but, given the broad dispersal of the ***Ogdoad story***, it would probably have been a site from where the gods originally migrated, the most obvious location of which is ***Aryan Scythia***, near the Black Sea region. It is quite possible that the time frame for this migration was 4000 bce, when the Bosphorus collapsed and the ***Ubaid*** fled south to ***Sumeria***. Later they became the gods of Egypt and it is feasible that the story of the "tilling of the sacred mound" migrated there with ***the Anunnaki*** - ***Ubaid deities***.

Venal or Venal?

The ***druids*** welcomed the ***Culdee*** into Britain as brothers in spirit and fellow druids. **Columba** called **Jesus** a ***Druid*** (of the order of ***Magi***) and the links between primal christianity and druidism are quite apparent. **Jesus**, (a harrower of hell like Orpheus-Bacchus) **Odin** and **Theseus** were born in caves and, like **Merlin** and **Elinus**, **Jesus** was buried in one, in a garden which was arguably a *Necromaniton*, or druidic sacred grove with a funerary cell. **Mary Magdalene** was initiated into the *Egyptian*

Therapeutate by **Jesus**.

She was twelve at the time and he was, according to the Bible, about thirty years old. The ritual employed was similar to that in which *Lazarus* partook, in that it involved symbolic death and resurrection. See Luke 8: vs 41- 56. Following her initiation and during the period of her early adolescence, as was common practice, **Mary** would have acted as **Jesus**' handmaiden or grail priestess.

Botticelli's *'Birth of Venus'* is described by **Graham-Dixon** as an analogy of the **Virgin Mary**. In the depiction of the red-haired Venus however, there is a supposed sexual analogy represented in the various folds of fabric and hair which are arranged by the painter to suggest the vulva which remains covered by her modesty. It isn't likely that the darling of the *Roman Church* would have been depicted in this manner. **Botticelli** wouldn't have got away with it in a period when **Gallileo** was being threatened with death for suggesting that the earth was an orbiting sphere. One could do virtually anything with the **Magdalene** however.

Common sense would, in any case, suggest that the ***Mary*** depicted was in fact the **Magdalene** and that the painting was a deliberate though esoteric attempt to record what was commonly known about her race, her position and her function, amongst alchemists and ***Rosicrucians*** during the *Renaissance* period. The suggestive folds were made in red cloth festooned with flowers and here we might have an intimation of the spiritual fertility of the vulva in *menstruus.*

Inasmuch as commentators have stated that **Magdalene** was a sacred prostitute or priestess of **Ishtar** (daughter of Hathor), this can be explained by this particular phase of her spiritual life where a certain type of congress, a secret outside the Cult, would have led to her being suspected of being a prostitute in some orthodox Jewish opinion, not being at the time married. It is very probable however, that the so-called ***rites of Venus*** she ritually engaged in with the ***Messiah*** have been confused with other definitions of the word venal, which pertains not only to sex, but to payment for any service or goods.

The confusion between the words ***Venus*** and ***Venal*** has led to the error where it was thought that **Magdalene** was a prostitute, who was "paid" for "*Venal*" services. In the Egyptian tradition of **Jesus**' ancestor **Solomon** however, **Mary** - a priestess of the rites of Hathor within the Egyptian Therapeutate - would, like **Sheba**, have been a young ***Shunnamite***, a donor of *womb blood* and the '***Water of Life***', a ***Lily of the Valley*** and a *Rose of Sharon.*

After **Jesus** death, **Magdalene** went to the cell and found it open. Rather, I would argue that in accordance with the traditional ritual that accompanied her station, she was expected to stay in the cell and commune with the ***Ka*** of **Jesus** in the underworld.

Few people actually knew the real reason why she went and the reason people might have assumed would have been expected of a *Priestess of an Egyptian Cult.* In ***Celtic*** countries and in ***Egypt*** this was common practice, as in the cases where it has been demonstrated that tombs had living quarters in them.

That she went to heal him of his non fatal wounds was a ***secret*** known only to an initiated few, in whose number the apostles, it seems, were not counted. In any case she was the first to "*see*" him, and in this she fulfils precisely the role of the ***Sibyl*** or ***shamanka***, the ***druidess of Cumae***, ***Medea of the Golden Fleece***, ***Ariadne***, and numerous other females, including the witch of Endor.
In Revelation 22: v.16

> Jesus, clothed as a ***Repha'im*** proclaims himself the Root and Branch of David, the Bright and ***Morning Star.***

Amongst other things, including being the ***Priest-King of Lucifer***, **Jesus** also proclaims himself as a ***High Priest of Hathor***, who is the mother of **Ishtar**, **Astaroth**, **Shekinah**, **Sophia** and **Venus**, the ***Star of the Morning***. It becomes increasingly difficult to see **Mary Magdalene** therefore as anything less than a central character in a collateral druidic cult of the dead, a priestess of the Ankou of Ishtar.

In such a capacity, as with the various cave dwelling *shamankas* in mythology, she would have acted in a twofold role both as a visionary and also as a guide and companion, a facilitator whose blood allowed access to ***the underworld*** or ***Cosmic Consciousness***.

Her ***essence*** and ***elan*** was the ***Dergflaith*** of sovereignty, the pomegranate wine of Persephone that gained the Bard of the Golden Bough, the Hero of Mythology, entrance to the land of Elphame, the Kingdom of Ankou. In this ritual capacity, Morgana, Melusine and La Filles du Lac et la Fonteine; followed her example and demonstrated a lineal descent as living goddesses, from at least one of the Ankh cults of antiquity.

In the bible the narrator says that a sword will separate the quick from the dead. The *sword* is the ***Spirit*** and the spirit, as we have seen, is also symbolized by the *tongue*, and by *fire*. In Latin a sword sheath is called a *vaginum*. It is the use of the "***sword***" which separates the quick, the living spirits; (the ***Elves***), from the dead or the dead in life. In other words it is the rite of the Maiden, the "*christos of salvation*" that gives life.

References to the ***Sword*** as the ***Holy Spirit*** in the bible include Revelations 1: v.16

> "Out of his mouth went a sharp, two edged sword....in his hand he held ***Seven Stars***", said to represent the seven churches of Asia (It is interesting to note the association here between ***Bacchus*** and ***the Pleiades***).

In **John of Patmos**' vision,
the ***Alpha*** and ***Omega*** figure: **Jesus**, is dressed in the garb of an *Angel* or ***Repha'im.***

> Hebrews 4: v.12 "The 'word' (pneuma/spirit) of God is a two edged sword".
> Ephesians 6: v.17 "Take the helmet of salvation and the Sword of the Spirit".

The story of the pentecost relates that the Holy Spirit descended upon the disciples like "*tongues of fire*" and this is a symbol which, connected to the foregoing, is especially relevant in relation to ***the Dragon***, whose fiery breath is a symbol of the ***Holy Spirit***, the "***Word***" ***of God***, the ***Torah***; or the Law of Destiny determining the progress of mankind's fate.

The ***sword*** is an ***Ankh symbol*** with the blade representing the tongue, the guard represents the grail dish or womb, the spiraled grip symbolizes the spinal column and the pommel (from Fr. *la Pomme*, the little apple) represents the ***pineal*** and its ***chakra.***

In the medieval ***Grimoire*** '*The Clavicula Salomanis*' the guard of the magical sword is constructed of two crescent moons back to back. The sheathed sword symbolizing Peace, represents *hierogamy* and *balance*, *oneness* and *union.*

The story of *Arthur and the Sword in the Stone* is translated by some to mean that **Arthur** became king because he knew how to extract iron from stone. As *smithing* was a part of *alchemy* and thus a kings science, it followed for some scholars that in order to become king, **Arthur** would need to convince people that he knew where iron came from.

The ***iron age*** had been extant for over a thousand years before the druids thought this story up. In a pre-industrialized society that depended on iron for everything and where nearly every moderately sized village had a smithy, **Arthur** would have already known how to extract iron from rocks and other people would have known that **Arthur** knew. The age of secret metal magic had long since passed by his time.

The *Sword-Stone tale* operates on two levels of organic, not metallurgic, alchemy and refers to the ***enthea*** resulting in *transcendence*, resulting in *sovereignty*. The stone is both the cubic stone of the ***Ankh Goddess- Priestess*** and the ***Lia Fail***, the stone of destiny, a representative symbol of the macrocosmic cubic stone of the Earth as the anthropomorphized ***Goddess of Sovereignty***.

The ***sword*** is both the ***tongue*** in the first instance and the Sword symbol of derivative integrity, cosmic consciousness and resultant personal sovereignty in the second. From such personal sovereignty comes the wisdom and creativity to administer the sovereignty of the nation, thus qualifying **Arthur** to be a king.

That he fluffed the job in the end is another matter. Even Goddesses have off days. They're only human after all.
The *sword in the stone* says that sovereignty rises from the womb of the Grail Maiden, the ***virgin Dragon Princess***.

The *Sword as Tongue* implies the method by which sovereignty is obtained. Elsewhere the pendant ***T*** bar of the ***Ankh*** glyph corresponds to ***Tau***, the Law and more precisely, the utterer of the Law, the Hindu *Lingham* or in Hebrew, the *tongue of the Repha'im*, the *fairy Bruidhe Bard* in Gaelic, whose spells, or words of cosmic law, bound men's fate and, like the ***Morrighan*** warrior or *valkyrie*, represented the ***Holy Spirit.***

In the foregoing examples the symbolism sometimes tends to overlap because of the adaptation of the glyphs over the passing centuries. Pure symbols like the ankh naturally evolve to become more complex with the addition of other components, whilst still retaining the originals, which can double up sometimes, as in the case of the addition of the ***T*** to the ***W***. On its own the ***T*** is already the *lingham* and *yoni* combined. Add this to the ***W*** as the *womb*, and the symbol becomes reinforced, as in the following breakdown.

To qualify the ***T*** component we have to separate this symbol into two parts. Being specific, the upright corresponds to the tongue as utterer whilst the crossbar, anciently dish-shaped like the new moon, represents the womb or uterus, also the utterer.

The ***Tau*** was given to the priest-king by the womb. He passed it on as spells or laws, with the tongue which drank the wisdom of the cosmic law from that womb. The cup/dish and stone, the moon or womb and pineal in this instance; being held by a statue of ***Melchizadec***, is situated outside the door of ***Chartres Cathedral***, along with a figure of the ***Magdalene***, which comes as no surprise.

The *Tau symbol* can be found in ***Scandinavia*** associated with ***Tir***, the *God of Law and Judgment* whose rune became in this century, the familiar crow's foot or upright arrow. The *Tir* mark was specifically the property of the king whose word was binding on all and so the *Tau* or *Tir* element of the ***Ankh*** is, like the *Omega* from which it feeds, a royal symbol, intimating again the holy- sacral nature of the ***Grail ritual.***

The symbol of the ***Chi Rho*** of these swan princesses, as a derivative, later form of the ***Ankh***, was known before Christ Jesus' lifetime, as was the ***IHS of Bacchus***, whose story is connected here via the ***Ankh Cross*** as a crucifix.

Chapter Nine

The Wheel of Fate

The adoption and modification of the ***Chi Rho Ankh*** by the Church was a late event and it is said that the *Chi Rho symbol* was based on the six pointed Gallic rune because, as we shall see, the symbol had such tremendous influence.

As we know this rune was the Sumerian symbol for the gods. It invariably preceded the name of any deity and therefore, as the ***Chi Rho***, in relation to **Jesus**, it was used to imply his divinity, not as the son of the Jewish storm and corn imp **Jehovah**, but as a ***God-King*** in his own right as a descendant of the ***Dragon Gods*** *of the Egyptians.*

The Church were and are past masters at assimilation for political ends, and the use of the ***Chi Rho***, like much else, must be seen as another way that the Church sought to be identified and adopted by non christian Europeans.

The *six pointed Gallic rune*, similar to the Norse rune Haegl would originally have been *eight spoked*, like the *Buddhist Wheel of Life* or the Tarot's Wheel of Fortune. In this guise it is the ***Web of Arachne***, the Web of Fate and the plan view of the ribbons of the Maypole dance.

The missing horizontal spoke of the ***Chi Rho*** is accounted for in its having been often carved into wood. Inevitably one spoke would always follow, and disappear into, the grain and so rune masters omitted it.

According to **Count d'Alviella** the ***Chi Rho*** is sometimes found situated in the loop of the Ankh itself. In Egypt the Chi Rho was known as the *Chrism of Philae*, or the anointing of pure love, which intimates the *Entheal* nature of the symbol, particularly in relation to the ***Ankh*** itself, which in some creative work has been thought of as the "*vampire cross*" being, as it is, the symbol of eternal life and youth.

Other examples have been discovered with the loop made of the ***Dragon Cross of Cain***. The ***Ankh*** was said to have migrated into the christian crucifix and this seems obvious when one remembers the ***Celtic Cross***, which would seem to support the foregoing, as does the pre-christian ***cross of Bacchus*** and the Albigensian (or Gaulish Fairy) use of the ***Ankh*** in relation to heterodox christian belief and ritual.

The ***Bethel stone*** was shaped like an ***Ankh*** and had associations with the various pine cone or dove capped pillars, the *Perrone* of the sacred groves. At later times the *Perrone* were capped by crosses and the name seems to be reminiscent itself of *Persephone*. Later still, in *European Heraldry*, one can see the *pine cone* column in the *Pyr of Augsburg*. In particular these columns were associated also with barrows and bergs.

In ***Belgium*** they were known as the *stones of Justice*, which again links them with the ***Tir*** or ***Tau*** and the ***Ankh***, whilst in ***Scandinavia***, according to the ***Saga of Gudrun***, they become the white stone pillars (Gita/Cita) on the barrows which were venerated by the peasants. The white stone, as a portable panacea features in the story of **St. Columba** and **King Brude of the Picts**.

The Goddesses of death and the underworld are again prominent here (in the transcendent sense, as with ***Persephone***, but one also remembers ***Mithras*** and the *World Bull* or *Minotaur* of ***Theseus***), and one can imagine the presence of the ***Bethel Stone***, as the *Perrone of the Ankh*, in the midst of the *Necromanitons* (a variant of the druidic grove of the Nemeton in Galatia, rel. to Nemesis or justice, the Tau or Fate), such as that built in ***Greece*** at *Ephyranus*, which had buried at its core, a subterranen cell for the rites which invoked the dead from Hades.

When thinking of ***Greece*** and ***Galatia***, it must be remembered that these were originally under ***Scythian*** (***Sidhean-Aryan***) ***overlordship***, manifesting draconian culture and subject to druidic law. These influences also helped to shape the Hindu, Sumerian, Egyptian and Judaic traditions, beliefs and iconographies, and it is therefore understandable that we find that there are many themes and symbols which these seemingly disparate cultures hold in common.

Within all these crosses and figures, there are held layers of meaning that can be interpreted to represent a close knit variety of rites or anatomical attributes within the strict parameters of their genre. Consequently, to settle for one simple explanation for any given glyph is simplistic, and at variance with the intentions of the ***Dragon Culture*** which invented them.

In the following figures the upturned crescent moon features, and this should be remembered in relation to the Galley or moon barque, which, accompanied by the Lion, is a prominent badge of the Scottish clans and features in the heraldry of *Leith*, near ***Edinburgh***, where the ship carries the figure of the "*Virgin Mary*" (**Magdalene**), another Ankh variant.

The ***Moon Boat*** is also said to be the origin of the *Genesis Ark* and with the symbol of the ***Templar***'s ***Anchor***, the crescent moon becomes the hull of the boat which carries the ***Ankh*** as its mast and sails.

The key to understanding this symbol is to refer back to the notes and remember that the virgin womb, (the crescent or new moon), carries the ***Ankh***, The ***An-Ka*** or ***Pneuma***, the secret of the *Benedicta Viriditas*, the Green Blessing of the Mouth - "The Fairy Gift" (also "the Dark Gift", "the Thirst", "The Hunger") of eternal life in this life (*transcendence*) and youth, the blessing of the virility of life regardless of age, as was said of anyone '*seeing the Grail*', that although their hair might turn grey, they would not age from that day forth (**Eschenbach**).

The migration of the ***Ankh*** and its collaterals are included in the following figures which are illustrated in the work of the **Count d'Alviella.**

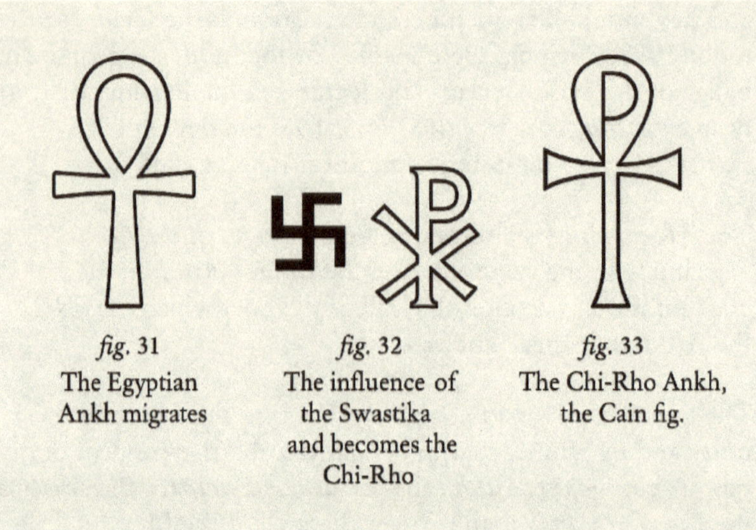

fig. 31 The Egyptian Ankh migrates

fig 32 The influence of the Swastika and becomes the Chi Rho. On the Chi Rho.

fig. 33 The Chi Rho Ankh, the Cain fig.

34 The cross of Bacchus and Ankh and the Celtic Cross. TheAlbigensian Ankh

fig. 35 The Ankh of Isis and Nephthys. fig.

36 The Fleur de Lys and the Gallic Haegl Rune

fig. 37 The Bethel Stone as Perrone or God-Stone. fig.

38 The Assyrian Bethel Stone.

fig. 39 The cuneiform symbol for the gods.

fig.40 The medieval Ankh of black magic.

Supporting material from D P Silverman, Richard Dufton, W H Matthews, Michael Grant, Oxford English Dictionary, Count D'Alviella, Ward Rutherford., Z. Sitchin.

The Lily and the Rose/The Dragon Tree

Being pertinent to the appreciation of the contents of the

following essays, the author here includes a brief word on the ***Dragon Tree*** or ***Dragontree***, which is a massive plant which grows in ***Persia*** and ***Gran Canaria***. Its Latin name is *Dracaena Draco* and it belongs to the genus *Lillaceae* or *Lily*.

Its ***resin*** is called ***Dragon's Blood*** and was used as a dye which the Romans called ***Lac***. Poetically therefore "the blood of the Lily is the blood of the Dragon", giving it especial ritual significance as a tincture for ceremonial robes and as as an epithet for the branches of the bloodline, as in a popular spelling of *del Acqs* as *Du Lac*.

In relation to the Greek word *derkesthai* there is, in Gaelic, a reminiscent word, *dergflaith*, which means '*red beer*'. The word *dergflaith* is used to describe the otherworld drink which conveys sovereignty upon a king. It is quite possible therefore, given the Greco-Gaelic connections in history, that one word has influenced the other. ***Derk*** and ***Derg*** might derive from a similar or common root and ***Flaith*** might be related to the Gaelic ***fola***, which is used in relation to the ***family*** and ***blood***. In which case ***Dergflaith*** actually might originally have meant ***Dragon's Blood***, being rather the blood of a dragon princess, conveying the *Derkesthai* ability

The Lily of the Valley

In relation to the discussion herein, the following is a brief discourse on the subject of the ***Lily***. For the purposes of this essay we will be concentrating on both the *Lilliaceae* and *Nymphaea Lotus* varieties which are regional variants of each other in ***Dragon Lore***.

The former, the Iris family, include the *Lily of the Valley*, whilst the latter are the species known as *Blue Nile Lilies*. Furthermore, for the purposes of providing an illustrative narrative we will concentrate here on *Hylas and the water nymphs*, a portrait by the pre-Raphaelite artist **John William Waterhouse**, whose depictions of ***water nymphs*** and ***Grail*** characters are somewhat prodigious. In alchemical lore we know that the lily represents the virginal seminal fluid of the vulva and the rose represents the womb blood. However the *White Lily of the Valley* produces red berries in Autumn that are reminiscent themselves of the droplets of *Virgin blood.* The ***Lily of the Valley*** is highly toxic and can be fatal, a reminder of the love that is death.

The virgin vendors themselves, like ***Melusine*** et al, are often described as water nymphs or naiads and in **Waterhouse**'s picture the naked, pale skinned, otherworldly ladies in the woodland pond are surrounded by and are wearing in their hair specimens of the *Nymphaea Lotus*, the "*lily sacred to the nymphs*". ***Hylas*** (Helios - the ***Sun Dragon***, representative of the Sephiroth of Kether or the Ajna Chakra) is a crew member of the ship ***Argo***, which, captained by ***Jason*** had been sculling around in ***Scythian*** territorial waters looking for the ***Golden Fleece*** which, like the *ark of the Covenant*, is a symbol of the

Holy Grail.

Having been at sea without a break for some time, it had been decided that, now they'd sailed back through the ***Hellespont***, they would put to shore on the island of ***Chios*** and seek for provisions and water. It fell to ***Hylas*** to wander off alone into the forest to look for a fresh spring. After a protracted peregrination ***Hylas*** entered in upon the scene where **Waterhouse**'s nymphs were bathing - and is depicted crouching on the banks of the woodland pool. Here we now see ***Hylas*** being tempted to enter the water and avail himself of the tender but fateful embraces of these emissaries of death.

Waterhouse painted his model of ***Hylas*** wearing a blue-black robe tied about with a red thread. This, the dreaded "*little thread of the Cathars*" was a memorial of the *Old Testament*, Hebrew scapegoats, one of which had a red thread tied about its horns, prior to its being pushed into the scorching desert to face its ultimate death, whilst the other was sacrificed. This double ritual was enacted because the Jews thought that the goat sacrificed to **Jehovah** was insufficient to take away the sins of the people.

The ***Goat*** was called ***Azazel***, a figure who was said to have been a fallen angel and whose name has several etymologies derived from its ritual functions but who is certainly "***Satan***" or ***Samael***. The red thread represented the sins of the Jews.

The symbolism is simple, the Jews ultimately laid all the responsibility for purging their sin upon ***Azazel/Samael***, when in the first instance, the *sin* belonged not to him who was their true creator, but to the usurper **Jehovah** alone. For this reason, as a memorial and to express their true allegiance, ***the Cathars***, the ***witches*** and the nobles of the blood wore the red thread.

The ***Cathars*** wore it as a belt about their black robes and the latter two groups wore it as a garter or 'points'. In this manner, for them it also represented the womb blood, the '***Rtu***' or '*red-gold flow*' of the virgin priestesses of the ***Kaula Vama Marg.***

On the ***Aziluth*** or imperial scale of the Kabalistic Tree of Life, red and black are the empress and emperor colours of the sephirah of Binah, the "sphere of understanding". ***Binah*** is ruled by Saturn or Chronos and its sacred plants are the lily and the cypress, whilst its sacred animal is the bee. Cypress was used in the Levant as an incense to celebrate weddings and mourn the departed, whilst the lily traditionally represents virginity and death.

Here we have the symbols of ***Enthea*** and the love that is death, with the bee describing the manner of such congress.
In **Waterhouse**'s beautifully evocative painting the nymphs are immersed in water, the element which is a *Scythian symbol* of the ***Daleth***, the door to the otherworld and ***Hylas*** is about to undergo a profound process of alchemical initiation.

The girls, whose watery embrace is said to spell death, are the ***shunnamites***, the lilies or virgins who are portrayed in the Song of Solomon. In their connection with water, the nymphs are thus depicted as the embodiment of the wells of living waters. Their deathly embrace is but the death of the ego, of the will and of desire. In uniting with them ***Hylas'*** soul will die and his mind, once stilled, will 'understand' and give way to the transcendent spirit of the cosmos. Such is the nature of this mystical process.

The ***nymphs*** are priestesses of Lilith, Diana and Persephone, they represent **Melusine**, **Magdalene** and the *La Belle Dame Sans Merci:* ***The Maid of Kent*** who was **Edward III**'s 'Queen of the Witches'. They are the Leanaan Sidhe, the Grail Maidens who, as perfect representations of the Goddess and the Muse, are the externalizations of man's longed for ***Anima***.

Enthea, divine union with these meremaids, is intended to facilitate the exultant union of the animus and anima which, via this external ***hierogamy*** or alchemical marriage, brings the death of the finite, isolated being, from whence emerges as if reborn, the universal spirit, unattached, undesiring and immersed in eternal love and life. In such terms the essence and the embrace of a ***Grail Maiden*** end all desire.

Hers is the embrace of death because her spirit and her energy enliven the tired spirit of the pilgrim and her beauty and completeness, her stillness and poise, are the sum of all that the initiate might seek. Her quiet, matter of fact acceptance which needs no striving for and is not gained by worldly show, infuses the stillness of the journey's end into the lover who, having to achieve nothing more to attain her transcendent love other than just to be, melts in her embrace and without barriers, melts his being into hers.

Her love is then his death, beyond which is ***Daleth***, the ***door to Elphame***, ***Oneness*** and eternal, silent understanding. Such is the watery grave to which ***Hylas*** has wedded his fate. The story of ***Hylas*** and the water nymphs links
the ***pineal*** and ***womb chakras***, giving a complete teaching picture of the Grail Process.

The Lotus Eaters

In Greek myth the ***lotophagi*** - the ***lotus eaters*** - to which ***Hylas'*** story is related, experienced a similar phenomenon in consuming the *Nymphaea Lotus* and lost their desire to return to homes which they had forgotten, along with all those emotional trinkets and fond memories which once possessed their hearts. (**Homer**: *The Odyssey*, IX - 90ff).

As an infusion in wine the petals of the Nymphaea Lotus are narcotic and bring about psychotropic effects similar to certain mystical states. In **Waterhouse**'s painting the nymphs are surrounded by and wearing these flowers in their hair. Their immersion in the lily bedecked water implies that their "*living waters*" or *seminal fluid*, the "***dew of their lilies***", had similar transcendent, psychotropic qualities.

The wearing of the lily on the head signifies that the source of the divine essence represented by the lilies in the pool originates with the ***pineal gland*** and the '*thousand petalled lotus*' of the ***Ajna Chakra***, which energizes it and the other cerebral glands. The water these swan maidens are swimming in is the "*sea of Binah*" and they are thus the daughters of understanding, witches of the waters of wisdom and the children of the Hive.

The nymphs are here seven in number and represent ***the Pleiades***, the fairy daughters of the ***Titan Atlas*** who were pursued by the ***Boeotian Orion*** or ***Osiris*** in an ancient ritualized form of the *Wild Hunt*. They became the seven stars of the constellation that bears their name and which, in a superimposed arc, adorns and suggests the *Ankh-like Cross* upon which ***Bacchus*** was crucified.

Waterhouse's nymphs therefore were also the *wild Bacchantes or Dionysic Maenads* who themselves hunted for and drank human blood in rites whose central feature was that of union with the divine.

Associated with these nymphs is the Romano-Celtic goddess ***Coventina*** (coven, covenant or union) who was depicted either alone or as a tripartite figure, bathing in a pool, surrounded by lilies. She is pictured in the act of pouring a jug of water into the pool itself. Her other name is ***Dea Latis*** meaning both *Goddess of the Mere* and also ***Bright Shining One***, which links her with ***the elves***. In this she shares the attributes of the cult spirit of the river wharf in Teesdale, whose name was both ***Verbeia*** and ***Latis***.

Related to the ***nymphs*** are the *Biblical Miriams* or *Marys*, and the *Tamarises* whose symbol was the Palm which represents the Sufi Tree of Life. Theirs was also the Pomegranate of Persephone, with which the Palm appears in mystical symbolism and the pool or oases adjacent to which the sacred Palm itself grows.

Miriam or **Mary** and **Tamaris** were the names of females who occupied specific dynastic offices within the royal dragon bloodline in Israel. In Hebrew the name **Miriam** is represented by the consonants ***M'R'Y'M*** and means '*bitter*', (defined here as sorrowful). From this we obtain *Mary, Mari, Marie, Marion, Maryon* or *Marian* and all these examples contain the ***M'R'Y*** or ***M'R'I*** consonant group. In the following passages we will encounter the ***Myr*** syllable group relating to myrrh, which is relevant here, particularly in relation to ***Tamaris***.

From ***Marion*** we obtain the "*Maid Marion*" of the ***Robin Hood*** cult, whose name and title equate with that of the *Virgin Mary* (**Magdalene**), to whom ***Robin*** and his band were devoted. In Egypt the name is *Mery*, as in *Mery Ataten* The name Mary or properly Mari is Indo-Aryan and means several things.

The component ***Mer***, ***Ma*** or ***Mar*** means,

i) A Mere or Pool

ii) The Sea

As ***Mari*** it is associated with the *Mori* orfates and is the *An* or *Ankhou* of the Basque witches. *Mari* is also *Mar Righ*, meaning royal pool or royal waters where *righ* defines royalty or kingship. Where king further relates to knowing and understanding, ***Mary*** as ***Mar Righ*** becomes,

i) the waters of wisdom

ii) Binah, the primordial sea

In ***Marian*** the syllables break down into *Mari* and *An*. *Mari* as we have seen means pool whilst An, the root of the names of many of the earliest ***Dragon Queens and Kings***, relates to the Grail and means fire or spirit, and so Marion means 'chalice' or 'pool of fire' which then renders the 'pool of the spirit'.

The sacred cups, pools, wells and fountains we have so far encountered all relate to the womb and the vulva. In this manner *Mary* or *Marion* means *'spirit in the womb'* or *'womb fire'* and it is in the latter instance that we have a direct reference to the ***Tantric***, ***Kaula ritual*** of enlivening or inflaming the ***chakra*** of the uterine region to produce the *'waters of life'* or, as the *Song of Solomon* puts it "***The Well of Living Waters***".

Mary's symbol is the white lily of the valley, the ***fleur de lys***. In relation to **Mary Magdalene** as the *Virgin Mary of Robin Hood*'s devotion, this is particularly relevant. In this cultic cycle there appears *'The One Ring that rules them all'* - the Draupnir or ***Andvarinaut*** - the "*Gold Dripper*" (or source of ***Rtu***, the red-gold thread or flow of the valkyrie womb) that belonged to Robin's father ***Aubrey*** or ***Oberon***, who is ***Alberich*** or ***Andvari***.

As "*The Well of Living Waters*", **Mary**'s relationship to **Jesus** becomes clearer as the *child handmaiden of the Messach*, the ***dragon god-king***. *Marie* is an ancient form of the word *Marry*, meaning: to join or unite with, as in alchemical marriage, divine ***enthea***, ***hierogamy***, the sacred marriage ritual of Solomon's Song, with which we will deal shortly.

The Hebrew meaning of *Miriam* is *'bitter'*- transf. "attended by pain or suffering: grievious (OE), hence of a state: Full of affliction, mournful, pitiable (1485), expressing or betokening intense grief or misery" (OED).

Here we are reminded of **Mr. Keats**'s 'palely wandering knight' and nanny ***Melusine*** as '*La Fontaine du Soif*' and 'the cup of sorrows'.

In many ***Dragon*** and ***Grail*** stories, the maidens inhabit or frequent pools or fountains in forest gardens. **Waterhouse**'s water-babes inhabit a forest pool. **Janet March** encounters the ***fairy knight Tam Lin*** by a rose-covered well in *Carterhaugh* forest, in a genealogical variation of Beauty and the Beast. **Solomon** has his **Sheba**, a well of living waters in a labyrinth garden bedecked with sacred *Pomegranate* trees and ***Melusine*** is the fountain and well in a garden maze in the *Forez*.

Relating these symbolic representations of the virgin priestess-goddess with works such as **Sir Richard Burton**'s "*Perfumed Garden*" and **Francis Israel Regardie**'s "*Garden of Pomegranates*", gives a clear picture of the forest as the pubis which is conceptually broadened by the maze in the dell on the hill, as the entrance to the otherworld, hidden within the *mons veneris*.

In the *Song of Solomon* we encounter the pubis as a *lock*, which like the *well*, is an old but well known European euphemism for the ***vagina***. In Chapter 5 vs 4 - 5 "My beloved put his hand by the hole of the door (the "lock"), and my bowels were moved for him (contractions): I rose up to my beloved and my hands dropped with Myrrh, and my fingers with sweet smelling Myrrh upon the lock".

Whilst earlier in Chapter 4 vs 12 and 16 "A garden enclosed is my sister my spouse, a spring shut up, a fountain sealed: A fountain of Gardens, a Well of Living Waters..." Throughout the *Song Sheba*, who is "black but comely" i.e. an Annis or

Persephone figure likened to ***Lilith***, remains a virgin. **Sheba** was described as "*the lily of the valley*" and thus, as her forest garden equates with the pubis, then the lily of her valley is the water lily in the valley of her vulva.

Naiads or ***mermaids*** are described as being semi divine and the handmaidens of the gods. This is aside from their usual mythic, pantheistic interpretation or symbolic representation as nature spirits, elementals or energy complexes, and such a description applies to the era during which these stories emerged, which was described by **Euhemerus** as the age when mighty men became deified and the gods were born of flesh and blood.

The ***Irish*** descriptions of their "*gods*", the ***Tuadha D'Anu***, mix the qualities of divinity with some very human sounding foibles whilst the descriptions of the ***naiads*** or ***mermaids*** present us with the qualities of human femininity but blended to a much greater extent with those of the divine. As we have seen, as handmaids to the gods and essentially young goddesses themselves, the ***naiads*** or ***nixes*** were the ***Dragon Princesses of the Grail***, the ***Ladies of the Lake***, water witches and meremaids.

They were the ***avatars***, the ***Sybils*** who supported the elder goddess queens and god kings, fed them, guided them to the otherworld and, in the embrace of death, empowered their beings with the integrity that gives birth to vision and wisdom: the wholeness that is sovereignty over self and consequently sovereignty over all things.

Such a condition releases creativity, but such a quality is not a product of ordinary human thinking, rather it is a phenomena which lies beyond thought and beyond the capability of mundane knowledge to encapsulate or describe, both of which are processes bounded by time and limited by definition. It is the still mind in union with the infinite, or more precisely that knows no distinction between it and the infinite, that becomes truly fertile and creative.

Such was the nature of true sovereignty, the state of mind that, in kingship, affected the people and the land through good management and foresighted husbanding. If the king was of the tinker or warrior variety, then he was by virtue of his birth and cerebral physiological capacity, barren and infertile, and incapable of transcending his nature. In consequence the land and the people suffered by virtue of their having a king who was no king at all.

Chapter Ten

The Rose of Sarai

Sharon is a level fertile plain between Jaffa and Mount Carmel in ***Israel***. In Hebrew the name derives from *Sharai*, a princess, from whence are derived Sarai and Sarah, which again were ritual offices in Judaism.

With regard to the word ***rose***, some dispute exists over exactly what that means and those who are authorities on the subject describe it as:

i) a crocus

ii) a polyanthus

iii) a narcissus

iv) a cistus

However, if you consult a gardening encyclopaedia you will find that the ***rose of Sharon*** is described as the *hypericum* or *St. John's Wort* which, interestingly enough, produces a red dye and is related to the *cistus.*

It is likely that in order to be described as a ***rose*** in the European translation of the Jewish bible, it would have had to have looked something like a rose, and in keeping with such an identification the ***cistus*** comes quite close in its foliate resemblance to the western, *red and white Plantagenet rose*, which we found growing unabated around *Janet March*'s well in *Carterhaugh Forest.* Furthermore the *cistus* is called the ***Rock Rose*** in Southern Europe and North Africa.

The ***cistus*** is white with deep, blood red blotches, like the dappling of menstrual blood. The ***cistus*** belongs to the family *cistacea* and is also known as the *gum cistus* whose botanical genus is *ladanifer* from which is obtained laudanum, the dream-bestowing prize of poets and visionaries across

Europe and the Middle-East, including **Thomas de Quincy** who, having taken it, were transported into the darkest, most terrifying realms of the ***Underworld*** or the highest reaches of ***Heaven***, both being the deepest recesses of their own psyches.

Sheba, as the *Lily of the (Nile) Valley*, the ***nymphaea lotus*** and the the ***rose of Sharon***: the *ladanifer*, was being likened unto a living, narcotic pharmacopoeia. As neither of these plants grow in Northern Europe, we have contented ourselves with the nearest familiar symbols, those being the virginal ***Fleur de Lys*** and the ***Plantagenet*** or ***English Rose***.

The ***Rose*** represents therefore the magical menstrual flow of **Solomon**'s beloved, whilst the name ***Sharon*** or ***Sarah*** means *princess*. The ***Rose of Sharon*** is therefore the ***Royal Blood***, the ***Sang Real***; and the San Graal, the Holy Blood of the Holy Grail or rosi-crucis. As the Latin *Ros-Sara* or rosary which is devoted to the Virgin Mary, the pure white Lily, which itself is the "dew of the princess" (OED).

The word ***Rose*** in Germanic means *Horse*, from *Hros*, a deity who is identifiable with the goddesses *Rhiannon* and *Epona*, who were symbolized by the white mare and immortalized in chalk, hill carvings across Britain.

By a lucky stroke of fate, or under the power of "the single poetic theme", as **Robert Graves** would have it, ***The Hros***, like *Slepnir (Yggdrasil)*, *Rhiannon, Epona* (and the Hindu *Breghi Moru*) were the goddesses who conducted the King to the Otherworld and to the goal of sovereignty.

This was exactly the job of **Sheba**, the ***Rose of Sharon***, and all the other watery nymphettes in history. So the ***Rose of Sharon***, whilst referring to the flower of the royal menses, also refers to the function of that fluid as a method of transport to the otherworld.

Again death is implied by *Hros* because *Epona* and *Rhiannon*, but especially *Slepnir*, are symbols of the white draped funeral byre carried by four men who, like *Slepnir*, have eight legs.

Slepnir, the white horse of ***Odin*** is Rhiannon, the ***elven*** mount of the Welsh *Arawn* or *Death*, the grim reaper who (like **Jesus** * who "*brings a sword to separate the quick from the dead*") scythes the spirit from the flesh. ***Arawn***, *Lord of Annwn*, in the story of '*Pwyll Lord of Dyfed*', leads a pack of red-eared, red-eyed hounds in the hunt for the red-eyed white hind, who is the virgin, ***elven*** princess who, like in the stories of Odin or Hearne the Hunter and the Wild Hunt for elf women at *Samhain*, is the source of truth.

* The image of **Jesus** as the grim reaper or Repha'im is consistent with his cultic role in the Egyptian mysteries. Significantly the verse that this passage is taken from refers to **Jesus** as coming with a sword, the spirit or Torah, to separate the "quick" - the divine, Immortal spirit, from the dead - the material soul or "dead flesh" of the unregenerate mind created from the "flesh" of mortal experience.
In ***vampirism*** the process of awakening the cerebral centers is called "*the quickening*".

In Indian love poetry the vulva has been referred to as "*the footprint of the deer*" and we may equate both the Hind and the Hros respectively with the physical and spiritual aspects of the Virgin.

The *Hart* or properly the hind in the thicket, so beloved of Graves, is the poetic truth hidden by the pubis, like the tangle of thorns that hides the castle, the enclosed fastness of the princess's virginity in *Sleeping Beauty.*

Rapunzel's tower, her inaccessibility, is likewise a symbol of the princess's virginity. The hounds of Arawn, Odin and Hearne, consistently in all these stories, represent the retinue of elf nobles who, in later times, were mimicked in the Wild Hunt by the race of the rustic youths around the maze for the virgin prize at its centre. Rapunzel's tower also represents her elevated consciousness as a Grail Maiden. By using her red-gold hair to climb the tower, in other words by following the Rtu or blood flow to, and consuming it from, its source - id est Rapunzel - both the witch; and the knight who supposedly rescues her, are able to climb to new heights of cosmic consciousness. Rapunzel's hair is both Ariadne's and Sleeping Beauty's red-gold thread of the menses. The knight has no intention of rescuing Rapunzel. She can't be rescued from a figurative narrative construct, she is a feeding female and the witch and the knight are the Dragon Queen and the vampire Prince who are her clients. The only way of 'rescuing' Rapunzel from the tower is to rape her, and rob her of her virginity and her transcendent vision which is symbolised by that tower. Some rescue attempt that would be.

Card 13 of the Major Arcana of the Rider-Waite Tarot is entitled "***Death***". 13 is the number of the Moon and specifically of the menstrual cycle. Riding *Epona or Slepnir*, the red-eyed white horse of ***Elphame***, the skeletal figure of the grim reaper rides across the field of life in a black cloak and full armour, trampling the noble and the humble alike under his horse's hooves. In his hand he carries the banner of the white rose of the spirit on a black field. However, this is not a funerary plant.

The ***white rose***, like the ***red rose***, symbolizes ***love***, but which in this case is *philea* rather than *eros*. The horse's reins and livery are black and adorned with skulls and crossbones, which we understand to be representations of the ***Baphomet*** or ***Holy Grail***. Behind him in the distance lie the twin towers that feature in another major *Arcana* card - "The Moon". Beyond the towers the sun is shining above the dark horizon.

The towers, the horns of the ***Sabbatical Goat***, represent the open legs of the priestess-goddess and the glow of the sun, like the *Hallowe'en* candle on the seesaw, or the candle between the goat's horns, is the glow of the red-gold of the virgin menses and the ***chakra*** or ***sephiroth of the womb***. This symbol is replicated in the second card, "The High Priestess", dealt with earlier.

This again is a card of "*the love that brings death*" and the ***reaper*** symbolizes, not physical mortality, but the victory of transcendence over mortal pomp and materialism and the life-that-is-death. In such a context therefore - Death as Initiation - the ***white rose*** of the spirit and pure love, is identical with the ***red rose of Sharon***, inasmuch as the red rose does not herein symbolize sexual passion, but the menses-smeared rose of the vagina's foliate aperture, contact with which brings the spiritual purity symbolized by the pale flower of Death's banner.

Like doves, roses are sacred to ***Venus*** who as ***Ishtar*** and ***Lucifer***, the "*bright and morning star*" is the bringer of light and enlightenment. ***Venus*'** emerald jewel, the hermetic tablet of destiny (also the *Lia Fail* of the ***Scythians***) is called the jewel in ***Satan*'s** crown which, when it "falls" or is reversed becomes the hidden "cubic stone", the dark, oozing monolith of the hidden Grail, concealed in the recesses of the body of the ***Swan Princess***, the ***naiad***, from whom one might obtain "blood out of a stone".

The reversed emerald tablet, the cubic stone darkened by its concealment, is the subject of two 15th century paintings - "*Livre du Coeur D'Amours Epris*" and "*Melusine by the Fountain*". In both these paintings, the image of a black marble block from whence flows a curious fluid, is repeated. In French legend *Melusine*'s *well and fountain* are the source of both joy and sorrow, much like the *Croix de Lorraine*.

This sentiment is repeated in "*Livre Du Coeur D'Amours Epris*", which warns that misfortune will befall him who drinks from the water that issues from beneath the stone. The knight in the picture, as in all stories connected with ***Venus' Jewel***, is further warned not to pour water over the stone itself.

Such would constitute christian baptism, which was viewed by the ***Bloodline*** as a defilement, and a debasement of their pure spirits by an invasive and hostile alien culture. Like ***Melusine***'s black stone, the one depicted in "*Livre*" engenders the "*Heart's longing for Lady Grace*" and consequently, like ***Melusine***'s, it is a fountain of thirst because, after one taste of its "waters" the ego's longing for material peace or security ceases but is replaced by the spirit's longing for ***enthea***, its westward journey home to the love that is death.

The Song of Solomon

The authorship of the *Song of Songs* is attributed to **King Solomon**, probably because the subject matter dealt with has an underlying Hermetic, esoteric character which accords with what is known of Solomon's ritual practices.

Less probably because he originally compiled it in its entirety. Nevertheless it is quite possible that he wrote certain aspects of the song which perhaps were added to later by subsequent poets or scribes. The overall syntax of the manuscript form of the *Song of Songs*, compiled circa 450-400 BC, is *Aramaic*, and was deposited in the *School of the Temple of Solomon* in Jerusalem.

The original piece is said to have derived from early oral sources and belongs to the genre of ancient Egyptian love poetry. The song also bears a striking resemblance, from a secular point of view, to near eastern love poems.

The ***Temple School*** was probably destroyed and its teachers dispersed during the destruction of Jerusalem by the Romans. A number of christian Nobles were said to have fled ***Palestine*** at that time which led, it is further attested, to the introduction of ***vampirism*** into Central Europe.

This isn't strictly true, but a new wave or variation of the cult could have been reintroduced then. It is also very likely that many *kabalists* and rabbis also fled and settled in less hostile districts in Europe following the destruction of the Temple.

In this way could be explained the appearance of "*Solomon Schools*" in places like ***Hermannstadt***, ***Toledo*** and ***Carpathia***, which one assumes were outposts or exiled cells of the original Temple of Solomon School in Israel.

It was from one of these institutions, renowned for alchemy, kabala and Hermetic lore that ***Dracula*** was said to have "*ridden the dragon*", meaning that he was the principal graduate. Following this illustrious academic career ***Dracula***, who claimed to have derived his name from his apostolic priesthood of the ***Egyptian cult of Draco***, embarked on a reign that was marked by his overt practice of vampirism.

Solomon was what some might call a pagan and a great deal of fairy lore and a great many gods from Eurasia filtered into and influenced Jewish culture during **Solomon**'s reign. The *christian bible* tends to blame this state of affairs largely on **Solomon**'s choice of wives, who were said to have brought these strange abominations with them. This explanation doesn't however take into account the fact that **Solomon** himself was deeply committed to and involved with Hermetic sciences and dark magic.

Solomon had, as wives, 700 royal princesses gathered from all over the near east. In addition to these he had a further 300 concubines and these comprised his Harem. A rather excessive and self indulgent amount of women simply for the purposes of providing one man with a variety of copulatory partners.

We are then obliged by our own curiosity to ask why **Solomon** kept so many girls around at such a large cost. If we take another look at the word *herem* we will find the answer. From the OED we learn that the English word '*Harem*' is taken from the Arabic *haram*, and means a sacred or prohibited place.

The term sacred could only be attributed if the *haram*, the building, or more appropriately the institution within the building, were in some way spiritual or religious. In the Oxford Companion to the Bible it states that the word harem has a cognate in the Hebrew *herem*, which is translated into the English *ban*.

Specifically the *herem* or *Harem*, as a *ban*, was something set apart for cultic use, to be used only by priests, and thus a ***Harem*** is understood to be spiritual and holy, not simply a royal bordello or an amusement arcade.

Such a reflection brings into question the actual purpose of Arabic and near eastern *herems* in general, particularly in the light of the fact that, in Arabic mysticism, the Sufic "tree of life" is a *Tamaris* or *Palm tree*, beloved of the Phoenix, whose leaves comprise of the many-eyed tail feathers of the *Yedzidic peacock god of Mesopotamia* - ***Shaitan***, who was worshipped in rituals of blood.

"He feedeth amongst the lilies" ***Song of Solomon***, Chapter II, vs 16: Sheba enjoins Solomon to feed amongst the lilies until the break of day, like a young hart on the mountains of Bether. A lily is a virgin and thus Solomon by night feeds amongst the Virgins, the virgin princesses of his "Harem".

The medieval kabalists proposed a sacred code as a key to translating the hermetic secrets of the Song or "*Canticle of Canticles*" as it was also known, whilst some commentators have asserted that the work was derived from (Egyptian) cultic origins and was part of a rite of sacred marriage, a fertility ceremony and a ritual to ward off death. (**James M. Reese**).

These three components together adequately describe, in its entirety, the organic-alchemical rite of ***vampirism*** which is itself a sacred marriage, a union of ***enthea***, intended to open the mind to creativity and transcendent perceptions, thus stimulating spiritual fertility and increasing longevity, or warding off death if you like.

The *Song of Solomon* is a ***Blood Rite***, a communion where the wine, the blood, of the virgin goddess is drunk. This rite remained in the ***House of David*** until **Jesus ben Panther**'s time when it was re-instated by him as an exoteric ritual for his disciples. **Solomon**'s harem was a blood farm and the females in it were there to feed him, to increase his wisdom and lengthen his life.

Sheba seems to have been the first lady amongst many and throughout the discourse she continues, like them, to retain her virginity. In taking a closer view of the evidence we will inspect the following passages. Chapter II vs 16-17; Chapter IV vss 12-13; Chapter IV vs 15; Chapter V vs 5; Chapter VII vs 9 and Chapter VIII vs 2.

> Chapter II vs 16: "My beloved is mine and I am his, he feedeth amongst the lilies".
> vs 17: "Until the day break and the shadows flee away, turn, my beloved, and be thou like a roe or a young hart upon the mountains of Bether".

As we have seen, feeding amongst the lilies is feeding from the ***blood*** and ***water*** of the young virgin brides.

The hart on the mountain symbolizes the young king in his glory and the medieval symbol of the young stag drinking from the ***Grail*** is directly related to these verses.

> Chapter IV vs 12 "A garden enclosed is my sister, a spring shut up and a fountain sealed".

Sheba is a virgin throughout the Song and her maidenly attributes attract various epithets. In this verse we find the three main Grail symbols associated with the priestess: The ***garden***, the ***well*** and the ***fountain***.

Here these are enclosed and sealed indicating **Sheba**'s maidenhood and her guardianship of an "underground" (hidden) stream or source of arcane vitality expanded upon in the next verses.

> Chapter IV vs 13 " Thy plants are an orchard of pomegranates (Grove: cf. Avallon) with pleasant fruits; camphire and spikenard".

Whilst the Indian *spikenard* (*spica narda*) was used by **Mary Magdalene** to anoint **Jesus**, the *pomegranate* is a standard symbol of the virgin vulva and womb and **Sheba**'s garden of pomegranates has in its midst:

> Chapter IV vs 15 "A fountain of gardens, a well of living waters..." which cause those who are asleep to speak as we shall see.

The living waters in other scriptural references is related to the Holy Spirit, as is fire. Water as we remember was the element through or over which one travelled to *elphame* in Celtic lore.

Elphame here equates with the ***Underworld*** or ***Otherworld***, the kingdom of ***heaven*** or ***samadhi*** and the living waters contain in their droplets the secret of eternal wisdom and the gift of transcendent awareness, god consciousness. The *Holy Spirit*, the *Shekinah*, is of the feminine gender and a female gift therefore.

In alchemy ***blood*** and ***semen*** are the *primae materia* or first matter of the great work. Sadly however, many think that only men have semen (an ignorance of female anatomy and physiology that has caused a great loss to our womenfolk) when in fact women also have it and this semen, from the *well of living waters*, is what alchemical texts are actually referring to.

Those who are familiar with the ***Templar story*** concerning their ***Lord of Sidon*** will recollect that the skull which comprises the skull and crossbones motif, as a symbol of the ***Baphomet*** - the ***Holy Grail*** - is derived from the skull which was placed between the thigh bones of the *Templar's dead wife*, butting up against where her vagina once was, nine months after an act of knightly necrophilia.

The wife's name in the story was **Yse de Maraclea** or ***Isis*** (of the clear waters: *Mara-Clair*). The skull, the ***Templar***'s "son", represents ancient wisdom from beyond the grave and that, in its positioning between the woman's thighs, such wisdom is obtained by uniting in ***hierogamy*** with one of the Goddess-Queens of the death cult of Ankou - Isis.

Such a union, similar to that expounded by the ***Scythians*** in relation to ***Epona*** or ***Rhiannon*** results in the birth of the ***Templar***'s son: the skull; the wisdom from beyond the mortal realm. This wisdom is directly related to the feminine principle, hence the proximity of the skull to the vulva, denoting the interconnection between the ***pineal gland*** and the ***womb***, the well of living waters.

> Chapter V vss 4 - 5: " My beloved put in his hands by the hole of the door and my bowels were moved for him".
> vs 5: "I rose up to open to my beloved; and my hands dropped (dripped) with Myrrh, and my fingers with sweet smelling Myrrh (vaginal mucus), upon the handles of the lock".

The hole of the door is the keyhole, the opening of the vagina, whilst the handles of the lock are the labia.

The door is *daleth* or *delta D*: the door to the mysteries and the triangle of the "all seeing eye of god" (that looks into the darkness) which in Hebrew is called ***Ayin*** or ***'The Devil'***, whose number is the same as the numerical rank of **Ishtar** or **Venus** in the assembly of ***the Anunnaki*** gods - 15.

In verse 4 the beloved manipulates the maiden and her "*bowels*" (a common word used in classical literature which referred to the deeper internal organs, not just the intestines) are moved for him. In other words *she orgasms*, her womb contracts and in so doing she rises and opens her vulva for him to drink the blood or seminal fluid discharged by the spasm.

In references to the ***Fisher King***, it is said that he drank the contents of ***the Grail*** through a golden straw. Very importantly, when thinking of the construction of this device, we should remind ourselves of the shape of both the *Ankh Cross* and the *Crux Ansata*. Such a device would have been inserted into the virgin's urethra to the depth of about one inch, whilst the partner in the rite inserted his or her finger into the vagina and massaged the "roof of the mouth" or the uppermost wall of the channel nearest the opening or 'mouth' of the vagina, behind the pubic bone.

After a few conducive minutes perhaps, orgasm would occur and the fluid from the gland would discharge itself through the straw, either into the waiting mouth of the recipient, or into a "*Grail Platter*" or dish held next to the vulva. In one publication the dish and the straw were confused with surgical instruments that the author thought were used for castration. This is not the case. The symbol of the ***Grail*** as a *Dish* is related to its use as a collector of blood or female ejaculate and is sometimes symbolized by the ***crescent moon*** (see above).

If we read Chapter V vs 5 literally, the maiden has been asleep with her hands in the spice jar and her fingers are covered with myrrh oil as a result. She then hears her lover at the door and, rather than noticing her mistake and wiping her hands, she goes straight way to open the door and covers the handle in grease.

Such an interpretation makes no sense whatsoever. If she had been asleep with her hands (plural) in the ointment, she must have either been a contortionist or a devotee of an odd form of nocturnal skin care therapy. In any case, if it were not a pertinent symbolic aspect of the narrative, there would be no justification in mentioning it. Therefore by its very inclusion in the text, we are obliged to look for a meaning that transcends the literal interpretation.

Myrrh (Latin: myrrha. Greek: murra - murra) is a gum resin produced from several species of the *commiphora balsamodendron*, also known as *commiphora myrrha*. The oil of myrrh is produced from the seed which is known as *myrospermum pubescens*, and the etymological link here to female ejaculate should be meditated upon. ***Myrrh*** or the "*myrrh tree*" is also a name for the plant called sweet cicely or *myrrhus odorata* (related to chervil) but, as a name it is further applied to any tree producing this type of resin.

We should bear this in mind as we look at ***myrrh*** as a word in itself. Although the Latin species classifications are late, deriving from ***Linnaeus***, in many instances the original names from whence they came are Greek. We notice that the word ***myrrh*** begins with the letters *myr* and there is a group of plants and substances whose names begin with this syllable that are relevant to this discourse. Firstly we encounter the plant *tamariscus* and remember the name ***Tamaris*** which was applied to princesses of the House of David.

Tamariscus or ***tamarix*** grows in sandy conditions in west Asia and is known by the Latin name *myrica*, a name which also applies to the bog myrtle: *myrica gale*. The ***Myrtle Tree*** is found in a medieval Italian story about a fairy lover who is the spirit of the plant, which lends itself to the idea that the story was extracted from far earlier sources and that the ***Tamaris Princess*** was the original "***fairy lover***" or in Gaelic the *Anam Cara* or *Leanaan Sidhe*. Myrica-tallow or myrica wax are produced from *myrtle trees* whilst the substance *myricin* is the insoluble component in the wax that ***bees*** produce to construct *HIVES*.

In the ***Tudor*** song "*The Nut Tree*" the tree in question will only bear a silver nutmeg and a golden pear. The *nutmeg* is known by its Latin name as *myristica* from the Greek word *murizein - murizein*, meaning "*anoint*".

Nutmeg contains the chemicals which, when refined are known as ***MDMA*** or "***Ecstasy***". In trials conducted on the *Nile Lily* or *nymphacaea lotus* the plant produced similar euphoric, but less strident, effects to those experienced by users of *MDMA.*

Nutmegs produce an oil with this drug in it and the association with *anointing* and the *Christos* is quite telling. The golden pear on the "***Nut Tree***" is a pomegranate which was often called by the former *epithet.*

In Old French *pomegranate* was spelt *pome grenat*, meaning "*apple of many seeds*" from the Latin *malum granatum*, and here we return to the Avallon connection and the pomegranate as the original perhaps of the later regional and literary variation - the Druidic and Edenic apple trees.

The pomegranate belongs to the family *myrtaceae*, whilst its partner on the legendary "*Nut Tree*", the ***nutmeg***, is of the family *myristica fragrans*, the "*musk smelling nut*". ***Musk*** is a name given to any group of scents which are produced by the *sex glands* and used as sexual attractants.

Returning to the ***Song of Songs*** we now find that the ***pomegranates*** and ***myrrh*** in the narrative are etymologically related via ***Myr***, to a whole series of plants and substances within grail lore which are associated with the *sephiroth*, with *psychotropic states and with the sex organs.*

Perhaps the ***myrrh*** of the '***Song of Songs***' is the oil of the "*Musk Smelling Nut*", the ejaculate, which then becomes associated with the sweet wine of the pomegranate, the menses, thus forming the partnership between the ***rose of Sharon*** and the ***lily of the valley***.

Again we are reminded here of the Irish story of the blood red nut that fell every 28 days into the *Well of Nechtan* (the pure one) to be consumed by the salmon of wisdom - the ***Ichthys*** of the New Testament. From there we travel back to the *Orchard* of *Pomegranates* in the garden of the Well of living waters.

> In Chapter VIII vs 2 Sheba says to Solomon " I would lead thee and bring thee into my mother's house, who would instruct me; I would cause thee to drink of spiced wine (nutmeg?) of the juice of my pomegranate".

Notice "*my*" and the singular *pomegranate*, as opposed to the fruits plural. She is not inviting him in for drinks and she is not referring to a beverage here, but the blood and mumae of her vulva. Pomegranate flowers, seed cells and juice are red, like blood.

> In Chapter VII vs 9 "And the roof of thy mouth like the best wine for my beloved, that goeth down sweetly, causing the lips of those that are asleep to speak".

The euphemistic "roof of the mouth" is the region by the opening or "mouth" of the vagina, behind the pubic bone, where the semenal duct is located which secretes ejaculate through the urethra.

The chemicals in these secretions increase perception and wisdom, enabling those who were "asleep", meaning unregenerate or untranscended, to speak with the words of the quickened or resurrected Spirit.

Sheba, the ***rose of Sharon*** and the *lily of the valley*, describes herself as black but comely. In so doing she has initiated a tradition where many scholars down the centuries have confidently stated that she was from **Sheba** in Ethiopia.

However, the constant, relentless reference to "my sister, my bride", whatever anyone says about terms of endearment in Biblical times, indicates that **Sheba** was the daughter of **Bathsheba** and as a consequence, the ***sister of Solomon***.

This is hardly surprising as he descended from a *pharaonic bloodline* where brother-sister marriages were de rigueur.

The reference to her being *black* relates to her other epithets as ***Sheba-Lilith*** and ***Sheba-Venus*** or ***Ishtar*** (Inanna) which associate her with her ancient dragon ancestry, and to her forebears Lilith (Diana), Inanna, Kali Azura, Hecate and ***Black Annis*** who, like **Sheba**, is associated herself with wells and labyrinths, and who was a principal figure of veneration in the ***Cult of Ankou***.

Solomon conversely is described as having skin as white as marble. In exoteric, uninitiated and therefore "*best-guessed*" vampire lore, it is said that such a complexion is equated with their being bloodless.

Nothing could be farther from the truth. Recent laboratory tests confirm the ancient inner tradition by showing that any animal injected with large amounts of ***melatonin*** turns paler in colour. **Solomon**'s complexion, like that of the ***vampire*** of legend, is as white as marble because, like they, he fed constantly from melatonin-rich royal, female virgin blood.

A lot of the additional etymological associations here are retrospective and poetic. Nevertheless the central theme of the story stands up to a classical alchemical interpretation whilst the Latin and Greek word relationships add a quality of resonance to the picture and further echo **Graves**' concept that the ***Cosmos*** has meaning and intelligence, expressing itself through a single poetic theme of interconnected meanings, the like of which inspired the ancient *Hermetic Table of Magical Correspondences.*

George Riley-Scott (*'Phallic Worship'*) points out, and is supported in his view by other academics, that,

<u>the Bible has been altered</u> down the ages to suit the ambitions of the translators of the day.

This being the case we must remember that much of *the Bible* has been cleaned up and passages dealing with incest, along with various other unseemly practices, have probably been given a narrative reworking to suit the sensibilities of various pious audiences and patrons.

An example of this might be found in Chapter VIII vs 1 which says,

> "Oh that thou *wert* as my
> brother, that sucked the breasts
> of my mother!"

Wert is printed as an italic - *wert*, denoting a translators insert. Remove this and you get a different picture.

Chapter VIII vs 5 claims that Sheba was born "Under the Apple Tree" and suggests that she was spoken for when she had no breasts. If she was a virgin, "a wall", says Chapter VIII vs 9, **Solomon** would build a palace of silver upon her, but if she were a door, he would board her up with cedar.

Sheba replied by saying that she was a wall and her breasts thenceforth were the towers of the palace that **Solomon** built upon it. The edifice of **Solomon**'s glory, the palace of his wisdom, was built upon the virginity of **Sheba** and the essence of the womb of the princess born under the apple tree, reminiscent of ***Avallon*** and sacred to the ***Druids***.

If the ***Song of Songs*** can be seen as a deliberate contribution to the poetry of the ***Dragon culture***, which has at its centre the maiden's ***labyrinth***, the ***Garden of Love***, then the *Song of Songs* begins to make sense as an Hermetic, alchemical vampire allegory of the love of the ***dragon prince*** for his ***maiden***, a sacred chemical wedding which is the source of his power and sovereignty.

Chapter Eleven

Who's Who in Heaven

We turn our attention now to the weighty problem of identifying the gods. Some mistakes have been made in the past when people tried to cross match the pantheons of contemporary civilizations. For example the Egyptian goddess ***Hathor*** became identified with the Roman goddess ***Venus*** and so on.

The mistakes are easy to make because the ***Goddess Hathor*** was actually originally the **Sumerian Nin-Khursag**, the Mother of **Inanna**, who is also known as the **Akkadian**

Ishtar, the **Semitic Astaroth**, the **Greek Aphrodite**, the **Norse Freja** and finally the **Roman Venus** etc.

As we know the positions of the gods in the various pantheons and their attributes and relationships to each other, we can re-identify who they really are. Surprisingly we find that all the separate pantheons of the Aryans, the Sumerians, the Egyptians, the Greeks, the Romans, the Vikings and so on, all appear to be derived from a very ancient family genealogy of "gods". These gods furthermore seem to stem from the ***early Sumerian pantheon***.

However, recent research confirms that the original Sumerians were ***descended from the Ubaid***, a proto-Aryan, Pictish culture which originated in the region encompassing ***Carpathia***, ***Transylvania*** and the ***White***

Mountains where the Greek gods originated, which later became known as ***Scythia***.

It is suggested therefore that the ***Sumerian gods*** (the ancient deific royal family) were imported with the ***Ubaid Picts*** from ***Transylvania***, ***Carpathia*** and ***Scythia***. Scholars relate that the name *Sumer* is pronounced *Shumer*, the *sh* for s indicating a linguistic relationship with early *Goidelic*, and thus it is closely related by pronunciation to the *Gaelic Sumaire*, meaning, as we know, a ***vampire*** and a "***reptile***" - a ***Dragon***.

Reminiscent of the racial term "*Gallic*" (Gaelic) the word *GALL* in Sumerian means "*navigator*" (*nautonnier*) and implies *guardianship* and *overlordship*. In **Barker**'s *theory of Cybernetics*, (management systems) the entity or mechanism controlling any system, be it social or mechanical, must operate at a technologically (or genetically) higher frequency or capacity than the system that it controls, otherwise chaos will ensue and the system will spin out of control. This guiding entity or facility, is termed in cybernetics the '*nautonnier*' or navigator.

In Gaelic, the language of the ***Nautonniers***, stated by many scholars to be, in an early form, a *precursive language of the Aryans*, the dialectic u is pronounced i when it follows a consonant at the beginning of a word, and so the first syllable of both ***Sumaire*** and ***Sumer*** would then have been pronounced *Shee*, directly related to *Sidhe* and the ***Sidheans*** or ***Scythians***. Both would then be pronounced the same - *Sheemar*.

And indeed evidence for just such a case lands in our laps from the pages of the *Bible's Book of Genesis*, where it states that "the cities of *Babylon*, *Akkad* and *Erech* are in the land of ***Shin'Ar***". ***Shin'Ar*** is ***Sumeria*** and so our *Shee* pronunciation finds credence in the very word of God itself!

Furthermore if we look at ***Shin'Ar*** with "our vampire eyes" (apologies to *Anne Rice*) and remember the ***Ubaid origin*** of ***Sumerian*** and hence, via *Akkadian*, the "Gaelic" origin of Hebrew as well, we will see *Shin* as *Sidhean* and *Ar* as *Arya. Sidhean* was the name of **King Elinus of Albany** in the 7th century A.D. His full name was ***Gille Sidhean*** (Jille-She'en) meaning Steward of the Fey. *Sidhean* was pronounced with the dh remaining dialectically silent as it sometimes does in Sidhe or Shee, giving us Sheen for Sidhean.

The *Ar* component can be found in ***Takla Makan*** where it forms part of the phrase *Arshi Cantu* or *Arya-Sidhe Canto* (Tocharian 'A'), the devotional, "power-wisdom" language of the ***Aryan Scythian*** inhabitants of western ***China*** (Aryan Sanskrit: China [soft *ch* - as in the French word - *chat*] or ***Shin'Ar!)***, who were named the ***Tocharians***.

It would appear then that the 'Ar-shi' phrase used by the eastern ***Scythian-Aryans*** to describe their spiritual language is reversed and repeated in the Hebrew name *Shin'Ar*, or *Sidhean-Arya.* And what does ***Shin'Ar*** mean? Exactly the same as it means in ***Sumerian*** - ***SU.ME.*** - Lord of the Powers.

In addition the Sumerian ***SI*** means righteous, pertaining to a god - (related to the Gothic - guth [and hence the *Goths* and the *Godthi* druids of the Danes] - one who has power over the fate or destiny of others, a fairy). ***SHU*** in Sumerian means ***Supreme***, also used in relation to the gods so ***SHU.MER*** would, in any case, mean Supreme Lords, which is the same as Power Lords (*Arya-Sidhe*) whilst the word supreme is related to ***Uber*** and therefore denotes a ***Vampire*** and an ***Overlord*** - A Guardian.

If the ***m*** in either *Sumer* or *Sumaire* was originally intended to be ***mh*** then both *Sumer* and *Sumaire* would have been pronounced *Shiva* or *Sidha*, both of which are connected with ***the Elves***, the Aryan god '*Siva the Destroyer*' and the ***siddhis*** - the powers. ***Sumer*** is thought to mean "land of the guardians".

A ***guardian*** - a "***Watcher***" - is an ***overseer***, and from this meaning we obtain the ***Scythian*** word ***uber***, meaning a ***vampire*** or ***Overlord*** (by association, we also obtain from "*watcher*" the word ***Nefilim***, which relates to the ***Anunnagi*** or ***Anunnaki***).

Here we remember again the proto-Sumerian *Ubaid Pictish culture* which migrated in about 5000 BC from ***Scythian Carpathia***, a land which had a ***Dragon Culture*** also as early as 5000 BC. Monumental stone carvings of winged serpents from 3500 BC have been found in ***Transylvania***, along with a "proto"-Sumerian script dating back as far as 8000 BC. The figures incorporated on the clay tablets found at ***Tartaria*** in ***Transylvania*** are almost identical with Sanskrit and early Egyptian pictograms.

Tantalizingly, the Goidelic ***mh*** couplet is exactly the same as the Goidelic ***bh***, both of which are pronounced ***v***. It isn't fantastical to suggest that both ***bh*** and ***mh*** lost their ***h***'s and have been substituted and re-substituted arbitrarily, one for the other over the course of the centuries. It has happened everywhere else, why not here? Further, the *mer* and *maire* syllables in ***Sumer*** and ***Sumaire*** are related in the Sumerian Me and the Gaelic Mor.

In Sumerian ***ME*** means *Lord* or *Master* (an Overseer or Overlord) and in Gaelic *Mor* means '*high*' (also related to mountain and thus 'dweller on the mountain' one who soars to the heights - a druid or Merlin) and is used as a suffix to the names of Scotic chieftains or kings as in - '*The Conor Mor*' - the High King (or Overlord) of the Clan Conor, for example.

If ***Sumer*** means *guardian* and thus *overlord*, then so does *sumaire* and the ***SU*** component thus means *'the Power'* - the Sidhe or Siddhi. ***ME*** is also, it seems, specifically related to wisdom and knowledge (the Aryas) and in both senses therefore the 'sumer' or 'sumaire', being one and the same thing - is a *derkesthai*, a **dragon** - a fact born out by every other piece of evidence you might care to mention. ***Sumer*** and ***Sumaire*** mean therefore - ***Lord of the Powers*** - ***SU.ME.***

The Ubaid culture was named after the place where in 1919 **H.R. Hall** discovered the ruins of an ancient settlement. Since then archaeologists made significant finds of blue-spiralled or labyrinthine decorated pottery and, up to the late 1960's, stone tools had also been found.

This "***Ubaid***" people who had been "*cast down*" (***Nefilim***) from their lofty abodes in the mountains of the North, fleeing south to *Sumeria* in about 5000 BC are now considered by academics to be the founders of Sumerian civilization.

According to **Zechariah Sitchin** - in 1852 the **Reverend Charles Foster** (*'The One Primeval Language'*) proved that all languages, including early Chinese and other Far Eastern languages, stemmed from one primeval source - thereafter shown to be *Sumerian.*

This is palpably untrue as we now know, because the Sumerian civilization and its language were brought to Mesopotamia by the ***Ubaid***, who were early "proto" (?) ***Scythian-Aryan*** migrants who fled the Black sea region at the onset of the first Flood.

It follows therefore that all languages stemmed, not from ***Sumerian***, but from the "proto-Sumerian" language of the early ***Scythian-Aryan Homelands***, examples of which we know were discovered in ***Tartaria*** in ***Transylvania***.

This language, called by most scholars "*proto Indo-European*" (and I wish they wouldn't), was called ***Gaelic*** by **Canon Beck** and other respected academics who were contemporaries of **Charles Foster**. The Very **Reverend Beck** quipped that this *Aryan Tongue*, the mother of modern Irish, was the language of the *Garden of Eden*. Proto Indo-European is thought to come from an earlier group called *Dene-Caucasian*, which tends to stress **Canon Beck**'s point even more.

Recent archaeological discoveries prove that there is many a true word spoken in jest! The present and seemingly vast differences in the varied languages that developed from "*Gaelic*" can be explained by one phrase - Chronologically Diversified Dialectics.

In the last four hundred years English has changed so much that the bulk of the resident British population would never be able to read **Chaucer** in the original script. Imagine what happens to a language over, for example, one millennium and several thousand miles.

From northern Mesopotamia to the foothills of ***Zagros***, archaeologists working in the area from the 1970's onwards, have ascertained that the ***Ubaid people*** had built cities which were the first to use: clay bricks, (cf: the Aryan, ***Mohenjo-Daro*** and ***Harrapo*** settlements of the Indus Valley: 2300 BC, which were controlled by ***Sumeria***) plastered walls, mosaic decorations, cemeteries with brick-lined graves, copper mirrors, beads with imported turquoise, copper-headed tomahawks, cloth, houses, and above all, monumental temple buildings.

However, south in ***Eridu*** - the first truly Sumerian city according to the ancient texts - nothing could be excavated from beneath the foundations of the temple of **Enki** that was any older than 3500 BC. This is clear enough evidence that ***Sumeria*** was founded by the ***Elven queens and kings*** of the ***Transylvanian Picts***, and the most up to date academic studies and archaeological discoveries corroborate this fact.

In the 1990's it was revealed by academics that the ***Ubaid priesthood*** wore leopard (***Panther***) *skins* (cf. **Jesus ben Panther**!) and tattooed themselves in a similar fashion to the ***British Picts*** and the ***Tocharian Aryans*** of *Takla Makan*. The pointy shamanic headdress, (worn by the god-kings and queens of the Indus pantheon as well), was also of Aryan origin, with or without the horns.

Moving from ***Romania***, via ***Anatolia*** to ***Mesopotamia***, the ***Ubaid*** left a trail of *Tells* or *Raths*, wall decorations, spirally decorated pottery and brick built structures. In Northern Mesopotamia, which has very little workable stone, they continued to use clay and plaster, whilst in the south, where rocks are plentiful, they built the ***Ziggurats*** or sacred mountains that reminded them of the holy peaks of their Carpathian homelands. When the ***Sumerians*** took over ***Magan*** or ***Egypt***, their *Ziggurats* became *Pyramids*.

In very little time at all after their arrival in ***Mesopotamia*** they had found and were working copper - centuries before other people's bronze ages. Their chief god-king **Enki** had been an adept at mining (earning him the epithet "*The Lord of Mining*" - ***Bel Nimiki***) and had, according to the later Sumerian texts, invented *brickmaking*, the planning and building of cities and metallurgy, which earned him the name ***Nidimmud*** - "He who makes things".

His fairy descendants since then have all earned epithets associated with mines and alchemy, such as Dwarves, Goblins, Kobelins, Trolls, Gnomes, etc., and, as in the case of the *Tuadha d'Anu*, they have always been renowned for their skill in many crafts and arts.

The place was called ***Al'Ubaid*** and was located just north or Ur, or Eridu as it was once called. The article ***Al*** in ***Al'Ubaid*** denotes that the location was named "*of the Ubaids*" and rather than the culture merely being named after its site of discovery, the actual site itself was named after the *Ubaids* in the first place, who had migrated south via ***Anatolia*** and ***Galatia***, from whence we originally derived the word ***vampire*** - the ***Uber***.

Although the meanings are self evident and the implications thereof are quite plain, It might be educative to meditate on the further implications of *Sumer* spelt *Subher* in connection with the ***Scythian*** (***Ubaid***) ***uber*** and the possible common European migration of the consonants ***b*** and ***p*** which give rise to our word super - as in supervisor - a guardian or overlord - an Ubaid.

In so doing and in heeding all above, we are left with the conclusion that the so-called ***Sumerian gods***, repeatedly symbolized by ***serpents*** or ***dragons***, are an *Aryan-Scythian* import of the earlier *Ubaid* settlers whose gods were the dragons incarnate themselves - the ***Uber*** or vampire queens and kings - the ***Ubaid Overlords***. The overseer or one who sees over or "beyond" is one who sees above others and one who thus sees clearly. One who sees clearly is a *derkesthai*, a ***dragon***.

That these ***serpent gods*** were later referred to by the *Sumerian* people themselves as ***the Anunnagi*** from whence is derived *naga*, a serpent or dragon god of the ***Vedas***, seems fairly conclusive. That the ***Nagas*** themselves were *Devas* - meaning *shining ones* - repeating the meaning of the name ***Anunnagi*** as shining ones (shimmerers - Sumerers) squeezes one into a corner.

Archaeological discoveries in the 1960's, of what was to become known as 'proto-Sumerian' script, dug up from ash pits in ***Transylvania*** should be compared with Tartarian traditions there, which assert that **Lilith** and her brother were born in ***Transylvania*** as a result of a mating between the "***Keshalyi***", the queen of the mountain fairies, and the "***Locolico***", the king of the dwellers of the underworld mounds, situated in the forests and plains.

This is echoed in the marriage of ***Nergal*** (*Nagal - Naga*) of the underworld and ***Eresh Kigal***, a netherworld goddess in whom one can see the prototype of *Persephone*. As with all ancient tales, the plot become confused but by looking at comparable stories, some light can be shed on the truth.

Eresh Kigal was not a lady or queen of the mountains, but ***Ninkhursag*** her grand-mother, was. It is interesting to see how the identity of the grandmother filtered down to the grand-daughter however, indicating that the myth of the region once included all the characters who elsewhere still feature in relationship to each other.

As interesting though is the possibility that we might find a clue to the triple goddess concept in the very grandmother- mother-daughter theme suggested by the muddling of characteristics in the *Transylvanian* story. It is quite feasible that triple goddesses are not solely depictions of the three stages of womanhood, the moon, earth or what have you, but the half-forgotten relationships of a holy dynasty.

As I have indicated above, in Greek mythology there is a relationship between Demeter, Persephone, Kore and Diana-Hecate. If we transpose this series into the Sumerian, we have Ninkhursag, Ningal, Eresh Kigal and Lilith as linear descendants.

In ***Transylvania*** the ***Keshalyi queen*** becomes ***Eresh Kigal***, and the **Lilith** of the Transylvanians and the Sumerians becomes the *Diana-Hecate* of the Greeks who, as a moon goddess, one might be tempted to turn into the Egyptian Isis, but stay your hand I say, and read on!

If we read descriptions of the "*Sumerian*" **Lilith**, taken from Hebrew sources, we discover that she, like her Grandfather **Enlil** (*Zeus*) and her uncles **Minos** and **Rhadamanthus**, and her cousin **Ariadne** of the labyrinth, had red hair and pale skin, and was called the *Alien Queen of the North*, indicating that both by her complexion and her stated geographical origin, she was a proto-Aryan or proto-Scythian. So the indications are that **Lilith**, along with the entire holy family of gods, was a ***Ubaid*** import from ***Carpathia*** who later became a Sumerian goddess.

It would be fair to say therefore that if **Lilith** was born in the mountainous regions that stood next door to where ***Zeus*** and ***Prometheus*** battled, (who were also identified with "*Sumerian*" gods), then so were her kin. It would then be simplistic to say that the gods of all the pantheons were descended from the Sumerian. It is more likely that they all, including the Sumerian, originated from the proto-Scythian Aryan culture.

As each group migrated and their descendants settled in their respective domains, becoming isolated by geography, and the passing centuries, from the source of their original spiritual culture, and also because of the inevitable influence of the belief systems of the aboriginal cultures that the migrants either vanquished or co-habited and integrated with, the names of their gods changed.

Table of Pantheons

Sumerian /Ubaid	Egyptian	Greek	Roman	Aryan/ Hindu
Tiamat	Gaia	Draconis	Rehu	-
-	-	-	-	Lama/Lhammu
Apsu	Uranus	Uranus	Ketu	-
Ashar	Cronos	Saturn	-	Mar'ishi
Anu	Iapetus	Kasyapa	-	-
Enki	Ptah	Prometheus /Aries	Mars	Mazda/Tvashtri
Enlil	-	Zeus	Jupiter	Ahriman/Dispater
Ninurta	-	-	-	Indra
Ishkar	-	-	-	Rudra
Shala	-	-	-	Tara
Marduk	Ra	Helios	Apollo/Mithras	Mitra
Inanna	-	Aphrodite	Venus	-
Lilith	-	Artemis	Diana	-
Kali Azura	-	Hecate	-	Kali Marg
Ningishzida	Thoth	Hermes	Mercury	-
Ninkhursag	Hathor	Rhea	Juno	-
Eresh Kigal	-	Persephone	-	-
Set	Set-Typhon	Typhoeus	-	The Nagas
Asar	Osiris	Orion	-	-
Ast	Isis	-	-	-
Horus	Horus	-	-	-
Nergal	-	-	Pluto	-
-	-	Poseidon	Neptune	-

Ham	Chem	Pan	Faunus	-

In some historical comparisons of the various pantheons, and indeed in the pantheons themselves, there will have been mistakes made because there was no understanding or overview of the relationships between the deities. In the case of the ***Vedas***, as **Sitchin** remarks, consistency and precision are not the hallmarks of this *Sanskrit literature*. Such an observation holds true for much of spiritual literature worldwide, as memory fades and the gaps are filled in to create myth out of history.

By a comparative study of the pantheons and beliefs, we may discover a consistent vein by which we may adjust all the pantheons, where such stem from a recognizable common source. One example is the case of the ***Aryan God Kasyapa*** who was the father of the ***Asuras***, the elder gods. One pantheon has him down as *Dyaus Pater* and identifies him with *Zeus*. *Zeus* or **Enlil** was the father of the younger gods, the Olympians who in the Aryan pantheon are called the ***Adityas***, who were also fathered by ***Kasyapa*** who fathered the elder gods which Zeus didn't.

Thus there is an anomaly which, I am pleased to report, is easily resolved when we learn that ***Kasyapa*** means ***Sky Father*** and so does **Anu!** In ***Sumeria*** the elder and younger gods are the offspring of **Anu** and the elder gods are led by **Enki**, whilst the younger gods are led by his brother **Enlil. Enki**'s followers are ***the Asher***, corresponding to the ***Asura*** of the Aryans, the *Aesir* of the Danes and the *Aes Danu* - the ***Tuadha d'Anu*** of the ***Irish***.

Chapter Twelve

Children of the Stars

Anu's father was **Asher**, ***Marduk*** was called ***Asar*** or ***Ra***, the grandfather of ***Osiris*** who himself was also called ***Ashur*** or ***Asar*** (As - Ar: 'Seeing Lord', a Naga or Dragon, A Merlin or Druidhe). These and their variants, including the Norse *Aesir* and the Gaelic *Scythian* (Aryan) *Aes Dan* mean "he who sees", (Ashshur - he who sees - [again: Ash Shar - 'Seeing Lord'] from segment six of an Assyrian clay tablet formed as a disc of eight segments, copied from an earlier Sumerian original - excavated from the ruins of the Royal Library of Nineveh) which is the very foundation and meaning of the Greek word ***derkesthai***, from whence we derive the word ***Dragon***.

In ***Aryan Samael*** or ***Ahura*** (Ash-ura?) ***Mazda*** is called *Tvashtri* or *Tv-Ash-Tri* and rumor has it that he, the elder brother, actually sired ***Indra*** who, when the pantheon is streamlined, turns out to be *Dyaus Pater*, which has certain ramifications when converted into Sumerian because *Tvashtri* "*the Fashioner*" converts as we have seen into **Enki-Nidimmud** "*The Craftsman*" whose brother isn't *Ninurta* (*Indra*), but ***Dyaus Pater*** or **Enlil**.

The conflict between **Enki** and **Enlil** therefore, might have been more deep seated than at first we realized, because it may not have been just simply the rivalry between two brothers, but the rivalry between a father - **Enki**, and his forbidden brother-son - **Enlil**. Such a conflict was played out between ***Zeus*** and ***Cronos*** (who had led a rebellion of the Titans against Uranus), but also between ***Zeus*** and ***Prometheus***.

In Aryan (ancient Scythian) the *Asuras* are also called ***Devas*** meaning "*shining ones*" and this epithet also becomes applied to both the members of ***the Anunnaki*** and the later ***fairies*** who descended from them. Earlier scholarly sources have the name ***Anunnaki*** translated also as the variant '***Anunnagi'***, meaning "*shining ones*" and here we have a relationship with the ***Vedic Nagas***.

From the *Sumerian Chronicles* we learn that the children of **Anu** were "***the Anunnaki*** who decree the fates" meaning that they themselves were also the *mori* or *fata*, the "*Fairies*" the *scale-armoured leprachauns* - the ***dragon kings*** who, in the Aryan Vedas appear alongside their divine companions and are referred to as ***the Nagas***, who became the snake deities of India who guard a submerged treasure, echoing the central theme of the grail and ring cycles.

The Grail and the lake represent the womb. The *Magic Ring* hidden in the lake and the red gold flow and the dew of the Grail both represent the life giving blood and mumae, the "submerged" or "hidden" treasure of the serpent tailed and swan's winged mermaids, the ***Naga goddesses*** of the north, whose *wouivre* or double-ended tails and wings are also to be found in representations of the ancient "*Aesir*" - ***the Titan**** or elder god - ***Typhon***, son of Gaia and Tartarus, whose other children included these *vampiric Lamias* - the meremaids or naiads, and whose name is closely associated with ***Tartaria*** in ***Transylvania***, the original home of the ***Dragon Queens and Kings***.

* Titan derives from the Sumerian ***TI.TI.AN*** which means:

1) The breath of life of Anu (the Sons of Anu - the Nefilim)

2) The Spirits of the Stars (the Star People)

Several thousand years after the contest between ***Typhon*** and ***Zeus***, Typhon's fairy descendants, ***Ygraine***, ***Morgana*** and ***Melusine*** were still portrayed in medieval church architecture with his wings and double ended tail, and a depiction of Melusine with these physical attributes appears as a supporter in the arms of the ***Imperial and royal house of Vere***.

In *Typhon* as a ***Dragon God***, we remember *Odin*, who himself was often portrayed as a *dragon or serpent*, a ***Naga***, and that he too was an *Aesir*, a member of the old, warlike order of gods. Odin is always associated with Yggdrasil or Yggd-Rad -Aes-Hel the World Ash of the Norse and here we will recall that the tree's name means Steed of Yggd or Odin and was a goddess who performed the same function as the queens of Avallon. As a serpent he is often seen entwined around the Aes Tree echoing the depiction of ***Samael*** as the ***Serpent (N'H'SH),*** entwined in **Lilith**'s branches.

Subtext - The Naga

At this juncture we must break off and study the ***Aryan Naga*** - the ***serpent devas***, guardians of treasures "hidden in water". We will do this by first looking at the Hebrew word *nahash*. this word means *serpent* (and thus dragon) and derives from the consonant root *N'H'SH - a snake.*

In *Hebrew Qabalah* and particularly and rather oddly, in relation to the Jewish practice of divination by birds or *Ornithomancy*, the serpent or ***Nahash*** is one who discovers hidden secrets or ***wisdom*** from the ***Raven***, the ***Dove*** or the ***Swan*** (Warburg Lectures, Universtity of London, private dissertation on Qabalah and Jewish Ornithomancy 1996).
The ***N'H'SH*** is *Enki-Samael* the *SU.HUR.MASH* (Capricorn - the Goat-Headed Sea Serpent) or *A.LU.LIM* (Ram of the "Glittering" [or Shining, as in Elven] Waters) is associated with Lilith of the Qlipphoth or "Abyss" (the APSU or watery deeps - ie lakes, wells, vulvas etc).

Closely associated with the relationship between **Lilith** and **Samael**, as outlined above, are the Raven and the Dove as birds of divination. In this context it becomes clear that these qabalistic, symbolic animals are meant to represent the *Valkyries, the Morganas and Magdalenes - the Ishtar priestesses* who are the Maidens of the Ring and the Grail.

The Dove, specifically the Turtle Dove or Barbary Dove is a soft brown colour and has a ring around its neck that lies open at the throat. This dove, specifically sacred to Venus, is a symbol of love and devotion. and is the bird referred to in the name **Mary Magdalene**. ***Magdal*** or ***Migdal*** meaning a ***dove***.

The ring around its neck is a torque, which, in Gaelic lore symbolizes, as do all rings, ***Kingship*** and therefore wisdom and *seership* - the *derkesthai* or ***Dragon Nature***. That **Mary** is named **Magdalene**, "of the place of the doves" which are sacred to Venus and thus Ishtar and mistakenly Hathor, means that she, Mary, was a priestess of this Goddess of 'Love'.

The link between the *raven*, known as the *Phoenix*, the *dove* and *Samael* is <u>alchemical</u>. At one level the raven and the dove are female and interchangeable, the dove or doves (in

Magdal: the place of doves or temple of the priestesses of Ishtar/Hathor/Venus) being the priestess or priestesses of Ishtar, the other - the raven - being the priestess of ***Morrighan***.

The *qabalah* specifically says that the raven and the dove are the same bird and in the Northern hemisphere the brown singing ravens of the ***Druids*** are obviously the Turtle doves or priestesses, brown *morrighans*, equivalent to swan maidens.

Samael, in his congress with them, obtaining the "*wisdom of the qlipphoth*" or the abyss - ie the waters of the deep. The Barbary dove or *Migdal* links the ring cycle to **Mary Magdalene** and thence **Jesus**. Both then are linked again to ***Hathor***, the raven Goddesses of the Druids, to ***An*** and the ***Phoenix*** of the ***Scythians*** and thence the Ring and the ***Dragon Orobourous***, called ***Janus*** by the Phoenicians and *Jormungar* by the Danes. Like **Enki** and *Chem*, *Siva* is the *woad painted Lord of the Goats.*

Jormungar - 'The Earth Spanner' : 'The encircler' or Vala of the Vedas, lives in the watery deeps and once upon a time long, long ago, Thor and the giant (Titan) Hymir went fishing for him. As bait they used an Ox-head which, as we have seen symbolizes the ovaries, fallopian tubes, womb and vagina of the virgin goddess.

Here again is a link between water, ***Samael the Dragon*** and virgins. The *Brown raven* or choral priestess of the Druidic cult is the turtle dove and the swan maiden because both animals are used in alchemy and ***Tantra*** to symbolize the ***brain***, the ***pineal gland*** and the ***Ajna Chakra***.

In ***Vala*** we have the original root of the words *Valhalla* and *Valkyrie*. It is now known, as we had suggested, that the *Valhallas* were forest halls. There were in fact built on mounds and displayed giant ***Dragon*** heads at each end. These were the dwellings of the *Vala Aes*, the ***Dragon Overlords*** of the forest and beneath them, lying in the *Creachaire* tomb- raths, were the remains of their ancestors, the Gods of Heaven.

The *Valhallas* were the dwelling places of the Gods of Heaven and Earth, the ***serpent queens and kings***. The *Great Hall* on the summit of the mound of the Otherworld was identical to the temple at the peak of the ziggurat. These Halls were where the ***Valkyries***, the singers of the Gods assembled. In this capacity these were sometimes called the brown ravens, meaning that they were still the ***Morrighans***, but assumed the magical, Grail role of brown Turtle Doves, the lovers of the Phoenix or Dragon God. Hence the Valhalla was also a variant of the Judaic Magdala or House of Doves.

The swan-serpent caduceus and the descended dove originate here and in placing the paten into the Grail both symbolize this love of the Turtle and the Phoenix. The *serpillion* is a swan or serpent necked dove depicted in medieval architecture and the link here is clear. In the association of **Lilith** with the abyss of the qlipphoth and the raven and dove who symbolize **Ishtar**, we have another link between Diana and Persephone and a clarification of the nature of Hades.

As the watery abyss, it is identified with the Gaelic Otherworld reached by water. The masculine nature of the raven is echoed in ***Machen***'s alchemical riddle where a serpent eating a serpent becomes a dragon (a serpent who eats its tail makes a circle and completes itself: it transcends) and a dragon eating a dragon (a transcended one drinking from another transcended one, **Samael** drinking **Lilith**) becomes a ***phoenix*** - a Raven King, Swan Knight/Prince, Dragon Queen, Rephaim etc.

The ***Phoenix*** in its final transcendent glory becomes a flaming, leaping star, an ***An***, or ***Shining One***. "The *Nahash* is taught by the Raven or the Dove" means that The Dragon Kings drink from Grail Princesses of the Abyss or Qlipphoth, the Tree of Life of the Left Hand Path - Kaula Vama Marg! The pool at the foot of Yggdrasil.

In the 'Phoenix and the Turtle' by ""William Shakespeare"" (I don't think!) there are mentioned the Turtle Dove, the Phoenix, the Raven, the Swan and the Screech Owl (Lilith). It is said that out of the Phoenix myth, ""Shakespeare"" (I don't think!) created a myth of his own. Not so. What he did was to expand the myth and fill it with its proper alchemical symbolism and demonstrate the purpose of the original story, that being divine union.

The ***Phoenix*** of myth, the only bird of its kind (symbolizing the **Oneness** of the All perceived by those who become united with **The All** and thus are alone) travels from its eastern paradise and makes a 'nest' of 'spices' (see Song of Songs) in an Arabian Palm Tree (A Sufic symbol and emblem of the Tamaris Princesses, read Lily and Rose again, back a few pages).

Having burnt up in its own fire (been consumed in the energy generated by enthea) it takes the ashes to the temple of the Sun at ***Heliopolis*** and lays them on the Altar. Other birds (ranks of druidism aforementioned) and men gather to rejoice and in *chorus* (***Cor***) they accompany the singing Phoenix as it soars to heaven and returns to its lonely paradise eg *Samadhi, Bodhisatva, Heaven, Transcendence, Enlightenment, Divine Union, Scythia!*

Summary: ***The Transcended Dragon King*** needs to drink from a ***Dragon Princess***, a fairy lover. He travels to Arabia, meets his ***Tamaris*** and drinks from her 'Nest of spices' and she bestows stillness and ecstasy upon him.

He is consumed by fire (the spirit or combined energy), is

reborn and takes his ashes, his mortal body, and lays on the altar of the Sun, symbolized by the ***Dragon***, *Lion, Hawk and Bull in Persian Mithraism* (***Mithras*** the mediator or Balance) to symbolize his achievement of the balance or nil point and subsequent oneness with the Cosmos. Everyone is seriously chuffed that he has managed to regenerate and won't be acting like a complete pillock and ruining everything now he has refreshed his sovereignty with a living goddess.

He can now go back to ***Scythia/Heaven*** and carry on reigning and being the wisdom and fertility of the land, end of story. Shakespeare's version describes beautifully the emotions of ***enthea*** and anyone who has experienced this divine union with another of the blood will not fail to be deeply moved, both with joy and sadness.

Again this is another *Solomonic*, ***vampire rite*** and proof yet again that vampirism is born of a love so deep that it tears the soul from the body, as this tale suggests. It also implies that the rite has to be repeated and that feeding must be recurrent.

The ***OTO*** call the '*Rite of the Phoenix*' the '*Mass of the Vampire*' for good reason. The ***Phoenix***, along with the other birds in Shakespeare's poem are called ***Bennu Birds*** and are identified with each other by Grant ('Magical Revival') and this is because all classes of druid are vampires and need to feed in order to remain transcendent.

The *Bennu Bird* or *Bird of Return* symbolizes a being that regenerates or must regenerate itself at regular intervals and the vampire itself bears an appellation that is named after this process. In folklore though the vampire, as 'one who returns' is mistaken for 'one who returns from the grave' instead of '<u>one who MUST return to feed and regenerate</u>'.

The ***Phoenix*** is symbolized in ***Transylvania*** by the double-headed Raven, brother of **Lilith**. This bird was adopted by the Hittites and came to symbolize the holy roman empire in the corrupted form of an eagle. This *Double Headed Raven*, the *Phoenix*, is the penultimate symbol of the dragon people. In the last process of its regeneration, the Phoenix becomes ***The Star***, the *An of the Anunnagi*, the *Elves or Shining Ones*: the ultimate symbol of the ***Dragon Race***.

The Serpent N'H'SH

In translating the word ***N'H'SH***, firstly we will take the Hebrew consonants back, via Phoenician, to their Sumerian roots and remember also that, in Sumerian, syllable groups could be reversed and yet still render the same meaning in an overall phrase. So, the N is Nun, the H is Heth (as opposed to He) and the SH is Shin (as opposed to either Sade or Samekh).

We check these through the Phoenician to ensure a continuity of shape in the correct pictograms as we venture back into the Sumerian and discover the following: Nun = Nag, Heth = H.A. and Shin = Salmunuz. Therefore from the Hebrew Nahash, we derive the original Sumerian Naghasalmunuz, Nagha Salmunuz or NAG.HA.SAL.MUNUZ., which translates as Drink (NAG) - Fish (HA) - Vulva (SALMUNUZ).

If this sounds a bit odd, the author explains that a fish is "of water" and so in Sumerian the equivalent to our letter 'A' means water whilst the 'H' is the article which stands for of. So the Hebrew N'H'SH - the Serpent - translates into the Sumerian "One (a dragon) who - Drinks of (the) Water (of the) Vulva".

One notices that in this phrase - ***Nagha Salmunuz*** - two things stand out. Firstly we have the Aryan word ***Naga*** spelt ***Nagha*** which would be pronounced with the gh sounding like a nasally, softly gargled ch (as in the Scottish word loch) identical to the Spanish x or g. According to the OED, 'H' which in Sumerian was H.A. evolved into the Greek pronounced as defined above, as an Iberian (Aryo-Scythian Celtic) x or ch.

In this way we can also justifiably spell ***Naga*** as ***Naxa*** and then we begin to understand the profound relationship between the Naga guardians of the Aryan pantheons and the Nixes or Nixas of western Europe who were, likewise, the female guardians of watery treasures, and like the ***Nagas*** or ***Naxas***, these *meremaids* or *Swan Maidens* were *Devas* or ***Shining Ones*** (***Anunnagi***).

The second thing we notice is that the Sumerian word for a *vulva* is *Salmunuz* and immediately the poetic connection between the '*Sacred Vulva*' (the *well of Nechtan* [Nixtan] - the pure one, the Nix or Nothing) and the ***Salmon*** (*Salmunuz*) of Wisdom that swims in the well should immediately spring to mind - as should the *Ichthys* - as being the vulva of the **Virgin Mary Magdalene**. Praise the Lord for the Single Poetic Theme!

In remembering that Sumerian can be reversed, we can look at the Hebrew *N'H'SH* again and see that if it is reversed, as was the custom in Hebrew Qabalah when rabbis were tinkering around with language looking for hidden meanings, it becomes *SH'H'N* which is pronounced *She'an*, 'of the Powers'. Furthermore the numerical or *gematric* value of N'H'SH in Qabalah is 9 which is the number of *Yesod*, the sephirah of the Moon, whose Phoenician God was the Sumerian SIN or SHIN - She'en.

The symbols associated with *SIN* included the ***Axe***, the ***Labrys*** which is a device which, as we know, depicts the Vulva. The Axe symbol, prevalent in *Mittani* and Minoan Cretan culture became the spinning Hammer of Thor (the swastika) who as Zeus, was the wielder of the lightning bolt which, in northern Europe, was symbolized by the Norse 'Sig' Rune. Sig -

the lightning bolt of inspiration (cf. Mead of Inspiration) - is the *Greek Sigma* which is the *Hebrew Shin*, last consonant of *N'H'SH*, and SIN - Sumerian god of the Moon.

Sig is the serpentine lightning bolt that courses down the Qabalistic Tree of Life. In one sense it represents **Enki-Samael** entwined around **Lilith**. The upturned crescent moon is also said to be associated with Samael (Sumaire-El) and, in an ancient Sumerian picture reproduced by Langdon, the moon as a dish is depicted next to the ***Star of Anu***, below which is the serpent N'H'SH entwined around the tree, symbolizing **Lilith**.

Finally we must consider ***Tiamat***. Her name - ***TI.A.MAT*** - means life-water-maiden. This translates as "maiden of the waters of life" and it is then clear that her name indicates she was both the first known matriarch and virgin priestess - the "feeding mother" - of the vampire dragon queens and kings. The mother of the Elven dynasty, she was the generatrix of a vampire lineage of goddess-queens and god-kings spanning seven thousand years.

She was a ***Nagha*** or ***Nixa*** and it is from her that **Lilith**, and all the ensuing Grail Maidens, including Sheba and Morgana of the Apple Trees, Tamaris, Mary Magdalene, the Princesses of Avallon, Melusine, Niniane and Ygraine owe their identifications as "Trees of Life". Consequently we can say that ***Tiamat***, the first Tamaris - the Maiden who gives the Waters of Life - was also the *Tir Mat* or *Tir Mata*, the first "Tree Mother" of the Lords and Ladies of the Forest, the Druids and Druidesses - the ***People of the Trees*** (***of Life***).

Of the younger gods of the Aryans, the ***Adityas***, two - ***Tara*** and ***Bhaga*** - stand out prominently. As we have seen **Ulick Beck** and several other scholars have traced the origin of the *Scythian-Irish Tuadha d'Anu* to the same region as the Aryans, and have gone as far as saying that they were one and the same.

Interestingly we find that the goddess ***Tara*** - wife of ***Rudra***, ***Indra***'s charioteer, appears in ***Eire*** as ***Tara***, the Hill or Rath of ghosts in County Meath, Eire. ***Tara*** was the sacred centre of the united Irish kingdom and was the seat of the Danaan Kings of Tara during the Iron Age.

Some scholars attribute the name of Tara in Eire to some complicated sounding god name which I find implausible in the light of the fact that a ***Goddess Tara*** already existed in the ***Scythian-Aryan*** pantheon.
Whether ***Asura*** or ***Aditya***, ***Danaan*** or ***Milesian***, all of the ancient Goddess Queens were the source of sovereignty associated with sacred mounds and it seems therefore entirely appropriate to name a Sidhe rath, a portal to the otherworld and thus the source of sovereignty, after a goddess who would herself have represented sovereignty.

In the case of ***Bhaga***, or ***Vaga*** as his name would have been pronounced in Gaelic, scholars think that he became the Slavic god Bogh, a word which came to mean "god" in Thrace, where the Danaan Fir Bolg were once exiled, prior to their return to Ireland. In Fir Bolg we either have the title "men of God", meaning druids, or we have, as is commonly thought, "men of the bags" which means "men of God" anyway, because the "bag", specifically the "Crane Skin Bag", was an accessory of the Godthi's and the Druid's: the "men of the gods".

Myth or reality?
Considering the foregoing, it is interesting to note that in **Tolkien**'s '*Silmarillion*' - the background mythology that supports his '*Lord of the Rings*' - we find a vocabulary and etymology that includes the following words - Ainur, Ainu, Vala, Maiar, Eldar, Ea.

Tolkien's word *Ainur* means the "*Holy Ones*" of which the singular is ***Ainu***. There are two orders of these gods in his mythology - the *Valar* and the *Maiar*. The plural ***Ainur*** and the singular ***Ainu*** are clearly derived from the Sumerian father of the gods - **Anu** and ***the Anunnaki***, whilst *Valar* appears in the Aryan pantheon as *Vala* "The encircler", reminiscent of the *Orobourus*, the alchemical Dragon Ring that **Tolkien** wrote so much about. We will also remember the Val-Kyrie at this juncture.

The word *Maia* is spelt *Maja* in Spanish and denotes a female line of nobility and royalty. The 'i' was originally 'j' and came, along with the word majesty, from the Latin majes or majus, a variant of which is magi or magus, from the Greek magos - magos, a bloodline member of a caste or genetic strain comprising of individuals heritably steeped in magic, (OED), in other words the Arya - or *Scythian Derkesthai* - The **Dragon Goddess Queens and God Kings**.

At this point we return to the concept of the ***derkesthai*** and the bloodline of the dragon god-kings - the ***Asuras*** and the ***Anunnaki***. In the '*Silmarillion*' Maia becomes Maiar and it accords with the ancient concept of deific royalty - Maia - which, related to Mana is the 'spirit of the gods carried in the blood', the attribute of a goddess-queen or god-king of the Dragon who are in themselves collectively an 'order of the gods' - the 'elves' - the shining ones - or 'gods incarnate'- the Devas and Avatars.

The 'spirits of the gods - the ancestors - carried in the blood' we will remember are the spirits summoned from the 'deeps', the subconscious, by the witch, (Vampire or Druid) who gains her or his name - *wicce* or *wicca* - from the ability to yield or bend to, or rather to draw to the surface of consciousness, these spiritual intelligences and their wisdom from her or his ancestral, and thus genetic, inheritance. In other words their waking consciousness is pacified or "yields", to allow the older spirit, or racial memory, to give voice.

Avatar is a word **Tolkien** includes in his *Silmarillion* as Aratar the eight most powerful of his Valar or order of old gods which, it seems obvious, were intended to mimic the Egyptian gods of the Ogdoad, the eight ***Anunnaki*** who tended the Holy Mountain after the Black Sea flood.

Another of **Tolkien**'s words similar to ***Avatar*** - ***Avathar*** - to him means "*The Shadows*" which he uses as a name for a land near his '*Bay of Eldemar*'. Comparably, in our world, an Avatar is a 'god made flesh' - a Dragon King or Queen who often occupied tombs and would have been thought of as a "shadow", a spirit of the otherworld, the realm of the Shining Ones.

So in the Vala and Maiar we have two orders of gods taken from the Dragon tradition itself whilst, according to the legends of Tolkien's elves, the word Eldar became used as a name for the three elven kindreds, one of which Tolkien named the Vanyar, who appear to be the Vanir Gods of the Danes, cousins of the Tuadha d'Anu. Tolkien's largest variety of wicked Orcs he named the Uruks and ***Uruk*** a City State of ***the Anunnaki***. The *Orcs* he said were once fair elves who had been imprisoned and tortured in the Land of Mordor.

'Eldar', explains **Tolkien**, means '*People of the Stars*', echoing a traditional Gaelic epithet for the *Tuadha d'Anu* and also one of the original meanings of the name ***Anunnaki - People of the Stars***.

Of men, **Tolkien** concurs that they are the second, younger race which his elves called the Atani, (Adamae) a name, says **Tolkien**, that later became the Edain, obviously the children of Eden. Again we have a borrowing of Dragon Lore where the Elves, the ***Children of Anu***, the Anukim or Repha'im of the Old Testament, appeared first, followed by our ***Adamae***, or the Atani as Tolkien would have it.

Edain is obviously Eden, whilst he uses Eä as a name for the Earth which in Sumerian is the name for the dragon god of the 'Earth and Waters' - Enki-Samael, the leader of the elder "Eldar" gods - the Aesir. **Tolkien**, in his epic works, with their plethora of borrowed names and borrowed linguistics and their elder and younger races, is obviously writing about the family, particularly when one peruses his vocabulary and discovers the name Avallónë, a haven and city of the Eldar - the Elves - situated on 'the lonely isle' - Tol Eressea, which was drawn across the ocean and rooted finally in the Bay of Eldemar, adjacent to Avathar - the land of Shadows: our Avalon or Otherworld.

The various names by which our planet is known all stem from the word ***Eridu***, which was the first city founded by **Enki-Samael** in Mesopotamia. As a variant of ***Eridu***, in the Silmarillion, Tolkien has Eriador and his Elven word for Earth is Arda, which is also derived from Eridu.

Nicholas de Vere
XXIV - VII - MCMIC

The House of Vere: References

The Duchy of Angiers

and

The Royal House Of Vere

Vere of Blackwood

Introduction

Published comments concerning the House of Vere

Vere-de-Vere stalked into the English vernacular as a playful term meaning the grandest, proudest, most historic, indisputably aristocratic and absolutely creme de la creme of Anglo-'Norman' antiquity.

In fiction the expression is used for characters of, or assuming, unquestionable ancient lineage - and with good cause.

In the Middle Ages, owing to plagues and battlefield mortality, the average noble dynasty in England lasted not more than three generations. The de Veres, however, managed to maintain a line of twenty earls of Oxford over 561 years*, (*our note: The senior descents in the male line today reach back 1300 years). Lord Thomas Macaulay, Victorian historian supreme calls this family:

> "The longest and most
> illustrious line of nobles that
> England has seen".

Vero Nihil Verius (nothing truer than truth) is the family motto granted by **Queen Elizabeth I.** The family crest was already the Blue Boar.

The Falling Star of Vere

A legend lingers round the acquisition of the de Vere (star) badge. In the version as told by Leland, Aubrey was 'at the Conquest of the Cities of Nicque, of Antioch, and of Hierusalem' and:

> "In the year of our lord 1098, Corborant, Admiral to the Soudan of Persia was fought with at Antioch, and discomforted the Christians. The Night coming on in the Chace of this Bataile, and waxing dark, the Christianes being four miles from Antioche, God, willing the saufte of the Christianes shewed a white Starre or Molette of fyve Pointes, which to every Manne's Sighte did lighte and arrest upon the standard of Albrey, then shining excessively".

The mystic star from this miracle became the de Veres' badge, which they wore on their shields from then onwards - quarterly gules and or, in the first quarter a mullet argent. Later heralds argued that it was merely 'a mullet with a difference' as always used to distinguish a younger son from an elder. Others said that it was not a star at all, but the rowl spur, from the French word mollet, which could have been held up as a pre~arranged sign to muster supporters and was caught in a ray of sunlight. "But for the de Veres the badge was simply God pointing out the family's near~deity".

From Verily Anderson,

'The Veres of Castle Hedingham'.

The House of Vere

"The noblest subject in England, and Indeed, as Englishmen loved to say, the noblest subject in Europe, was Aubrey de Vere........who derived his title through an uninterrupted male descent, from a time when the families of Howard and Seymour were still obscure, when the Nevills and Percys enjoyed only a provincial celebrity, and when even the great name of Plantagenet had not yet been heard in England. One chief of the house of de Vere had held high command at Hastings; another had marched, with Godfrey and Tancred, over heaps of slaughtered Moslems, to the sepulchre of Christ. The first Earl of Oxford had been minister of Henry Beauclerc, The third earl had been conspicuous among the lords who extorted the great Charter from JOHN. The seventh earl had fought bravely at Cressy and Poictiers. The thirteenth earl had, through many vicissitudes of fortune, been the chief of the party of the Red Rose, and had led the van on the decisive day of Bosworth. The seventeenth earl had shone at the court of Elizabeth I, and had won for himself an honourable place among the early masters of English poetry.........".

Baron Thomas Babbington Macaulay, Lord Macaulay of Rothley Temple (1857).

See source profile.

Professor Vivian Greene:

" The Counts of Anjou: Princes of Anjou"

Sir Bernard Burke, Ulster King of Arms,

when speaking of the Vere called them

singularly and in plural:

"The Princely Noble"

"The Race of Vere"

(Extract from 'Vicissitudes of Families', page 424 line 12 and page 426 para 2 line 12)

G. E. Cokaynes Complete Peerage Volume X

Page 208

OXFORD

II. 2.AUBREY (DE VERE) IV, EARL of OXFORD, hereditary Master Chamberlain of England. 1st s. and h. by 3rd wife, **(a)** b. 1163 or later. **(b)** While still a boy he attested his father's charters for Colne Priory **(c)** and a charter of Ranulf de Mandeville for St. Osyth ; **(d)** and he witnessed 7 more of his father's charters for Colne **(e)** and joined him in attesting a number of other charters for that priory **(f)** and 2 other charters. **(g)** Early in 1190 he Was with the King in Normandy. **(h)** He obtained the Bolebec fief with Isabel the heiress, **(i)** and together they gave a tenement in Wavendon to Woburn Abbey. **(j)** On 21 Feb. , 1190/I he confirmed his father's foundation of Castle Hedingham Priory, and at the request of his father and mother gave it his church at Castle Hedingham and the wood at Gosfield; **(k)** but at Michaelmas in that year he owed 100 marks for what was imposed on his men for burning the nunnery. **(l)** Within the years 1191-9, he witnessed a charter of John, Count of Mortain (afterwards King), for Rouen Cathedral. **(m)** In Dec. 1194 he suc. his father, and in 1195 as Aubrey de Vere junior, he rendered account for £100 for his relief............

Footnotes

(a) Item in comite Alberico Alberici comitis de Ver filio, simile naturae miraculum vidimus. Cum enim pater ejusdem, matre jam Praegnante, filia scilicet Henrici de Essexia, ob ignominiosum patris eventum jam ad divortium modis omni elaborasset, partu prodeunte; quem pater in oculo casuali laesione sustinuit, eadem parte defectus in filio parentavit (Giraldus Cambrensis, OP. cit, p 132). Albericus Comes Oxeneford. His testibus Alberico filio meo et Herede et Roberto Henrico Filiis meis (Colne Cart., no.42).

(b) There is no proof that his parents did not cohabit between 1163 and ii or 1172; for his mother's age cf p.206, note "e."

(c) His Testibus Alberico filio meo Radulpho de Ver. Radulpho magistro Alberici (Colne Cart., no.38; cf Idem, no. 45) That Aubrey had a master proves that he was a boy at the time.

OXFORD

III. 1214. 3. ROBERT (DE VERE), EARL OF OXFORD,

Hereditary Master Chamberlain of England, being 3rd but eldest surv. S. of the 1st Earl, by 3rd wife.

Footnotes

(1) His afilliation is proved by his attestations to 4 of his father's charters Colne, e.g. "His testibus Albrico filio meo et Roberto fratre ejus" (Colne Q no.46). He has always been described as the 2nd son, but in the 3 charters for Colne Priory.................

OXFORD

Footnotes

..........................which are witnessed both by **Robert** and by his brother **Ralph**, his name precedes **Robert**'s (Idem, nos. 36, 41, 85).

(a) On the assumption that Robert was the 3rd son; after 1172 if his parents did not resume cohabitation before I 171. He seems to have been with his brother Aubrey in Normandy in Aug. 1197 (Landon, op. cit., pp I20~2I)

See Source Profile.

'The Royal Genealogies'
Table CCXVI

ther *Heathen* Nations whom he conquer'd, to receive the *Christian Faith*, and so made the
Grand Revolutions of *Europe*.

[illegible]

Tabular Section of the above right
Milo: Count of Anjou

...ushold under Dagobert III.
...an Kings of *France*.

N. N.

Leutbergis his Concubine.

...lomannus King ... the *Soissons*. 768. ... 71. Wife *Gerber*... a *French* Woman.	**Gisela** an *Abbess*, born 757. † 812.	*Talendus* was beloved of the Empress *Hildegardis*.	*Bertha* Wife of *Milo* Count of *Anjou*.
...udolph a Count of the *Franks*.			*Rolandus* the General of Charlemain, † in *Spain* 809.
Fastrada the third Wife of Charlemain, upon the Death of *Hildegardis* 783. † 794.			

(Page 450 'The Royal Genealogies' The Rev. Dr. James Anderson, D.D., M.A : **Milo I de Vere** was **Count of Anjou**, (hence eldest *son* of Melusine/Melouziana de Scythes /Maelasanu: The Dragon Princess).

See Source Profile.

THE MADNESS OF KINGS

A count of Anjou came back with a new wife, a strange girl of extraordinary beauty but she kept very much to herself. Unusually in so religious an age she was reluctant to attend the Mass. When she did go she always hurried from the church before the consecration of the host. Her husband, who was puzzled by her behaviour, told four knights to keep watch and to try to delay her departure from the church. When she got up to go, one of them trod on the hem of her train. As the priest raised the host to consecrate it she screamed, wrenched herself free, and still shrieking, flew out of the window, taking two of her children with her. In reality the countess was the wicked fairy, Melusine, the daughter of Satan, who cannot abide the consecration of the body of Christ in the Mass. It was from the children that she left behind that the counts of Anjou and the Angevin kings of England were said to be descended.

(Of the Plantagenet Branch):

So devilish an ancestry accounted for the demonic energy and passionate ill-temper by which these princes seemed often afflicted. 'We who came from the devil', John's brother, Richard I, was reported as saying caustically, 'must needs go back to the devil. Do not deprive us of our heritage: we cannot help acting like devils.' 'De diabolo venit et ad diabolum ibid', commented St Bernard of Clairvaux, 'From the devil he came, and to the devil he will go.'

Professor Vivian Greene

Cependant, apprenant plus tard que Geoffrey a brule l'abbaye de Maillezais et tue son frere, le Comte maudit son epouse. Il l'acuse publiquement d'etre "tres fausse serpent". Le secret est devoile. Melusine doit regagner L'Autre Monde et s'envole transformee en DRAGON.

Christine Bonnet, Lusignan.

The Duchy of Angiers

Angiers was a Ducal principality in the Comite region of Anjou. In the work of The Rev. Father Sabine Baring-Gould Angiers is referred to as the country where the Princess Melusine was a native. Angiers is now the city of Angers in northern Anjou. As a Ducal principality its rulers constituted a regnant royal house who, in the case of the Vere, were also the Counts of the region in which this 'city state' was situated.

See Source Profile.

Vere Princedom

Although Merovingian culture was both temperate surprisingly modern, the monarchs who presided over it were another matter. They (The Sorcerer Kings) were not typical even of rulers of their own age, for the atmosphere of mystery legend, magic and the supernatural, surrounded them, even during their lifetimes. If the customs and economy of the Merovingian world did not differ markedly from others of the period, the aura about the throne and royal bloodline was quite unique.

Sons of the Merovingian blood were not 'created' kings. On the contrary they were automatically regarded as such on the advent of their twelfth birthday. There was no public ceremony of anointment, no coronation of any sort. Power was simply assumed, as by sacred right.

But while the king was supreme authority in the realm, he was not obliged - or even expected - to sully his hands with the mundane business of governing. He was essentially a ritualised figure, a priest-king, and his role was not necessarily to do anything, simply to be. The king ruled in short, but did not govern.

Even after their conversion to Christianity the Merovingian rulers, like the Patriarchs of the Old Testament, were polygamous. On occasion they enjoyed harems of oriental proportions. Even when the aristocracy, under pressure from the Church, became rigorously monogamous, the monarchy remained exempt. And the Church, curiously enough, seems to have accepted this prerogative without any inordinate protest. According to one modern commentator: Why was it [polygamy] tacitly approved by the Franks themselves?

We may here be in the presence of ancient usage of polygamy in a royal family - a family of such rank that its blood could not be ennobled by any match, however advantageous, nor degraded by the blood of slaves ... It was a matter of indifference whether a queen were taken from a royal dynasty or from among courtesans...

> The fortune of the dynasty rested in its blood
> and was shared by all who were of that blood.

And again,

> 'it is Just possible that, in the Merovingians, we may have a dynasty of Germanic Heerkonige* derived from an ancient kingly family of the migration period'.

Extracted and expanded upon by Henry Lincoln, from 'The Long Haired Kings'
by J. M. Wallace-Hadrill; Fellow of Merton College Oxford.
* Fritz Kern, Gottesgnadentum und Widerstandrecht (1954).

The House of Vere are descended in various lines from the dynasty of Meroveus and consequently share this Germanic Royal Blood Tradition. Prince Milo de Vere - married to Charlemagne's sister - and as Head of the Imperial House and Chief of the Imperial Army, was himself an Imperial Prince.

The Descent of the 'Imperial and Royal' House of Vere of Anjou

700 -2000 a.d.

Ex libello **Genealogiae Comitum Oxoniensium**

Official de Vere family records

Repetit genus á Noe. Deinde á Tideo Graeco. Insuper á Vero nobilis Romano Postremo á Milone comite de Genny, alias Gisney (GUISNES).

- 760+ AD Milo de Ver: Duke of Aungiers and Duke Leader of Great King Charles house and army (son of Rainfroi: de Ver) - Milo married Bertbelle, sister of Great King Charles Charlemagne.

- 800+ AD Rouland de Ver (son of Milo and Bertbelle): Held the titles of the "Earl of Palatine", "Earl of Maunce and Bleuys", "Governor of the Marches of Brittany" however, he was killed by warring Pagans at Rumcidevale. 800+ AD Baldwine de Ver: became "Duke of Maunce" after his brother Rouland's death.

- 800+ AD Milo de Ver II (ii) (son of Milo [i]) Held title of the "Earl of Genney or Gisney or GHISNES" given to him by Charlemagne, he married Avelina the daughter to the "Earl of Nauntes" and they had two sons, Nicasius and Milo(iii).

- 800+ AD Nicasius de Vere : married Agathe daughter to the "Earl of Champaign" and gave issue to Otho "de Vere" who later became the "Earl of Genney".

[Nicasius de Ver Erle of **Genney** sonne to yong Milo
Erle of **Genney**.
This Nicasius had to wyfe Agathe the dowghtar of the
Erle of Champain.
Of Nicasius cam Otho de Vere Erle of **Genney**, maried to
Constance dowghtar to the Lord of Charters]

Excerpt from Stow MSS, British Library, London

- 800+ AD Otho de Vere: married Constance daughter to the "Lord of the Charters" and gave issue to Amelius de Ver.

- Amelius("Aldolphus") de Vere: Earl of Genny (GHISNES or GUISNES) married Helena daughter of

Earl Bloys

- His son:
  - Gallus/Guillaume (Guy Blanc Barbe) de Vere: Earl of Genny (GHISNES - GUISNES) married Gerbrudis daughter to the Lord Cleremont. (Gallus - Guillaume went with Aubri and the King to England). Descent to Godfroi de Bouillon and the Counts of Boulogne.

- Manasses de Vere: Earl of Genny married Petronilla daughter of the Earl of Boleine.

- Their son:
  - Alphonsus (Alberic) I de Vere: Earl of Genney, Count of Ghesnes (Genny, alias Gisney or GHISNES or GUISNES) married Katarine daughter to Arnalde Earl of Flaunders. And was a "Counsellor (earl of the Witan) to Edward the Confessor".

The Vere Earls of Guisnes

In the matter of the succession of Robert de Vere to the earldom of Oxford in the reign of Charles I, the title was contested for by Lord Willoughby de Eresby. Several Judges of the day were appointed to guide the Lords in legal matters regarding this succession. Leading them was the Lord Chief Justice of England, Sir Randolph Crew. Robert de Vere won the case and the Crown vouchsafed the earldom of Oxford to him.

The summing up speech delivered by the Lord Chief Justice before the House of Peers (The House of Lords) was recorded as part of the judicial process (Sir Bernard Burke) and its comments are therefore part of English Law.

On Saturday 1st April 1626 Sir Randolph Crew addressed their Lordships saying:

> "This great and weighty cause, incomparable to any other that hath happened at any time, requires great deliberation, and solid and mature judgement to determine it, and I wish that all the judges of England had heard it - it being a fit case for all - to the end we all might have given our humble advice to your Lordships herein.
>
> Here is represented to your Lordships certamen honoris, and, as I may well say, illustris honoris, illustrious honour. I heard a great peer of this realm, and a learned, say, when he lived there was no king in Christendom had such a subject as Oxford.
>
> He came in with the Conqueror, Earl of Guynes; shortly after the Conquest, made Great Chamberlain of England above five hundred years ago, by Henry I., the Conqueror's son, brother to Rufus; by Maud, the Empress, Earl of Oxford; confirmed and approved by Henry II., Alberico comiti, so Earl before.
>
> This great honour, this high and noble dignity hath continued ever since in the remarkable surname of De Vere, by so many ages, descents and generations, as no other kingdom can produce such a peer in one and the self-same name and title.................And yet let the name and dignity of De Vere stand for so long as it pleaseth God"

That the Vere were Earls of Guisnes before 1066 is recognised by British law.

With thanks to Miss C. Shelton; the House of Lords Archivist, for the primary sources consulted.

- 1000+ Albery II de Vere: Earl of Genney wed - Beatrice Sister to King William the Conqueror. Alberic went with the King to England. He used the motto,"Albri Comes" which some say is "Albery of truth cometh", de -of ; Ver- true. Albery is also Aubri, Albury, Alberic (in Latin); Alphonsus (in Greek). He built "Hedingham Castle". At the time of the general survey, Alberic de Ver was already noted as a person of ancient and noble descent (Domesday Book). Leland, stated or deduced that the pedigree of this family was from "Noah", Meleager, who slew the Caledonian boar, and Diomedes, who was at the seige of Troy. - N.B. Caesar and Charlemagne.

  Alberic held a number of lordships in several countries in England and particularly 14 in Essex; where Hedingham was his castle, chief seat , and head of his barony. His wife was Beatrix, daughter of Henry Castellan, of Baurbough but others say King William sister, by Sibilla, daughter, and heir Manasses Count of Ghisnes (GUISNES); by whom he had a daughter Rohesia, married, first, to Pagen Beauchamp; and after; to Geffery de Mandeville, earl of Essex; and five sons,

- Geffery, Roger, Robert an William.

  This Alberic, styled Aberico senior, took the habit of a monk; and was buried in the church of Colne priory, which he had founded.

- Albericus, Junior, was successor to his father; and became so much in favor with Henry I that the said King made him great "Chamberlain of England", in fee;

Patent extracts:

"H Rex Anglrorum, &c. Sciatis universi quoniam dedi & concssi Alberico de Ver & hereib, ' suis post eum de me & meis tenend' magistram camerarim ,eamtotius Anglie in feode & hereditate quare volo & firmiter precipio quod ipse & heredes sui eam jure hereditario teneant cim omnibus dignaitatibus & libertatib'& honorisicentitis ad eam pertinentibus, ita bene &libere & honorisice sicat Robertus Malet vel aliquis alius ante vel pst cum inquam melius & nonorisicntius tenuit, cum liberartionibus & hospiciis curie mee que ad ministerium cameratieae pertinent" Test. &c.

- ....to hold the same, with all the liberties and privileges thereto belonging, as fully and honourably, as Robert Malet (Robert de Vere or Veer who had been banished and disinherited), had holden that said office.

This Alberic was also justice of all England in that king's reign, but about the 5th of king Stephen, was killed in a popular turmult at London; leaving by Adeline his wife, daughter of Gilbert de Clare, or, according to Collins, in his Extinct Peerage, daughter to Roger de Ivery, three sons; viz. Alberic,

n.n canon of St. Osyth, in Essex;

- Robert lord of Twiwell, in the county of Narthampton; Geffery, who, the 12th Henry II, certified his knight's fee to be nine deveteri seossamento and three de novo, and then resided in Shropshire; and William; (constituted "chancellor of England", by Maud the empress), and Juliana, Hugeot Bigot, earl of Northfolk. Alberic the third, succeeded his father, and was so considerable a person, that Maud, the empress, in order to engage him to her interest, confirmed to him the office of great chamberlain, and all his father's estates, with diver other inheritances, likewise the earldom of Cambridge, if the earldoms of Oxford, Berkshire, Wiltshire, or Doreseshire. all which grants, Maud's son, Henry II, confirmed, and constitutes him Earl of Oxford, with the grant of the third penny of the pleas of the county; a perquisite then belonging to the earls of this kingdom. He died the 6th Richard I. having been twice married:

First, to Eusamia, daughter of Sir William de Cantilupe, by whom he had no issue;

secondly: daughter (api) to Lucia, daughter and heir of William de Abrincis
(by his wife, daughter and heir of William de Archis), by whom he had sons.

From 'The Itinerary' of the Reverend John Leland 1503 - 1552.
Dictionary of National Biography.
See Source Profile.

Aubrey (Alberic or Oberon) III de Vere

Had several issue including:

Robert de Vere. The historical claimant to the earldom of Cambridge and Huntingdon, heritor of the lands of FitzOoth or Hood. Robert, 'a Templar', was outlawed by King John and lost all his lands and castles. Robert was the historical Robin Hood, Robin Goodfellow or Puck, (see Shakespeare [Edward de Vere]: A Midsummer Night's Dream, commentary; Robin's father Oberon or Alberic the Elf King descended [via Melusine] from Morgan la Fey and Julius Caesar).

Aubrey's eldest surviving son:
Ralph de Vere.

Ralph de Vere, founder of the Veres of Scotland

The first Aubrey de Vere on record (in Britain) came to England with William the Conqueror. .... He is usually held to be a Norman, though he may have been a Breton; he certainly had strong Connections with Brittany. Before the Conquest he was described as one of the barons of Conan, Count of Brittany, and after the Battle of Hastings he or his son (a second Aubrey) was allotted lands in Essex by the overlord there, who was Alan of Brittany, now called Alan, Count of Richmond in Yorkshire.

Like all civil wars, the conflict between the Empress Maud and King Stephen was a very troubling one. It was really a fight between Normans and Flemings for the English throne; and since Stephen's wife was the Flemish Matilda, Countess of Boulogne, those Flemings already in England naturally flocked to her side. For reasons best known to himself Aubrey III de Vere sided with the Normans; he got his reward when the

Empress Maud created him Earl of Oxford.

It has been said, I think correctly, that before a man could be given an earldom he had to have another honour.

Among those who supported Stephen and Matilda against the Normans was Alan Earl of Richmond, and Aubrey III's second son, named Ralf, went against his father and fought for Stephen in the army of his own overlord. The first officially recorded de Vere in Scotland was a Radulfus (or Ralf) who was holding estates in Lanarkshire during the reign of Alexander II. In 1160 Conan, Earl of Richmond, had married Margaret, sister of the King of Scotland, and it seems likely that this may have been the time when his follower, Ralf, was awarded his lands there. We may note that when Aubrey III died, he was succeeded as Earl of Oxford by his first son, Aubrey IV; but when that son died childless the earldom passed to a third son, missing out the second son, Ralf.

With thanks to Mrs Beryl Platts, author of 'The Scottish Hazard'.

'Descent of Scots Family'

The Scottish descent of the Senior line of the Vere of Oxford.

The Scottish name Weir is derived from the Norman-French de Vere..... Alberic de Vere... accompanied the Conqueror. Ralph or Radalphus de Ver was the first of the name on record in Scotland. As Ralph de Ver he was taken prisoner at Ainwick in July 1174. As Radulphus de Weir, he witnessed a Charter of

King William, between 1174 and 1184. and as Radulph de Veir he gave a bovate of land in Sprowston, Roxburgh, to Kelso Abbey. As Radalphus de Vere he witnessed another Charter by King William to the Abbey of Lindores. He also witnessed another undated Charter of King William's to William de Hala, Herd (Errol.) The same, or perhaps a succeeding Radulph de Ver, or de Uer witnessed about 1204 a grant to the Abbey of Arbroath, and before 1214 another Charter by William the Lion. The Weirs of Lanarkshire claimed to be descended from this Radulph.

..................Richard Wer, Lanark, rendered homage to Edward I in 1296. Between 1398 and 1400 Rothald de Were, Baille of Lesmahagow, had a Charter from Patrick, Abbot of Kelso, of the lands of Blackwood, Mossiygning and. Durgundreston. and in 1497 Abbot Robert granted Rogerhill and Brownhill to Robert Weyr for services rendered...

The English 'Weirs' (however) are descended from a progenitor who dwelt at a weir or fishing dam.

The Scottish Weir crest is (was in 1700's) a demi-horse in armour proper, bridled and saddled

gules. The motto is Nihil Verius.

Source:

From Dr. George Black.

The senior descent of the Scottish Branch of Vere of Oxford continued

Source - 'The Surnames of Scotland', New York Public Library Edition.

Primary sources in italic.

WEIR............As Ralph de Vere he was taken prisoner at Alnwick along with William the Lion in 1174 *(Bain, I, p. 174)*.He witnessed a charter by King William '*de decimis episcopatus*' of Moray between 1174-84 *(REM., 2)*, and as Radulph de Veir or Veyre, within the same period, he gave a bovate of land in Sprowestun, Roxburgh, to the Abbey of Kelso, his brother Robert being one of the witnesses *(Kelso, p. 177)*. The same or perhaps a succeeding Radulph de Ver or de Uer witnessed a little before 1204 a grant to the Abbey of Arbroath *(RAA., I, 11)* and before 1214 another charter by King William *(Panmure II, 126)*

WEIR

Tartan: Weir (also Hope-Vere)

Motto: Vero Nihil Verius (Latin: Nothing Truer than Truth)

......**Ralph de Ver**, from whom the **Weirs of Blackwood**, Lanarkshire, claim descent, was captured, with King William I (the Lion), in 1174 whilst besieging the castle of Alnwick in Northumberland. Others of the name held land in Lesmahagow, Lanarkshire, in the fifteenth century.

Major Thomas Weir (1599 - 1670) born at Kirkton House, Carluke, was burned at the stake in Edinburgh for .....witchcraft. His sister was hanged the next day for her part in some of his activities.

'Scotland and her ***Tartans' Alexander Fulton.***

*(**Major Thomas Weir** was the grandson of **William of Stonebyres** and **Elizabeth Hamilton**. His father Thomas married the witch, Lady Jane Somerville. **Major Weir** was posted to Ulster in 1641 and, by family tradition, had some connection with the Tyrone descent. For Somerville see below).*

'Of The Fesse' Chapter X. From the Archives of:

The Lyon King of Arms of Scotland.

THE Sirname of *WEIR* is ancient with us, as Sir *James Dalrymple* obferves in his Collections.

Ranulphus de *WEIR* is mentioned in the Regifters of *Kelfo*, *Paifly*, and *Murray*, to have lived in the Reign of King *William*, and *Thomas* de *Weir* in the Reign of *Alexander* II. Of this Sirname there are feveral Families in *Clydfdale*; the two principal of which are thofe of *Blackwood* and *Stonebyres*.

SIR *George WEIR* of *BLACKWOOD*, Argent, *on a Fefs* Azure, *three Stars of the* firft, *with the Badge of* Nova Scotia *in the Dexter chief Point*, as the Knights *Baronets* ufe; and for Creft, *a Demi-Horfe in Armour proper, iffuing out of a Wreath of his Tinctures, bridled and fadled* Gules; and for Motto, *Nihil verius.* His Grand-father was of the Name of *Lawry*, who married the Heirefs of *Weir* of *Blackwood*, and took upon him the *Name* and *Arms* of *Weir*.

The Scottish Clan and Family Encyclopedia

'(The Armigerous Clans and Families of Scotland)'

Weir

Arms (of Blackwood LR 4/94)[1]

Argent, on a fess Azure, three mollets of the first

Crest

(As Oxford)

Upon a chapeau Gules furred Ermine

a boar standant Azure armed Or.

Motto

(As Oxford)

'Vero Nihil Verius'

(Nothing Truer than)

1. Lyon Roll of Arms.

Ralph de Ver was captured along with William the Lion at Alnwick in Northumberland in 1174. He witnessed a charter of his king of lands in the bishopric of Moray sometime between 1174 and 1184. He also donated land to the Abbey of Kelso, and his brother Robert was a witness. The Weirs of Blackwood in Lanarkshire, who were to become the principal family, claim descent from Ralph de Vere.

(The claim is upheld in the Lyon Rolls as evidenced above).

Senior descent of the Veres of Scotland and Eire

'Baltredus' (Ralph/Ralfredus) de Vere

Who opposed his father in the Flemish war, was disinherited and fled to Scotland with his Liege Lord Conan of Brittany in approx 1165. Conan married the sister of the king and Ralph was given his lands in Lanark. He was a witness to a charter of King William, The Lion of Scotland 1165 - 1214. Ralph and William were captured after beseiging the Castle of Alnwick in Northumbria in 1174.

Had a son:

Walter Rory de Vere

Who had a son:

Ralph (Rudolphus) de Vere

Confirmed his father's donation to Kelso Monastery. Died at the end of the reign of Alexander II of Scotland 1214 - 1249

Had a son:

Thomas de Vere

Living in 1266. Witness to a charter of a donation to Kelso Monastery by Hemicus St Clan.

Had a son:

Richardus de Vere (de Were)

Living approx 1294. Laird (Lord or Baron) of Blackwood. Lanarkshire. Mentioned in a donation to Kelso Monastery

Had a son:

Thomas de Were (de Vere) of Blackwood

Proprietor of the lands and Barony of Blackwood, Lanarkshire. Died in the reign of David the Bruce; David II of Scotland 1329 - 1371

Had a son:

Brian (Buan) Were of Blackwood

Living around 1386. His 6th cousin, Robert De Vere IXth earl of Oxford, Lord of Hedingham, was Marquess of Dublin and Duke and Vice Regent of Ireland. Robert was effectively the Sovereign of Ireland during his lifetime and was permitted by King Richard to mint coins with his own likeness. Brian died in the beginning of the reign of King Robert III of Scotland 1390-1406

Had a son:

Rotaldus Were of Blackwood

Received a charter from Patrick, Abbot of Kelso Monastery; dated 1404. He was Baillie of Lesmahagow from 1398 - 1400. Died in the reign of King James II of Scotland 1437 -1460 Had a son:

Thomas Were (de Vere) of Blackwood

Had a son:

Robert Veyr of Blackwood

Died soon after receiving a charter of confirmation from Robert, the Abbot of the Monastery of Kelso dated 1474.

Had a son:

Thomas Weir of Vere of Blackwood

Married Aegidia, daughter of John, 3rd Lord Somerville (of the Dragon) in 1483. Acquired vast holdings of land and was patron of St. Mary's Church in Lesmahagow. Died in the beginning of the reign of Queen Mary of Scots in 1542.

Had a son:

James Weir of Vere, Lord of Blackwood

Married Euphemia Hamilton, sister of the Duke of Chatelherault, Marquess of Hamilton. The Hamiltons were the Heirs Presumptive to the Throne of Scotland during this period. James lived to a great age. He died in 1595. Had sons:

1. James Weir

Married Marriotte Ramsay, daughter of George, Lord Dalhousie, an ancestor of the Hope-Veres of Craig Hall. George Ramsay was created Earl of Melrose in 1618 and changed this to the earldom of Dalhousie in 1619. The 9th earl was Governor of Canada, Nova Scotia and New Brunswick. His son was Governor General of India.

They had issue:

a) George Weir who married Margaret Vere of Stonebyres with whom he had one daughter.

Marriotte Weir who married =

1. Major James Bannatyne (a sept of the Stewarts of Bute).

2. William Lowry by whom she had a Son George who became

Sir George Weir Bt. (descent to Hope-Vere of Blackwood).

The Hope-Veres died out in 1974.

b) Robert Weir of Craighead sold or assigned his estate in 1610 and moved to Monaghan House in Co.Fermanagh, now renamed Hallcraig House. Robert married the sister of the alchemist Sir David Lindsay.

From Robert various branches descend.

Robert had sons, the eldest surviving son was:

Alexander who married Anne, Daughter of Sir John Dunbar (Graham descent) of Derrygonnelly, Co. Fermanagh.

Their eldest son:

Alexander married Sarah, daughter of Captain Goodwin and secondly, Elizabeth, daughter of Sir Paul Gore Bt.

Their eldest son:

Robert Weir of Hallcraig married Anne, daughter of Captain Carleton of Tullymargy

Castle.

They had a son Captain Alexander Weir of Hallcraig

(from whom the senior branch of the House of Vere descends to Nicholas de Vere's ducal kinsman - The Mac An Mhaoir - who is of matrilinear Stoughton-Collison descent)

and a daughter from whence Captain Noble Weir of Hallcraig who married Catharine Graham (descent from the Grahams of Scotland 1600) and had issue:

('Burke's Irish Landed Gentry' 1891-1915; 'Burke's Landed gentry' 1974; 'Burke's Peerage, Baronetage and Knightage' 1957; Burke's Dormant and Extinct Peerages).

Vere of Tyrone

Robert, who by Rachael Stewart had their eldest son,

Robert Weir of Desertcreat, Tyrone who married Sarah Graham,

and by her had their eldest son:

John who moved back to Scotland where he married Mary Logan of Logan in Galloway. The Logan families have held their lands in the Stranraer Peninsula since the 1100's, whilst others of that name held Restalrig. Two Logan

Knights, Sir Walter and Sir Robert Logan, were killed in Spain whilst taking the heart of Robert the Bruce to the Holy Land for burial with Sir James Douglas.

Their eldest son:

Thomas Logan Weir married a Gael, Anne Grant Macdonnell of Inverness. They had male issue, the eldest of which died without heirs.

The second eldest and surviving son:

James Weir of Vere of Lewes who married Natalie Hopgood, daughter of George Collison Hopgood, Esquire and Julia Harding of Godalming, grand daughter of Captain George Butcher of the 11th Light Dragoons, of Windsor Castle and Osbourne House; Tapetiere to Queen Victoria.

They had an only son:

Nicholas Thomas Logan Weir of Vere (Nicholas de Vere)

The relationship between the Head of the House of Vere and Nicholas de Vere; who is Head of the Tyrone Branch, is 3rd and 6th cousins. Found in only 3% and 6% of the clinical samples tested, both share two sets of rare genes each and Nicholas de Vere has an extra set of these genes from the matrilinear descent which supports the Collison descent from Norfolk in his own line and echoes the selective and exclusive royal and noble marital alliances which have continued throughout the history of the House of Vere.

Parish Records for Ulster 1820 - 1845, United Kingdom Government Registers for Births, Marriages and Deaths 1845-1997.

Notes

The House of Vere are latterly of Flemish extraction and the former senior, Scottish Branch; Hope-Vere of Blackwood, traditionally observed the Flemish law of Noblesse Uterine, and matrilinear and family inheritance in accordance with Scottish Law, which historically supports blood descent.

The Titles of Princeps Draconis and Prince de Vere, currently held by Nicholas de Vere, are acknowledged by the British Government's Department of Internal Affairs: 'The Home Office' and are registered with them as 'Official Observations'. The House of Vere in the senior line acknowledges these titles accordingly.

Nicholas de Vere, though recognising both, does not claim to be either a member of the historical British royal bloodline or of its peerage in any sense: and does not claim any status or rank suggestive of such or appertaining thereunto. The Vere princedoms are not modern, socially derived titles; either assumed or bestowed, for or by, political expediency.

The princedom of Vere is a genetic quality carried in the historical blood royal. Established in Angiers as a Royal House arising from sacral-regal origins rooted in antiquity, The House of Vere is recorded in a single name and in an unbroken line for over 1300 years, and consequently is one of the oldest surviving royal houses in Europe.

Source Profiles

- 'Histories of England' - Baron Thomas Babington Macaulay, Lord Macaulay of Rothley Temple, (1800 - 1859). Politician and historian. Educated at Trinity College, Cambridge he became one of the acknowledged intellectual pundits of his age. He entered the Supreme Council for India in 1834 where his famous 'Minutes on Law and Education' had a decisive influence on the development of the sub-continent. He was Secretary-At-War 1839-41 and went on to write his acclaimed, best-selling 'Histories of England' between 1849-1855.

  "He used a wide range of manuscript sources with great skill, and modern historians neglect his reconstruction of events at their peril", Margaret Drabble CBE, Morley College.

- 'The Dictionary of National Biography' - designed and published by George Smith (1824-1901) The Dictionary was first published in 1882 with Sir Leslie Stephen

  (1832-1904) as editor. The DNB in its original form included biographies of all the national notabilities from the earliest time to 1900. The work has been continued by the publishing of decennial supplements. Stephen was succeeded as editor by Sir Sydney Lee and their names appear jointly on the title pages of volumes XXII to XXVI (1890). In 1917 the Dictionary was transferred to Oxford University.

- 'Myths of the Middle Ages' - Reverend Father Sabine Baring Gould, Lord of Lew Trenchard, Devon, (1834-

1924). Baring-Gould travelled the Continent extensively and was educated at Clare College, Cambridge. An Antiquarian and folklorist, Baring-Gould; a prolific writer, was the author of numerous works including 'Mehalah', which Swinburne compared to 'Wuthering Heights'.

- 'Burke's Peerage' - properly 'A Genealogical and Heraldic history of the Peerage and Baronetage of the United Kingdom' 1826 -1947, first compiled by John Burke in 1826 and published anually after 1947.

- 'The Itinerary' - Reverend John Leland, (1503-1552). "The earliest of modern antiquaries" Leland was educated at St. Paul's School and Christ's College, Cambridge. He studied in Paris, took holy orders and by 1530 was involved with the Royal Libraries. From 1533 he appears to have received a commission to search the monastic and collegiate libraries for old authors. He made a tour through England between 1535 and 1543 intending his researches to be the basis of an opus magna on the 'Histories and Antiquities of the Nation'. His notes were first published at Oxford University by the historian Thomas Hearne (1678-1735) as 'The Itinerary' in nine volumes in 1710-12. Lucy Toulmin Smith produced an edition of 'The Itinerary' in 1906-10 in which she noted that the descent of Vere was included as an extract from Folio 42 of the original work which was preserved in Stow's original collection.

- 'Stow MSS' - John Stow (1525-1605). A collection of manuscripts first collated in 1564. Stow transcribed manuscripts and was the first person to compose historical works based on a systematic study of Public Records. He assisted Parker with editing historical texts and his chief publications were 'The workes of Geoffrey

Chaucer' (1561); 'Summary of English Chronicles' (1565); 'The Chronicles of England' (1580) and a 'Survey of London'. An edition of the collection was published by Strype in 1720 and the fullest edition of the original work was C.L. Kingsford's, which was published in 1908.

- 'Complete peerage of England, Scotland, Ireland, Great Britain and the United Kingdom, extant, extinct or dormant' - George Edward Cokayne MA, born in Russell Square, London in 1825; the son of Dr. William Adams LLD and The Hon. Mary Anne Cokayne, neice and co-heiress of Borlase, 6th Viscount Cullen. Complying with his mother's wishes Cokayne changed his name by royal license on 15th August 1873.

  Cokayne was educated at Exeter College, Oxford. Barrister; Lincoln's Inn (1853); Rouge Dragon Pursuivant-of-Arms (1859-1870), Lancaster Herald (1870-1882); Norroy King-of-Arms (1882-1894) Clarenceux King of Arms from 1894. His 'Complete Peerage of the United Kingdom...' in 8 volumes was compiled between 1887-98 and published by George Bell. Holding Library: Trinity College Dublin.

- 'Royal Genealogies' or 'The genealogical tables of emperors, kings and princes from Adam to these times' by Dr. James Anderson DD., MA., (1680-1739). Anderson was born in Aberdeen where he was also later educated and took his degrees. He was appointed Presbyterian Minister for Swallow Street and Lisle Street, Leicester Fields in London between 1710 and 1734.

  Described as "a learned man" Anderson; who was a Freemason, was assigned the task, in 1721, of compiling an authoritative digest of the 'Constitutions' of the fraternity (see: Entick's edition of 1747; page 194 et seq). As Grand Warden of the Grand Lodge in London he presented his work to the Order in 1723. It has appeared in numerous subequent editions and has been long recognised by English Freemasons as the standard code on its subject.

Editions were translated into German and also appeared in America in 1855, as facsimiles of the earlier English Version. The work by which Anderson is chiefly remembered; 'The Royal Genealogies', was first published in 2 volumes in London in 1732. Anderson based this work on the earlier 'Genealogische Tabellen' of Johann Hubner. See below.

The relatively later tables of the 'Genealogies' were considered by Sir Stephen Leslie (Dictionary of National Biography) "to be of use (i.e. a valid historical source work) in relation to the genealogies of continental dynasties and houses", (Re: Vere). 'Royal Genealogies': Holding Library; Cambridge University.

- Genealogische Tabellen' - Johann Hubner. Properly: 'Der Genealogische Tabellen zur erlauterung der politische historie vom anfange biss auf diesen tag continuiret', published in one volume, Leipzig 1719. Holding library: Glasgow.

- 'The Collections' - Sir James Dalrymple. 'Collections concerning the Scottish history, preceeding the death of King David the First, in the year 1153. Wherein the soveraignity of the crown and independency of the church are cleared; and account given of the antiquity and purity of the Scottish-British church, and the novelty of popery in this kingdom. With an appendix containing the copies of charters of foundation of some churches; with genealogical accounts of the donors and witnesses'. First Published in Edinburgh in 1705 by the heirs and successors of Andrew Anderson sold by John Vallange and Mrs. Ogstoun ...[8], LXXXVI, [4], 432, [4] p. (8o) Holding Library: Durham

- 'The surnames of Scotland, their origin, meaning, and history' : by Dr. George Fraser Black. Published in New York in 1946 : The New York Public Library. Holding Libraries: Cambridge ; Edinburgh ; Leeds ; Liverpool ; Nottingham ; SAS ; Sheffield

---

Primary Sources

- Family Archives of the House of Vere of Fermanagh and Clare.
- Colne Priory MSS, Kelso Abbey MSS, Paisley Abbey MSS, Arbroath Abbey MSS.
- Charter 'De Decimus Episcopatus', Moray.
- 'The Plantagenet Chronicles' Thomas de Loche (1130) and Jean de Mortimer (1164-1173).
- Sir Randolph Crew's summary - House of Lords Archives.
- Roll of Arms of the Lord Lyon King of Arms of Scotland (a Government Office), Lyon Court, Edinburgh, Scotland.
- Arden, St. George and Glover Rolls of Arms, ref: College of Arms (a Government Office), London, England.

- Parish Records and Census Returns for County Tyrone - Public Records Office, Belfast, Northern Ireland.
- Parish Records and Census Returns for Wigtonshire - Scottish Records Office, New Register House, Edinburgh, Scotland.
- Registry for Births, Marriages and Deaths for Cumbria, Kent, East Sussex, Hertfordshire and West Sussex - St. Catharine's House Records, Preston, Lancashire, England.
- Home Office Policy Review Committee, Whitehall, London, England.

www.ingramcontent.com/pod-product-compliance
Lightning Source LLC
Chambersburg PA
CBHW030600170726
48283CB00002B/406

* 9 7 8 1 9 1 9 3 0 9 8 0 4 *